FITZ:

ALL TOGETHER NOW

FITZ:

ALL TOGETHER NOW

by

TOM FITZPATRICK

DAVID McKAY COMPANY, INC.

New York

To Kelley, Tom, and Mike

CONTENTS

PREFACE

I remember the night Tom Fitzpatrick walked briskly into the *Sun-Times* newsroom after running with the rampaging Weathermen through the dark, elegant streets of Chicago's Near North Side.

He wasn't even winded. That's because Fitzpatrick jogs all the time—*hut, hut, hut* around a muddy little track crammed in among the high-rises of the Near North Side. So he was in better shape than the window-busting Weathermen and the not-so-hot-in-pursuit policemen; and he knew the territory. It helps explain why Fitzpatrick ended up in a newsroom that night instead of in a jail.

With twenty minutes to go before deadline, Fitzpatrick sat down at a typewriter and began unfolding this extraordinary tale of what it's like to be at the center of moving chaos. I sat at the news desk, where we put the paper together, watching page after page being dropped in the basket by copy boys.

Fitzpatrick captured the feel of the Weathermen's determined energy, seemingly galvanized by the very outrageousness of their Idea—that they would bring down the power Establishment with a temper tantrum. He caught the bewilderment of policemen who couldn't quite believe what was happening and the fear of bystanders who were out strolling with their dogs.

I walked back from the news desk to where Fitzpatrick was clacking away, wondering how to avoid breaking his train of thought while reassuring him to keep writing. It was past deadline and his story was already twice as long as the space available for it. In a nonchalant mumble I said, "Let it run. Take whatever you need."

Fitzpatrick looked up briefly with a glance that was one part appreciation, two parts annoyance, and ten parts disbelief that anyone should feel it necessary to reassure him about a story sure to win a Pulitzer Prize.

Fitzpatrick wrote on, and the edition was fifteen minutes late. He also won a Pulitzer Prize for the story.

When the award—tops in journalism—was announced months later, I was surprised and excited. Fitzpatrick wasn't. He had bet a couple of the regulars at Riccardo's bar that he would win. When told of the award, he matter-of-factly said it was a good choice, in fact the only one that could have been made if the Pulitzer Prizes weren't fixed. (You have to make allowances for that last little bit of suspicion; Fitzpatrick has lived in Chicago a long time.)

He is also filled with a healthy dose of Irish bravado and, I might add, some talent. He knew he had produced an award-winning work of journalism because Fitzpatrick is a master of his craft. Recently I was talking down my nose to him about one of his columns which was less than a show-stopper and had run far back in the paper. He interrupted to express his surprise that I had run it at all.

Fitzpatrick has a remarkable ear for hearing what people are really saying and an eye for the telling detail. He follows no suffocating rules of story structure, but sets a scene to fit his subject. He can be very rough on people who try to put him on. Otherwise, he is quite unpredictable in how he will react—an invaluable trait for keeping a column fresh. Sometimes, Fitzpatrick lets a story tell itself with little personal embellishment. That was the case with his account of the Weathermen's rampage and the power of the telling had an impact long before the Pulitzer Prizes were announced.

Mayor Daley is the keeper of the keys in Chicago and he, for one, was enraged by the story. I don't think he quite knew why, which might explain his morning-after news conference. The mayor could express his wrath only by bellowing at Fitzpatrick for having called the Weathermen "kids" instead of "hoodlums." I think what really upset Hizzoner was that Fitzpatrick had so vividly evoked an activity clearly impermissible in the mayor's world view and therefore not worthy of any discussion.

I knew a young Weatherman at the time and he didn't like the story either. It made the Great Night's events appear too much a crazy kid's stunt rather than an auspicious beginning of the revolution. He was a drop-out from Brown University with an interesting case of lost identity. He used to stop by my house Saturdays and Sundays and discuss the philosopher Wittgenstein with bewildering complexity.

I understand he is back at Brown doing very well in philosophy; Mayor Daley still has a firm grip on the keys in Chicago; and Tom Fitzpatrick is still writing one of the best columns in modern journalism.

James F. Hoge, Jr.
Editor,
Chicago Sun-Times

INTRODUCTION

I really owe Billy Goat Sianis a lot more than I ever admitted when he was alive.

Toward the end Billy Goat drove most of his customers crazy. He ran his saloon as though he were a visiting emperor. A favored few would be summoned to his table to hear Billy Goat tell stories of his boyhood in Greece and the golden days when he ran a saloon on West Madison Street, across from the Chicago Stadium.

One of his last acts was the unveiling of what he called his "Wall of Fame." On it were the portraits of the men Billy Goat considered the greats of the Chicago newspapers in his time.

Not surprisingly, Bill Goat's portrait was placed at stage center in dimensions that dwarfed all the others. A lot of us had never seen many of the other members of Billy Goat's pantheon of heroes.

A few days later, Billy Goat led me proudly to the wall. One by one, he pointed them out with the crutch he always had with him by this time. Most of the top-ranking executives of the four papers in town had made it. So had the gossip columnists. There were a few others, too. One was the chauffeur of Don Maxwell, then the editor of the *Chicago Tribune*.

There was one face missing. Tom Morrow, in his time, a great columnist for the *Tribune,* wasn't there. This was astounding, because Morrow's columns had helped to make Billy Goat the financial success he was.

I asked him why Tom Morrow had been omitted.

"There's no room," Billy Goat said, shrugging his shoulders.

"Billy," I said, "this is your show. You can pick whom you want. But how can you figure the editor of the *Trib*'s chauffeur rates over a man you admit helped you more than anyone else?"

"Let me tell you something you should know," Billy Goat said. "Someday you may get to write a column yourself. Look at the columnists I have on my wall. They all still have columns. Tom Morrow is dead. Once a columnist stops writing, he's no more important to me than a dishwasher who doesn't show up for work."

Billy Goat gave me a shrewd smile. He poked me with his crutch.

"One more thing," he said. "Cheer up. There's a much bigger turnover in dishwashers than there is in columnists."

This is what I know about being a columnist. If I blow this job a lot of people who are friends now will become very hard to reach by phone. That will be okay with me. Billy Goat has prepared me.

How did I ever get to be a columnist with an attitude like this, you ask? It was easy. I worked on all the papers there are in Chicago for ten years. By that time I had created such an impression that I was describing myself on job applications as a "freelance writer."

Then, early one evening, I had the following conversation with Jim Hoge, a hunch player, who on this occasion probably thought of himself as a patron of lost causes. He is also the editor of the *Chicago Sun-Times*.

"Would you like a job?" Hoge asked.

"Yes," I said.

"Can you stay sober?" Hoge asked.

"Reasonably so," I answered.

I took the job. A year later I won the Pulitzer Prize. That changed the ballgame. So now I'm a columnist. Jim Hoge has survived all this. He's still the editor.

I'm glad about that. I never wanted to be editor. We ought to become what we admired when we were young. Jimmy Cannon and Red Smith were my idols then. So were John Lardner, Meyer Berger, and Bob Considine.

And then, not too many years ago, the *New York Herald Tribune* let Jimmy Breslin roam free, and that opened up everything for the rest of us.

There are other people in Chicago who have helped me a lot, too. Bob Cromie of the *Tribune* gave me the first break I ever had. Mike Royko once got me a job as a baseball writer on the

Daily News. Herman Kogan encouraged me when I was down. So did Jim Peneff, Dick Takeuchi, Ray Brennan, and Wendell Smith. I still owe them.

Tony Gieske and Barbara Kerr helped me put this material together. I couldn't have done it without their help. Tony's the most gifted unemployed newspaperman I know. Barbara kept us both out of O'Rourke's Pub for a whole month. I owe them, too.

So here I am. Some people tell me I have the best newspaper job in town. Well, I like it better than any job I've ever had. It's what I'd always wanted to be when I grew up.

FITZ:

ALL TOGETHER NOW

CHAPTER 1

THOSE GREAT STREETS

ONE NIGHT OF RAGE

*This one won the Pulitzer. I knew it would be a night of run-
ning. That afternoon I jogged only two miles instead of the usual
three. It was a good thing. That night I ran five miles with the
kids.*

*Funny how these things work out. We had lots of stories about
the rampage in the paper already. Jim Hoge, who is our editor, said
try writing a piece that would explain just how it was in the middle
of the riot.*

*It was only minutes to the deadline for the four-star final. I knew
the piece would have to run long. I had no time to look it over.
All there was time to do was type.*

*After I had written about seven pages, Jim came over to my
desk. "Keep writing," he said. "It's going to be a good piece. Take
all the space you need."*

*The two pieces that follow describe a riot by rock fans in Grant
Park. Incidentally, there is one unifying element in all three pieces.
We have a policeman who turns out to be a hero and a man of
honor, First Deputy Superintendent James Rochford.*

Bad Marvin had been standing in front of the fire he had made
of the Lincoln Park bench for thirty minutes, shouting to everyone
in the crowd and warning them how bad he was.

It was 10:25 P.M., and I kept looking to the north where the police had set up their command post in the Lincoln Park Cultural
Arts Center.

Deputy Chief Robert Lynskey had told me he'd be coming to the park at 10:30 to see how the situation was developing.

"Maybe we won't even have to tell them to leave," he had said about two hours earlier. "Maybe by that time they'll all be tired and want to go on their own."

But they weren't tired, and now about two hundred of the kids began racing out of the park, heading toward the Chicago Historical Society.

Bad Marvin started running, too, brandishing a long piece of burning board in his right hand.

"*Viva* Che," he kept shouting as he ran. "*Viva* Cuba."

"Bring the war home now," screamed a girl running alongside him.

She was so caught up with running in the dark that she ran right into a large tree outside the Historical Society and collapsed in a lump, the first casualty of the night.

By now the main force of the group had reached North Federal Savings, at the northwest corner of North and Clark. It's a big, impressive building with large plate-glass windows, and here is where the tide turned.

Two weeks before, in a similar march south on Clark, the kids contented themselves with shouting insults.

This time it was different. A tall, skinny kid in a white helmet ran a little in front of the crowd and tossed a rock through one of the large windows.

The sound of shattering glass hit everyone in the group like an electric shock. You are not alone when you're in a group like this. From now on, it was going to have to be a wild ride. And if you were going to find out what happened, you had to go along with it.

The first rock was soon followed by a second and a third and then cheering.

Watching the rock-throwing and the wild applause and seeing the motorists on the other side of North Avenue jumping out of their cars and running for cover, it suddenly hits you that everyone has gone insane.

The first thing you look for is the police. Certainly, those blue lights are going to be shining all over in seconds. Incredibly, they're not.

The only thing for a man to do who has thrown a rock through the window of a bank is to run away, and as the three or four who threw them began running, everyone else began running, too.

Now everyone is shouting at the top of his lungs, and it's amazing how many of them have come out of the park with rocks in their hands.

"Ho, Ho, Ho Chi Minh!" they're shouting. A blonde in the front row is waving the Viet Cong flag.

Once on Clark Street and heading south, the kids have taken over the entire street. The street is narrow enough to create an echo as the windows start exploding on each side of the street.

Three rocks go through the windows of the Red Star Inn, and apartment windows on all sides are falling.

One girl, who can't be more than seventeen, has a heavy stick about three feet long in her hands. She displays an amazing technique with the vent windows of cars parked along the street. She gets the first seven she tries, and the man in the white helmet behind her gets four back windows in a row before missing one.

By this time, you have already learned one important rule about running with mobs who are tossing rocks: you have to stay up front and stay right in the street with them.

If you get on the sidewalk, you'll never see the rock that hits you instead of an apartment window. There is a risk in this, too, because you must time your moves so that you get away from the whole outfit as soon as you see the line of police forming ahead of you. The police still aren't in sight and the wild march goes all the way to within fifty yards of Division Street.

And there the police were waiting.

They were lined up across the street, and they weren't saying a word. It was a sight so formidable that you couldn't blame the kids when they turned and ran back north on Clark and then turned east on Goethe to escape.

Goethe was where it really got bad. It's a very narrow street where people like to park their cars.

Nobody who parked there Wednesday night, however, was happy Thursday morning. Every car window for a two-block stretch was smashed, and so were the lobby windows of a high-rise apartment on the corner of Dearborn and Goethe.

The kids knew it was all over for them, but they kept on the attack. Anyone who wanted to still had a chance to escape, but the kids ran south on State, heading for Division again. They had to know the police would have moved over from Clark and would be waiting.

"Hurry," they kept shouting. "Make it fast, and we'll beat the cops to the corner."

How did they ever think they were going to run four blocks in the time it took the policemen to ride two blocks in their cruisers?

And now, as we're heading into the eye of the storm at Division Street, I see a beautiful thing happen. It's Bad Marvin, the guy with the flaming stick who was bragging to everyone how bad he was going to be. Bad Marvin is running away, and his torch has burned out.

It always makes you feel good when the tough-talking guys cave in, but now what does happen is not good. All the kids who have been wound up tight from listening to all the inflammatory speeches in the park are the ones who are going to take it in the head.

"Charge!" one little kid screams as he runs for the police line. "Charge!" the cry comes back as about a dozen more follow him.

Anyone who tells you he can see everything that goes on at a moment like this is not telling a straight story. It comes at you in little pieces, and if you're lucky you can put a few of them back later. But you never get it all.

The squadrons are in the intersection and kids are being thrown into them as quickly as possible. One policemen is leaning over a squad car holding his head. He's been hit by a rock and he's bleeding and he's mad. But the kids aren't stopped yet. Some of them head east to Lake Shore Drive. Another group turns back and races west along Division.

This was the first confrontation. You will see three more at different intersections before it ends at Crilly Court on North, just west of Wells.

There are only about fifty kids left, and this is the time it scares you.

Walking in the middle of the street, you're amazed to see cars heading toward you as if they mean to run you over. This is something new. For an hour, every motorist on the Near North Side has run for his life.

The cars are filled with policemen. Some in plainclothes, some in uniform. As they leap out, you can see at least three of them have their revolvers drawn. The others are wielding clubs.

The kids run, but they don't have a chance. It's all over with them now.

They have been asking for a confrontation all night and now they finally get one.

Within minutes the street is cleared, and Deputy Superintendent James Rochford is walking toward Sergeant James Clark of the eighteenth District to get a final report.

But there is no smile of triumph on Rochford's face. He's been through this same thing during the Democratic National Convention, and he didn't take any delight in it then, either.

"All right," Rochford says to Clark. "Get the men to clear the street. Let's just all get out of here."

ROCK CONCERT RIOT

In July 1970, Sly and the Family Stone was scheduled to perform a free rock concert in Grant Park. The concert was scheduled by the city as part of a public relations campaign to woo back young people after the disaster of the Democratic Convention.

Here's how it backfired.

Make no mistake about this one. This was a tougher and more vicious battle than any that Chicago police fought against the demonstrators during the Democratic National Convention of 1968.

The police came out of that one with their reputation tarnished by charges that they had overreacted. They have been hypersensitive ever since.

Monday night, the police hopelessly outnumbered by thousands of frenzied rock fans, had all they could do to escape with their shields intact.

It was close all the way. There were times when it seemed the only way the police could save their own lives would be to begin shooting to kill.

This is not an exaggeration for dramatic effect. It was that close, because if this mob had finally gotten the upper hand, I truly believe it would have stoned policemen to death.

The rock festival fans had a reason for all this, of course.

Monday was a hot, muggy day in Grant Park, and many of them had been on hand long before the 4 P.M. starting time for a concert by a group called Sly and the Family Stone.

When Sly and the Family Stone didn't take the stage for the assembled thousands, the mood of the crowd turned ugly.

"This is the fourth rock concert I've been to," Helen Lozowsky, eighteen, said later, "and it's the fourth time they haven't come on stage.

"Those people who had the loud-speaker on stage kept buggin' us. First, they'd tell us that Sly was on his way in a police van. Then they'd tell us he was in a helicopter hovering up above the bandstand. Then they'd say he was underneath the stage and afraid to come out. Anybody would get mad at that kind of treatment."

"Yeah," said Sheri Meltzer, eighteen. "Sly is chicken. He's afraid to come on stage whenever the crowd gets too big. That cat don't know where his head is."

That was how the battle began. Unhappy rock fans began tossing rocks and bottles at the empty stage and finally surged forward, knocking down a snow fence in front of it and overwhelming the Andy Frain ushers.

The police moved in to protect the ushers. The sight of the police inflamed the crowd, most in it viewing any man in a police uniform as a mortal enemy.

That's how the battle began. It went on that way until after dark.

The demonstrators at the Democratic Convention never could produce the numbers this crowd mustered. Police estimates of the crowd at the start of the battle were in excess of 75,000, and it was a crowd made up of both blacks and whites. There were very few black demonstrators at the convention.

They were pitted against no more than four hundred police officers, and the crowd must have sensed it had the upper hand and that it would be impossible for police to surround and subdue it.

The field of battle was that naturally shallow soup bowl that is Grant Park, just north of the bandshell.

It was a battle that went on for four hours, then with the rock fans being driven as far north as Buckingham Fountain and counter-attacking and driving the police south to the band shell.

This was a crowd that was in a frenzy, exhorting one another to "kill the pigs." They had shouted this at the convention, too, but that crowd was almost always on the defensive. This crowd was on the attack right up until the moment that the police made their final move shortly before 9 P.M.

I lost count of the policemen I saw with bloody mouths, bloody shirts, and hands and legs dripping blood from thrown rocks and broken bottles that had hit them after traveling in long, high arcs.

It was dark when First Deputy Superintendent James M. Rochford stepped in front of a line of two hundred helmeted policemen and waved his baton with the red tassel as a signal to advance.

Rochford, in his dress blues and soft cap, made a beautiful target as he marched twenty yards in advance of the line.

Several rocks came close to hitting him, warded off only by a deft move of his baton. One thrown bottle smashed against the baton, too.

"Move out!" Rochford kept shouting, "and stay together."

"Any policeman that I see throwing a rock," shouted Deputy Superintendent James Riordan, "will be suspended. That's after I deal with him first.

"I want every man to arrest anyone he finds in the park on this pass. If they haven't moved out, they go in the van. Let's go."

The police line began moving slowly and the rock fans kept tossing the rocks. Still the line of police went forward, and here and there they began falling to the ground.

It was like a scene in one of those movies about the Napoleonic wars where the soldiers keep advancing even though they are such easy targets.

After walking about one hundred yards, the police line broke and they began trotting . . . then running full speed ahead.

Now the night was filled with screams and groans from both sides. I had never heard a policeman scream before Monday night, but the pain in the man's broken wrist must have been unbearable.

"My hand's broken!" he shouted. "Help me back. It hurts. Oh, my God, it hurts."

His right hand was covered with blood that seemed to be gushing from a large hole in his wrist.

Thirty feet to the east, another policeman screamed and fell in a heap, on a burning railroad flare that the rock fans had somehow added to their arsenal for the final skirmish.

Two other officers rushed to pull him off the flare.

"Oh God," said one policeman. "Look at his face."

"I saw it," shouted another policeman running up to the trio. "One of those bastards hit him right in the center of the face with a piece of concrete that weighed about five pounds."

I walked over to the policeman to see if I could read his name on the gold tag on his breast.

After looking at his face, I forgot about the name tag.

Coming from the other direction, three policemen were dragging one of the rock fans through the battle lines to place him under arrest.

His face was just as bloody as the police officer's and he was screaming for mercy.

A girl in bell bottoms and with long hair was running alongside the policemen, screaming at them as they dragged her friend to the paddy wagon.

"Lousy bastards!" she shouted. "Pigs! You're just rotten pigs!"

The policemen who had been hit in the face wasn't making a sound anymore. He was propped in the arms of two other officers, sitting on the grass.

He was a big, heavy-set man, but now he looked like a broken doll that someone had splattered with ketchup.

I hope someone doesn't come around to me in the next few days to tell me about police brutality.

I stood with them as they dodged the rocks and bottles and watched their fellow officers being carried to the rear after being struck.

I saw them bristle with anger as they had to stand by and watch the rock fans turn over autos on Balbo and set them afire.

And during the one big retreat, when they turned and fired more than one hundred warning shots in the direction of their attackers, I felt for the first time that I was on the losing side in this battle.

If someone can show any justification the rock fans had for their attack, I would be fascinated to hear it.

But I don't think anyone will come forward with an explanation other than that they were a vicious mob, hell bent on maiming and killing policemen.

ALL RIGHT, FRANKIE, DROP THE GUN

One day in April 1969, Frank Kulak, a forty-two-year-old ex-Marine, who had fought on Okinawa and in Korea, thought the war was on again. For six hours he began holding off what he figured were the enemy as they attacked his second-story apartment on Chicago's South Side.

Kulak had several rifles, two carbines, hand grenades, a grenade launcher, and an endless supply of homemade bombs. Two policemen were killed and four wounded.

"Life just pushed Frank into a corner," his brother, Harold, said, "Life pushed him too hard and he decided to fight back."

Here's how it ended.

You may wonder how I know what Rochford and Chief of Patrol John T. Kelly were talking about as they drove downtown to the Central police station. I was in the car with them. I got in because of one of those crazy breaks you get when you push for things you have no chance of getting.

"I need a ride downtown," I said to Rochford.

"What will all the other reporters say?" Rochford asked.

"They all have cars."

"Well, you'll have to ask Chief Kelly about it," Rochford said.

I walked to Kelly, who was standing at the open rear door of the police command car.

"Rochford said for me to sit back here with you," I said.

Kelly was too tired to react.

"All right," he said, "get in."

I had been in the car for five minutes when Rochford turned around and spotted me.

"My God," he said, "how the hell did you get in here?"

The lights from the television cameras were turned on just as Deputy Superintendent James M. Rochford reached a spot on the sidewalk in front of Brown's Funeral Home. Rochford, forty-seven, has balding red hair and a ruddy face. He has been a policeman twenty-three years.

Less than ten minutes before, he had convinced gunman Frank

Kulak to hand over his weapons and surrender after two policemen had been killed. But there was no elation on Rochford's face. He merely looked tired. Frank Sullivan, the police department's public relations man was at Rochford's side, explaining to him that everyone was waiting for a statement.

"I can't do it, Frank," Rochford said. "My voice is shot. We'll get Spiotto to do it. He knows all about it."

A heavy-set, middle-aged woman with a microphone in her hand looked incensed.

"I've never heard of such a thing," she said to Rochford. "Do you realize I've been standing out here in the rain for four hours?"

Rochford's face didn't change expression. He didn't bother to tell her he had arrived on the scene when Kulak was still running from window to window firing his two carbines at anything that moved and throwing hand grenades and homemade bombs out the window as fast as he could.

"I'm sorry," Rochford said. "I'm going to let all of you people talk to Chief of Detectives Michael Spiotto, who will fill you in as to the details."

Rochford stepped out of the glare of the lights, and Spiotto, a medium-sized man with a full head of gray hair, replaced him. Another woman with a microphone in her hand shoved it to the forefront now and shouted to Spiotto:

"Are you going to give this man a psychiatric test?"

Spiotto looked back in disbelief. Then he began to explain in a soft, patient voice that Kulak had surrendered to Rochford and that the bodies of two policemen had been found on the third-floor balcony. Spiotto spelled the names of each of the dead men carefully.

"During the course of the conversation with Superintendent Rochford," Spiotto said, "the subject admitted that he was the man responsible for the Goldblatt department store bombing, too, as well as another in this neighborhood either last Sunday or the Sunday before."

"Get all these bums out of here," came a voice over the crowd.

It was the man from inside Brown's funeral home. A wake was being conducted inside and, with more than 250 people standing in front, it was impossible for the mourners to get in.

"Don't you bums have any respect for the dead?" the man shouted to a uniformed policeman standing next to him in the doorway. "Get them the hell away from my place."

"Please," said the policeman, "it will only be a minute more."

Rochford was standing at the corner of 95th and Exchange, away from the mob scene. He looked down the street about five doors, at the building where he had just convinced Kulak to surrender.

There were bright lights from a fire truck on the front of the three-story building now. Commander Francis Flanagan and men from the bomb and arson squad were walking around gingerly examining what appeared to be dozens of unexploded hand grenades on the front lawn.

"Big job," said a uniformed policeman to Rochford.

"They're all big jobs," Rochford said, smiling back.

Rochford walked slowly to the middle of the street where his black limousine was waiting for him. He got into the front next to the driver. Sullivan and Kelly got into the back.

Kelly, who is fifty-seven and has white hair, looked tired, too. Rochford and Kelly had been in charge of the operation and both men had risked their lives to crawl into the building under fire.

Slowly, the limousine glided away from the crowd. There were approximately two hundred policemen at the scene and perhaps ten times that many people looking on.

"Looks like we got an awful lot of spectators," Kelly said.

"We have too many spectators," Rochford answered.

He sat with his arms folded looking neither to right nor left as he spoke now of the two dead cops.

"Some job, huh," Rochford said. "Schaffer's got a lot of kids. I remember his wife's a school crossing guard. At least she was the last time I knew."

Sergeant Robert Schaffer, Star 824, was forty-eight years old, just a year older than Rochford. They had been on Okinawa together in World War II.

Now Schaffer was dead, along with Detective Jerome Stubig, forty. Rochford and Kelly had found their bodies on the third floor of the building.

Kelly explained how they died when he was standing on the street corner. He didn't have to explain it again, because you'd never forget the look on his face as he said it the first time.

"It appears Kulak emptied a carbine into them at close range," Kelly said.

"Where did the bullets hit them?"

"I think it was about the area of the head," Kelly said quietly as though he didn't want to let the words come out. The big car moved easily along the Dan Ryan Expressway heading north for the Central Police Station at 11th and State.

Rochford had emerged from Okinawa as a hero, winning the Bronze Star with Oak Leaf Cluster. Now he was a hero again, but it was sitting like ashes on his tongue. He had been in charge and two of his men were dead. Others had been wounded.

"The thing you have to do is to get the shooting stopped," Rochford said now, almost talking to himself. "When I got there, he was shooting and throwing those bombs. I've never seen anything like it. Well, we got the shooting stopped and then we got his family on the walkie-talkies to start talking to him.

"From that point on, nobody was hurt. The thing you have to watch out for is that all along the line you have people urging you to 'charge him.' "That isn't the way to do it at all. You have to wait."

"You have to get a plan."

"That's right," said Kelly. "Anytime you're gonna charge, you have to figure that some men are expendable. You can't think that way."

"I knew you were right behind me," Rochford said now to Kelly. "I could tell it as I was running through that open space."

"That's a funny thing about it," Kelly said. "Here we are in charge and running out there like that. But that's the way it is. You can't ask the men to do something unless you're willing to do it yourself."

"Once we got into the building, it was just a matter of getting his confidence," Rochford said. "First we were on the floor below him and then I was at the foot of the stairs and he was standing at the top with the .45 automatic in his hand."

"What did you think when you saw him?" Kelly asked.

"I tell you the truth—I didn't know whether he was gonna shoot me or shoot himself," Rochford said.

"That's the fourth time I've taken guns away from guys like that. This one wasn't the toughest, though. I'll never forget the carpenter. He was really a problem."

Rochford was silent as the limousine passed White Sox Park. Traffic on the Dan Ryan was light.

"I suppose when we get downtown we should call in all the newspaper guys and give them the full story," he said.

"That's right," Sullivan said. It's his job to get the stories that make policemen look good into the papers as often as possible.

This night they had looked good.

CHAPTER 2

NO PLACE TO HIDE

THE DEATH OF MR. WEE FOLKS

If you are going to cover crime in the streets in Chicago, you will find yourself on the scene of many murder-robberies like this one.

Usually, they are reported in two or three paragraphs and used as filler on the obituary page. But there is a strong story in every one of them. This one was different from most, though. This time the gunman was caught and convicted.

Nathan, thirteen, tall for his age and with big luminous eyes, had never seen a man die. But now as Nathan peered through the window of the toy store on East 79th, there was Mr. Wee Folks on his back in the aisle near the cash register. The eyes of Mr. Wee Folks were closed.

"I thought maybe he just fell down and knocked over all those Barbie Dolls," Nathan said, "but then I saw Mrs. Wee Folks and I knew it was more than just that. Mrs. Wee Folks had this funny look in her eyes. Her mouth was open like she was screaming but the door to the store was closed so I couldn't hear anything.

"That's when I looked at Mr. Wee Folks again. He wasn't moving at all. He looked like he was asleep with his arms over his head. But I knew he wasn't sleeping. Right then I knew he was dead . . . and that's when I started running."

But for Mrs. Belle Lazar there was no place to run. All she could do was stand there looking at the body of her slain husband, Emanuel, sixty, and wait for the police and ambulance to arrive.

The Lazars had been running the Wee Folks Toy Shop longer

than anyone could remember. When the neighborhood turned black and the other white store owners moved out, Emanuel Lazar stayed.

He had no fear of remaining because he felt everyone in the neighborhood was his friend. They were, too, but the man who came into the store Friday afternoon was driving a black Caddy, and the license plates had been issued in Indiana, which is a long way from East 79th.

"This man came in and he said he wanted to get some toys for his baby," Mrs. Lazar told police, still unable to believe what had happened. So Emanuel went to the rear of the store with him. A few minutes later they came back to the front. Emanuel put two toys on the counter next to the cash register and the two of them were standing in the aisle. Suddenly, the man ordered my husband to put up his hands. Then before he could take any money the man began shooting. He kept on shooting."

Emanuel Lazar was shot four times in the chest and once in each arm. The force of the bullets knocked him over backwards, and he landed amid a small army of differently dressed Barbie Dolls.

The news spread rapidly along the street, and one of the first to hear about it was Joe Harrill, thirty, who operates the drug store just a few doors west.

"I just can't understand what's happening," he said. "A couple of weeks ago a man came in here with a gun, too, and tried to hold us up. You know what? I have this crazy girl working at the cash register and she refused to give him any money. Finally, when some other customers came in, the guy just cursed her and made a break for it."

Harrill had talked to Lazar only hours before the shooting.

"We were talking about holdups," he said. "There have been a lot of them on this street lately. All of us are worried. About a week ago someone threw a rock through Mr. Lazar's window. I told him he should put an iron grate over it like I have over mine.

" 'The day I have to do something like that,' Mr. Lazar told me, 'That's the day I'm gonna go out of business.' "

The men from the crime lab were in the store now moving around the Mother Goose books and the dolls and toy pistols, measuring angles and looking for fingerprints.

It was getting dark and the red neon lights of the sign in front of the building were blinking on and off.

There was a crowd of several dozen black youngsters in front of the store now and all of them were talking loudly about the death of Mr. Wee Folks.

"And he was such a nice man," said Columbus Murphy, sixteen. "I bet Mrs. Wee Folks is gonna close that store for sure now. We won't have any toy store 'round here no more."

It was almost two hours after the shooting. A big car pulled into a parking lot next to the toy store and Mrs. Lazar alighted slowly, returning from the police station.

A small woman with gray hair, she was wearing a black fur coat and blue slacks. Over her right arm was slung the red plaid blanket with which she had tried to warm her husband's body. Mrs. Lazar headed for the toy store to answer more questions for the homicide detectives.

The knot of black youngsters quieted as they saw her coming. You could tell they wanted to tell her that somehow it would be all right. But they didn't have the words. Nobody else did, either.

They watched, noses pressed to the windows, as Mrs. Lazar went to the aisle where the shooting had taken place. The Barbie Dolls were still strewn on the floor as they had been when her husband lay dying.

Nathan stood there watching the woman he knew as Mrs. Wee Folks tell the story again.

"You got to do somethin' for me," Nathan said to a man alongside him. "You got to promise not to use my name and address in your paper.

"If you do, that man's gonna come and find me and kill me sure."

That was February 1970—the death of a sixty-year-old white man who had run a store in the neighborhood more than 25 years and who believed everyone was his friend.

It came to an end in August of 1971 in the courtroom of Criminal Court Judge James J. Mejda.

On trial for the murder was Daryl Cannon, twenty-one, a six-foot-one-inch black man who reputedly had been a hit man for the Black P. Stone Nation and—ironically—a police informant on the activities of gang leader Jeff Fort.

At the conclusion of a six-day trial, Assistant States Attorney Joseph Witkowski reviewed the state's evidence.

He explained to the jury how Cannon had walked into the store and asked for a doll for a three-month-old child.

Mrs. Lazar had become suspicious and put her hand on the burglar alarm.

"You recall," Witkowski said calmly, "how Mrs. Lazar then heard her husband come from the rear of the store. You remember how she testified that Cannon said, 'Don't move or I'll shoot' and shot six times before he had stopped talking."

Witkowski whirled around to face Cannon, who sat erect in a chair next to his attorney.

"This man is a consummate liar," Witkowski shouted. "Look at his face. Do you see any sympathy or remorse for what he did? He's so low he has to climb to get to the bottom."

Amazingly, or perhaps just by reflex action, Cannon nodded his head in seeming agreement.

"He shot a little man, and by the time we find the gun he already has it reloaded. He's an ice-cold-blooded killer and the evidence shows he should never be allowed back on the street again."

The State's identification of Cannon as the guilty man was easy to follow. They had, Witkowski explained, heard that one of the Main 21 of the Black P. Stones was involved.

They brought pictures of the Main 21 to Mrs. Lazar and two other witnesses, who picked out Cannon with no hesitation.

But Cannon's side of the story was an impressive one as related by Jack Gerber, one of the most flamboyant lawyers in the city.

Pacing angrily in seeming outrage in front of the jury box, Gerber outlined a story of the police frame-up of a man who had been one of their chief informants but who had outlived his usefulness.

"My client went to the Gang Intelligence Unit and told them there was a rumble on the street and that both he and his grandmother were going to get hit because he had been informing on Jeff Fort," Gerber said."

"And what did they tell him? They told him there was no way out. They told him he must go along with them. If not, either they would get him or the gang would."

Gerber told them the policeman who testified against Cannon was not to be believed: "If he weren't a policeman he might be a thief and a murderer."

Gerber paced around to the other side of the court and placed his hand on Cannon's shoulder.

"Do I believe my client is telling the truth?" Gerber said. "I honestly don't know. But the police believed him when he was their informer. And I say to you now that it is better to let a guilty man go free than to send an innocent man away." Gerber moved around the room again to conclude his argument directly in front of the jury. "And now they not only want you to find him guilty," he said hoarsely, "but they want you to become murderers, too, by giving him the death penalty."

Cannon shook his head as if wondering at the injustice of it all.

A little while later, Judge Mejda had finished his charge to the jurors and sent them to deliberate on the verdict. As Judge Mejda outlined it they had three choices.

They could find Cannon innocent. Second, they could find him guilty of murder. Third, they could find him guilty of murder with a recommendation for the death penalty. Once the jury left the courtroom, Gerber's anger and outrage died.

"I never had a chance," Gerber said, smiling. "When you can't gain ground, you punt. He's one of the big triggermen and everybody knows it. I was just in there pitching, that's all."

Witkowski sat at a table in the court looking tired and drawn.

"I think we made a strong case," he said. "But you can never tell what a jury will do. You never know what they'll do about a death penalty. "But these people have got to make the choice. It's their neighborhoods that are being destroyed."

There were only a handful of people in the courtroom at the close of the trial. One was the defendant's grandmother. She looked very old and tired, but so had Mrs. Lazar when she testified.

It was three hours before the jury returned and announced a verdict had been reached.

The foreman of the jury stood up and handed a piece of paper to the court clerk. Jedge Mejda ordered Cannon to stand.

Then they read the verdict. It said that the jury had found him guilty of murder in the death of Mr. Wee Folks and that they were recommending the death penalty.

Watching Cannon standing there without expression, I couldn't help but remember what a man named Edmund Adams had said to me about Mr. Wee Folks there on that freezing sidewalk, back in February.

"You know something?" Adams said.

"He was one of the best sons of bitches on this street."

WHERE THE FIX IS—THEY PAY THEIR DUES

*The people who supply heroin to the pushers have gotten us all
into a hell of a spot. If we ever do get out, it will be only because
tough guys like Joe Corcoran and Wilbur Campbell worked their
hearts out.*

The lower part of the walls were covered with a bilious green
tile. The folding chairs lining the long corridor were cheaply made.
Some were orange. Others were green.

There is a reprint of a poem on the wall. It reads:

> *I do my thing and you do your thing,*
> *I am not in this world to live up to*
> *your expectations,*
> *And you are not in this world to live up*
> *to mine.*
> *You are you and I am I,*
> *And if by chance we find each other,*
> *It's beautiful.*
>
> Frederick S. Perls

There was a Coke machine at one end of the hall. Free coffee
was being served in one of the rooms.

Sitting in the chairs in the hall that now seemed like a stalled
subway train in a tunnel were thirty-six admitted junkies.

Some were sweating. Others had pulled their overcoats over
themselves like blankets to ward off the chills. A few were grimac-
ing from the pains in their stomachs. All going through heroin
withdrawal.

And all were sitting in their chairs at 8:45 A.M. Monday at the
Illinois Drug Abuse program's central intake station at 1919 West
Taylor. They remained there, taking tests and going through interviews, until 6 P.M. before receiving the methadone fix they needed
to get through the night.

The big black guy with the fur coat seemed high and he had
everyone's attention. He was bragging about being a pimp and how
three prostitutes were making him nearly $500 a day.

But then his tone changed abruptly and the sweat broke out on his forehead.

"Oh man," he said, "I'm so tired of rippin' around. I'm tired of stickin' myself and tryin' to outsmart the next man and I'm fed up with the ———— up to here.

"I just want to be normal for a while."

There wasn't a sound in the long corridor as the other junkies directed their attention to the big man.

"I'm here because I finally just got scared," he said. "I don't want to go to jail, and the only way I can stay out is to give it up."

There was still no one else willing to talk, and so he continued.

"You know what it is to hurt twenty-four hours a day for two weeks? It's been that way with me, waitin' that long to get on the methadone program.

"The pain, man, I just can't even touch my sides, they hurt so much."

The big man put his two large hands to his side and then grimaced.

"My wife brought me to a hospital emergency room Sunday because the pain got so bad. They put me on the table. I just lay there. I couldn't move, I hurt so.

"The nurse, she took one look at me, and saw the marks on my arms. 'You ain't sick,' she said. 'You just a junkie.' "

The big man and the others were enrolling in the methadone program as their last-ditch solution to kicking junk. Methadone is long-acting narcotic that has to be taken only once a day to relieve withdrawal symptoms.

Addicts can get it free, thus relieving the necessity to hustle on the street for ways to satisfy heroin habits that cost them an average of $75 to $150 a day.

The doses are supervised by doctors. After the patient gets the heroin out of his system, the doctors reduce the supply of methadone gradually. If the cure works, an addict of twenty years can be cured in perhaps three years.

But none of it comes easy.

"You have to pay a little dues, man," Wilbur Campbell explained a little later in the day.

Campbell paid his. He was a junkie until he was forty-two. He kicked the habit, and now he is one of the most valuable men on the staff. In charge of dispensing methadone to addicts, Campbell works more than sixty hours a week at his job.

"It isn't easy to kick," Campbell said, "especially if a dude is carryin' a stick [shooting with a needle] when he comes in.

"You got to figure the average man has been using drugs seven days a week for twenty years or so when he comes here. He's got a whole life style built up around it.

"His friends are all into it and it's awful tough for him to quit unless he changes his whole environment. Only if he has the desire will he make it."

Campbell is warm and friendly, but he doesn't smile when he talks about dope.

"You can't tell anything by the way they act the first day. They're so scared and sick they'll do anything to get a fix. It's how they act in the weeks to come that will tell it.

"They got to come here six days a week and they got to take urine tests three times a week to prove they're stayin' clean. It's when those things start happenin' that you know they're really sincere."

The administrative director of the clinic on Taylor is Joe Corcoran, who, unlike most of the people who work in the clinic, was never an addict. But he has worked around them enough to know the ropes.

He is a wiry guy with a mustache and a broken nose that makes him look tough but with eyes that give away his compassion.

During a lull in the middle of the afternoon, Corcoran sat alone in his office.

"You know, I've found this much out about addicts," he said. "When they get cleaned up and off the dope, most of them turn out to be the most sensitive, talented people you could imagine.

"They'd have to be sensitive. How else could they understand everybody else on the street so well all those years they spent ripping people off to support their habits?"

Corcoran is proud of the fact that most addicts can now be admitted to the methadone program within a week of their application.

"You hate to tell them to go away," Corcoran said, "you just hate it. When Wilbur Campbell came on the program we were so short-staffed, so low in funds, that he had to wait nine months."

"Do you know what that means? That's like telling a man to go and shoot up for awhile until you're ready for him.

"And that's such a risky thing. It does something to your head to work up the guts to walk in here. Everytime we have to tell people to go away we run the risk of losing them forever.

"How do we know how long a man has to live?"

The methadone, mixed with orange juice, was passed out in little paper cups shortly before supper time. It was dark outside now, and a cold wind was blowing.

The big man in the fur coat had a smile on his face.

"They tell me this stuff takes about two hours to catch hold," he said. "I'm gonna celebrate. I came as close to being in the county jail today as I ever want to be. My life is gonna be better now."

SIX HOURS OF HELL

It was the early morning rush hour on October 30, 1972. An Illinois Central railroad commuter express slammed into the rear of a local commuter train. Both trains were packed to capacity. When the toll was counted there were 44 dead and more than 300 injured. It was the worst train wreck in Illinois history.

The most dramatic single story of all was the six hour ordeal of two seventeen-year-old girls who were the last ones to be rescued from the wreckage.

"Please help us," Patricia cried.

Firefighter Billy Nolan from Snorkel Squad No. 1 heard the voice coming from the front end of the train.

This was the second Illinois Central train, the one that had slammed into the rear of the doubledeck highliner at 27th St. Monday morning.

Nolan made his way into the mangled wreckage. There were two girls there and they were pinned side by side.

"Are you in pain?" Nolan asked.

"I'm numb," Patricia said. "I can't feel my legs."

"Can you get us out?" Lisa asked. "Are we going to live?"

"Don't worry girls," Nolan said. "We have lots of equipment here. We'll get you out. We'll keep you safe."

The two girls, Patricia Wysmierski, 17, of 3446 S. Green Bay, and Lisa Tuttle, 17, of 8413 S. Colfax, had both been sitting in the front seat of the train, directly behind the motorman.

When the car in which Patricia and Lisa sat telescoped itself into the modern highliner, the impact of the crash flattened their seat.

Now they were pinned underneath the weight of the steel bulkhead of the motorman's cab and the pressure from the pushed-in front end of the train.

On either side of Patricia and Lisa were a middle-aged man and woman. They had died instantly. But the two girls didn't know this and no one ever told them.

Fire Captain John Wiendle approached the girls seconds after Nolan.

"Billy," he said. "You stay with these girls. It's gonna be awhile before we can get them out. Stay with them, Billy. Keep talking to them.

"If you don't they'll panic. If they go into shock, we'll lose them for sure. Stay with them, Billy."

Nolan went back to the girls.

"Did we crash?" Patricia asked.

"Yes," Nolan said. "I'm afraid you did."

"The last we remember," Lisa said, "was the motorman opening the door of the cab and telling us we were going to crash."

Wiendle is Nolan's boss on Snorkel Squad 1. He has been a fireman 23 years and he has been at many disasters. Wiendle was one of the first firefighters on the scene in 1950 when 33 persons lost their lives when a streetcar collided with a fuel truck at 63d and State.

He knows how fear can grip people who lay helplessly trapped after accidents occur.

Wiendle walked back to the girls. Patricia reached up her hand and gripped him around the wrist. Patricia's grip was surprisingly strong.

"Don't leave me," Patricia said. "You're not going to leave me, are you?"

"Don't worry, kid," Wiendle said. "We're not going to leave you. We'll get you out. I promise you that."

Wiendle turned and walked over to a spot a few feet away where Chief Deputy Fire Marshal Curtis W. Volkamer was waiting.

"Curt," Wiendle said, "those two kids are wedged in pretty good.

We're gonna have to be very careful with this job. We have the tools. We'll lift the door off them just a little bit at a time. Then we'll shore it up and move it up a few more inches."

Volkamer agreed. Then Volkamer departed to direct rescue operations at other critical points of the scene.

Wiendle returned to Patricia and Lisa. He explained to them that an aluminum blanket was going to be placed over their heads. He told them that it was being done so they wouldn't be burned or be overcome by fumes when the other firemen began using acetylene torches to cut the steel that was holding them captives.

"You won't be alone," Wiendle said. "Billy Nolan, here, is going to be under the blankets with you. I'm putting him in there with you because he's the gabbiest guy we have at our station and besides that he's got seven kids of his own."

Just before the aluminum blanket was placed over the girls, Dr. Joseph A. Cari, one of the Fire Department's physicians, stepped forward and gave each girl an injection to kill pain.

Shortly after the blankets were placed over the girls, Lisa looked at Billy Nolan and asked:

"Am I going to be all right? Am I going to have my legs?"

Nolan told Lisa not to worry. He assured her she was going to be all right.

Wiendle's voice came through to the girls now from the outside.

"We're going to use the torches now," he said. "If it gets hot let us know right away. We're using a hose to run water on you all the time to keep the heat down. If you hear any screeching noises, that will be the equipment we're using to pull steel apart.

"Girls, we're going to tell you about every noise before you hear it. Don't worry now. We have this thing under control. You're going to be safe. It may take a little time, but you're going to be safe."

"Please hurry," Patricia called back. "Please get us out as soon as you can."

It went on this way for two hours.

Fire Department Chaplain Matthew McDonald made his way under the aluminum cover about this time.

"Girls," he said, "I'm here to administer the last rites of the church."

Patricia glanced over at Nolan in panic.

"Isn't that what they give you when you're going to die?" she asked.

This was a tense moment for Nolan. His stomach knotted up but he thought quickly.

Nolan gave the two girls a smile.

"That may be the way it is with some chaplains," Nolan said, "but this guy just needs the practice. Go along with him, won't you?"

Twice more during the six hours that Patricia and Lisa lay trapped, it became necessary to administer more morphine injections to kill the pain.

Outside, Wiendle and Chief Volkamer and more than a dozen other firemen worked ever so carefully, making sure the huge weight was pulled off the girls bit by bit.

Rescuers had two concerns. If they lifted weight off and it fell back, the girls would be killed. If they lifted the weight off too quickly, that could kill the girls, too, because the weight of the train was now acting as a tourniquet on their injured legs.

Finally, at 1:40 P.M.—almost six hours after the crash—Patricia called out one more time: "Are we coming out soon?"

The aluminum cover was pulled back and the light came through to the girls. It was like being removed from a locked closet.

Wiendle stood there smiling. So did the dozens of other firemen.

"You're coming out right now," Wiendle said. "It may hurt a little so grit your teeth, girls. You're coming out."

Within minutes, Patricia and Lisa were placed on stretchers and carried to waiting helicopters. They were the last survivors to be rescued. The flight to Billings Hospital was a short one. For Patricia and Lisa, this part of their ordeal was over.

HE WANTED TO DIE

This piece explains itself. Read it and you won't be surprised to know the pilot put a gun to his head and killed himself the next day.

In the pitch darkness, firemen in raincoats stood at the southern tip of the Meigs Field runway staring down into the swirling black water.

The wind blew so fiercely the firemen in the raingear and the policemen in short-sleeved blue shirts braced themselves against it in order to remain in one place.

The water on the runway was ankle deep.

Perhaps 50 uniformed men stood there. Each one stared silently at the bobbing searchlights of the police and fire rescue boats less than 50 yards offshore.

Two policemen had just walked up to four firemen who were among the first on the scene. The policemen held their shoulders up the way people always do to keep off the rain.

"What happened?" asked one of the policemen.

"It's just silly as hell," a fireman said. "He came right down this runway and went off it and right into the lake."

"Where's the plane?" the policeman asked.

"Well, it should be right about where the boats are. But with this wind it's hard to tell."

John Casey, the 1st District fire marshal, stood about 25 feet away from the group of firemen and policemen. The rain was falling so heavily that even the raincoated firemen sought shelter next to their fire trucks.

Lightning occasionally lit up the area, showing the outlines of McCormick Place about 150 yards to the right of where the rescue workers were waiting.

Casey talked about what had happened with two other fire department officers in white fire hats.

"The pilot is out," he said. "He's safe. They picked him up in a boat and took him to Mercy Hospital, I think."

"Who was he?" someone asked.

"I don't know yet," Casey said, "But I'm afraid there's people still in that plane. I'll know more when the ambulance gets back."

Casey and all the other firemen and policemen huddled in the rain, waiting. There was nothing anyone could do. The plane was in the water and the water, though only 25 feet deep, was so black and so choppy, that even the powerful searchlights on the boats were no help.

A helicopter hovered above. The noise of the wind and the rain, and the crackling of the lightning and the thunder were so disorienting that no one noticed the helicopter until it was directly overhead.

"What the hell is he doing?" one fireman asked. "He can't see anything, either."

Casey received a message that the ambulance was heading back down the runway. He walked to the edge of the runway and signaled for it to stop in front of him.

The driver, Fireman Eugene Chucta, got out.

"Yes, sir," Chucta said. "The pilot said he got out through the door. He says he got his belt off as the plane was going into the water. As soon as he hit he says he opened the door and got out.

"He says the plane went right down. He was in the water right above the plane when the police and fire boat picked him up."

"What was he trying to do?" Casey asked.

"He told me he was trying to beat the storm. He wanted to get back to Davenport, Iowa, where he lives."

"How is he?"

"He's all right. But I could see he was going into shock. He told me, 'My wife and my three kids are in the plane. I saw them when I went through the door. They were still in there with their seat belts on. It all happened so fast.'

"Chief, when he said that I could see in his eyes how he felt. When he told me that I felt the same way. God, I felt sorry for him."

"What's his name?" Casey asked.

Chucta consulted a clipboard, which he held inside the ambulance so it wouldn't get wet.

"Dave Robert Utroska, 30. He lives at 112 W. Marlow Street in Davenport."

"Did he say anything else?" Casey asked. "Did he explain what happened?"

"He told me he just ran out of runway. From then on he just kept saying over and over: 'I should never have taken off. I should never have taken off. My wife and my kids are still in there. I saw them. They were still strapped in. I saw them as I went out the door.'"

Casey walked away and went off the pavement and onto the grass that runs to the edge of the field.

He stood there staring out at the lake and the rescue boats. By now the plane had been located and the scuba divers were bringing up the four bodies.

A second fire department officer in a white hat walked over and stood next to him. Firemen see death more than the rest of us. They can handle it better.

"I never get over the wonder of it," the second officer said. "You never know who's gonna die. There were five people in that plane. How could anyone tell which one of them would come out of it alive?"

CHAPTER 3

LOVE LETTERS

The best thing about having a column is that you can write about people who you'd never otherwise be able to get into the paper. These people are here only because I thought you might like to meet them, too.

JACK BEGUN

"The thing about me," Jack Begun was saying, "is that people don't go for me right at the start. Maybe I come on too strong or somethin' and so that puts them off.

"But, after awhile, I start growin' on people and they love me. Take my grocer. He's a very important man in my life and at first he couldn't stand me. But I need him to cash checks and by now I've grown on him to the point where he thinks nothin' of cashing a hundred-dollar personal check.

"The reason this is important is I have to go in there and get dough from him every so often to make a deposit in my checking account to back paper that would otherwise start bouncing very high in the air in other places around town."

The sheer artistry involved in these financial manipulations is a scource of joy to Jack Begun, who was standing now at the bar in Billy Goat's tavern with a tall glass of seltzer in his hand.

Begun does not drink and he does not inhale when he smokes. But in all other areas, he is the most outrageous man you are ever likely to encounter.

He walks fast. He talks fast. He thinks fast, and whenever you're around him all you can see is the continual whirring of his hands in the air as nonstop dialogue keeps bombarding you.

He's a strain. But there's one thing you have to give him. He does grow on you.

Begun will not reveal his age. He sports a year-round sunlamp tan and there is no gray in his hair but he does have mileage on him and this he admits.

He grew up on Chicago's West Side with what he likes to call "the Mafia mustache guys" and the "tough Jews" like Barney Ross and Jackie Fields, the prize fighters, and U.S. District Court Judge Abraham L. Marovitz, who was the smartest kid in Begun's Riis Elementary School class.

Begun went on to become a star Maxwell Street clothing salesman, a shrewd boxing manager and promoter (the Zale-Graziano fight in Chicago Stadium), a restaurant owner, a gossip columnist for a throwaway weekly, a theatrical flack, and now back again to being a star clothing salesman.

Once he even ran for mayor against Dick Daley. This was in 1963, and it all started when King Solomon, one of Jack's old fighters, came to him with the proposition.

"There's a guy out on the West Side who's got it in for Daley," the King told Begun. "My guy's got some good action goin' and Daley's been leanin' on him.

"So my guy's willing to invest $35,000 in your campaign if you run for mayor against Daley. He'll give you a salary of $400 a week, buy you lots of billboards, and give you a brand new gold-painted car with your name on the sides in big letters."

Begun takes up the story:

"So now I'm runnin' for mayor and I'm runnin' very good, too. I'm gettin' some ink in the columns and everything is nice. I am also collectin' the $400 a week and this is even nicer.

"Well, one day I get a call to go out to see my sponsor. He's in the hospital but he's tellin' me how the car has been ordered and I'm gonna get it as soon as they can put the special paint job on it.

"Next week I get another call. My guy ain't in the hospital no more. He's dead. My campaign is over and I'm lookin' for a job again."

Jack took a quick sip from his glass of seltzer water. Quick, so that nobody could get a chance to talk, just enough so that his pipes got a chance to cool a bit.

"That reminds me a' somethin'. You know this death thing used to get me . . . tear me up inside. Like the other day my friend the Baron and I were supposed to go to Dick Axman's funeral.

"Dick was my friend a long time, and he was very good for the wrestling shows during his time. First thing that happened, the Baron couldn't go. He got a contract that morning to hit some guy over the head with a chain to remind the guy he still owed $1,300 on a note.

"Well, I couldn't blame him because those jobs don't come so often anymore and the Baron has to show how dependable he is.

"Wait a minute, now, I'm gettin' away from what I wanted to say. It's about this dyin' thing. You see, I thought about it again the other day when I went to see them plant poor Dick and I told his widow about it and maybe it was some consolation.

"You see, I've realized that we're all comin' back again. So as much as I miss Dick now, I know he's comin' back for another time around.

"Of course, next time he may come back as a cow or a horse and maybe I won't recognize him right away, but sooner or later I'll know who he is and it'll be nice to have him around again."

A man started to ask Begun if he felt the same way about money but there wasn't enough time for the question to be completed.

"Now wait a minute," Begun said, "I'm doin' the talkin' and it's very impolite to interrupt when a man is tryin' to give you the benefit of something he's been thinking about for a long time."

He hunched up his shoulders and launched into the subject of money.

"You see, I've been what I call a little millionaire two times and I've now been broke three times but I'm on the way back up. I'm gonna make it all the way back, too, because I'm the greatest clothing salesman there is.

"I'm every bit as good now as I was back in the old days on Maxwell Street when everybody knew I was the best sandwich man on the street.

"What's a sandwich man? What's a' matter with you? Ain't you ever been anyplace? All right, I'll tell you what a sandwich man is.

"We used to have two blue suits with a chalk stripe. One was wool and we had thirty dollars in it. The other was cotton and we had nine dollars in it.

"So you get these smart guys who want to come to Maxwell

Street and talk down the salesman and walk away with a bargain. All right. They're lookin' at the wool suit and they don't want to pay no thirty dollars for it.

"So I keep goin' down with them and finally they get under twenty dollars and they think they're pretty shrewd by this time but I got a surprise for them.

"The minute they go under twenty dollars in their negotiations, they're gettin' the sandwich. As soon as it comes time to put the suit in the box I pull the switch and they're walkin' out the door with the cotton suit which should sell for nine bucks, and that's what I mean by givin' them the sandwich."

There was a circle of half-a-dozen listeners around Begun now. This is not unusual because he attracts crowds wherever he goes and he never fails to put on his show.

One of them was a new face, however, and Begun didn't let an opportunity for some action slip by.

"Look," he said extending his hand toward the stranger, "my name is Jack Begun and I'm gonna give you my business card. I want you to come out to the store and see me and I'm gonna fix you up with a nice suit.

"Look. We only live once and that suit you got on right now ain't doin' a damn thing for you. So come see me and we'll do a little business."

The man did not smile, but he did shake hands. It looked as though it was going to take Begun at least another half hour of nonstop talking to grow on this guy.

ZIGGY CZAROBSKI

The clock on the wall behind the bar in Johnny Lattner's Marina City Restaurant read 6:16 P.M. Lattner was sitting on a stool in front of the cash register. He looked unhappy.

Lattner was peering toward a spot about fifteen feet in front of the bar where Zigmont Czarobski was poised on one knee singing a song called "April Showers" in his best Al Jolson manner.

Ziggy, who weighs in at three-hundred-plus, was once an All-American tackle at Notre Dame. Within the hour, however, Ziggy was scheduled to face one of the sternest tests of his forty-seven years. At 7 o'clock, Ziggy would walk into a place called Sully's on the Near North Side, step to the microphone in front of a group called the Will Mercier Affair, and give his first major singing performance, a repertory of Al Jolson tunes.

Ziggy had a bar strainer up to his mouth, using it as he would later use the mike as he moved toward the close of his last warm-up tune.

"Whenever April Showers come along . . ."

With this Ziggy removed his large Panama hat and stretched out his huge arms to their full extension, giving the nonexistent audience his best shot.

He looked over toward Lattner with a big smile on his face and his dark brown eyes twinkling.

Lattner did not smile back.

"Ziggy," said Lattner, "I'm really a little bit afraid about this. I don't know how it's going to come off. Quite frankly, you are not in the best of voices tonight."

"Nonsense, Lattner," replied Ziggy. "For an ex-Notre Dame football player you have remarkably little self-assurance. Let's get into the car and head for the field of battle. Mark my words, we have absolutely nothing to fear except fear itself."

That's Ziggy, telling the 1953 Heisman Trophy winner about fear. Ziggy seemed as elated by the prospect of the struggle to come as Lattner was deflated.

"Lattner," said Ziggy as the car headed north, "I regard this as the culmination of my singing career, a career which you well know got its start when I led the chorus for both "The Mikado" and "The Chocolate Soldier" while in Mount Carmel High School."

Lattner did not reply, raising his eyes to the heavens in a look of dismay.

"In fact," said Ziggy, "I feel just as elated tonight as I did for the senior prom at Notre Dame. You weren't around then but it was quite a success, too. You see, I saw this advertisement in the papers for a hearse for sale at $150, and I thought it would be a hell of a way to take my friends to the prom.

"I didn't have much money at the time, so I borrowed the dough from a friendly bookie in Elkhart and made a deal with George Connor and Marty Britz, my teammates, that they would chip in fifty dollars apiece. You know that part where they put the box, don't you? Well, I removed it and bought a secondhand couch from Brother Bookstore for five bucks so that we could all sit there in style.

"At the last minute I also had a siren installed, and let me tell you, we made quite a splash arrival at that prom. The only thing was that the prefect of discipline took an exceptionally dim view of the entire proceedings. He ordered me to sell the hearse, instantly, and I had to let it go for sixty dollars the very next day."

There are of course many stories about Ziggy, many of them equally colorful, and it was obvious Lattner had heard them all before.

He had heard the one about Ziggy getting off the train in California the first time he went out there with a Notre Dame team to play the University of Southern California. Ziggy looked around for a few minutes and then said:

"My God, I've never seen so many cars with California license plates."

Lattner had also heard the one about Ziggy bragging he had "graduated magna cum laude or whatever that means in Spanish," or the fact that Ziggy swears that the only time he ever went near the library was to sit on the steps as a senior to pose for a picture for the yearbook.

Lattner was parking in front of Sully's place now, and the two ex-football players climbed out of the car and headed for Ziggy's debut. Waiting inside were nearly two hundred people, all of whom had paid twenty-five dollars that would go toward the expenses of the International Special Olympics to be held here for the benefit of retarded children.

Among the first to greet them were members of the Chicago Bears and Cubs as well as such old Notre Damers as Paul Hornung and George Connor, the man from Ziggy's hearse. Ziggy and Connor shook hands warmly and then Ziggy laid it on him.

"Connor," he said, "I know you're a rich man now, and so I'd like to remind you that you still owe me fifty dollars for that hearse."

HANK OETTINGER

"Well, of course, the women are right, God bless them," said Hank Oettinger, who has always been my favorite demonstrator.

Hank was out there in the broiling sun, giving his support to the women's liberation movement just as he has marched and picketed in every demonstration worth the name since the 1930s.

"Men and women have exactly the same enemies," Hank said. "The enemy is the system. Why, I bet there are a hundred women in this crowd who'd make a better mayor than that Democratic machinist over in City Hall.

"Phyllis Diller would be a better Vice President than Agnew, though maybe not as funny."

If you have ever taken part in a demonstration in Chicago, then you have seen Hank Oettinger without knowing it. He's the middle-aged, rotund guy with the small mustache who looks vaguely like Oliver Hardy.

Hank began marching in Milwaukee, in 1932, when the hunger marches were the big thing of the day. He still recalls with pleasure the May Day marches in the late thirties that drew as many as 10,-000 marchers.

"In the 1940s," Hank was saying now, "we had marvelous demonstrations for the Second Front in World War II. Why, one time, we filled Wrigley Field to capacity.

"After the war we had a lot of tough strikes and I marched in the picket lines in them. When we got into the sixties it was the civil rights movement."

There have been many demonstrating highlights in Hank's career, but one of them came because he is such a natural put-on.

It was during a march against segregation in Chicago schools and Hank, who of course was supporting open schools, made up a sign indicating that he was a racial bigot.

Sun-Times photographer Jack Dykinga took his picture and titled it "Bigot." It won a prize.

"I think the greatest demonstrations I've ever been in were at the Democratic Convention," Hank said now. "They were just outstanding. I can't go by Lincoln Park at night without looking up at those lights in the paths and smelling tear gas.

"I'll never forget the speech Dick Gregory made the night he invited everyone to march out to his house with him. He told the crowd that if the young people of Germany had stood up to Hitler that way, there would be millions of Jews who would never have had to die.

"That was picked up by the *New Statesman* of London, but I never saw it printed in an American newspaper."

Hank nodded knowingly. He tends to keep a watchful and critical eye on the Chicago papers, and anything that doesn't meet

Hank's standards is likely to prompt him to sit down and send off a letter.

Hank is even prouder of his letter-writing, in fact, than he is of his demonstrating. I have to admit that he has written some damn good lines from time to time.

Once, Hank referred to Mr. Melvin Laird as "Secretary of Offense" and Hugh Hefner as "Everyman's Bosom Buddy" and Father James Groppi as "Christ on Concrete."

"I'm not the most prolific letters-to-the-editor-writer in the city," Hank said, "but I must have the highest rate of acceptance. Eighty-five percent of them make the paper."

Hank works full time as a linotype operator in a job shop, and he works the evening hours because it gives him all day to take part in demonstrations. His son is a doctor, and Hank is very proud of this.

"He's a good boy," Hank said, "and he loves it because I've still got the courage to show my convictions."

Hank has never been injured in any demonstration, but he has been heckled a lot.

"I bet I've been told a thousand times that I should go back to Russia. All I do is stop and explain to them very politely that I don't know anyone in Russia and I don't speak the language and I'd rather change things here."

Hank chuckled, and his round body bounced up and down.

"Then there are all the people who tell me to go back where I came from. I just tell them that I grew up in Crandon, Wisconsin, and I'm not about to go back to a little town like that unless Daley deports me."

BILL HOBAN, THE BALLOON MAN

Everytime I grow dissatisfied with my lot in life I think about my friend Bill Hoban.

Bill Hoban has the whole ballgame solved. You and me, we keep looking in the mailbox, wondering which creditor is going to pounce on us next.

If we don't pay the bill, the creditor will run to our boss and complain. If we don't borrow money to pay, we're out of a job.

That's not the way it is with Hoban. He solved all those problems. There is no place where you can send a bill to Hoban. In fact, there is no employer to whom you can complain.

Hoban is an independent businessman. He sells balloons for a living.

There are some who say that Hoban lives in an abandoned packing crate. Others maintain he sleeps in the rear booth of O'Rourke's saloon on North Avenue. No one is sure. The only thing I know is that there is no way to reach Hoban.

If he wants to see you, he appears.

Hoban is probably the biggest balloon seller in the United States. He is six feet, three inches tall and weighs 240 pounds. He prides himself on the fact that he is a very physical guy.

His father was a Chicago policeman for thirty-two years. His two brothers are also policemen, one in Chicago, one in Highland Park. Hoban, who is a graduate of the old St. George High School, doesn't often talk to reporters.

"The only scribes I've known," Hoban said, "have been guys who've had no ability to get anything straight.

"I don't know how you're going to write your article but try to get the damn thing right for a change, will you?"

We were sitting at the bar in O'Rourke's, and one of their finest bartenders moved in to ask Hoban about his thirst.

Hoban, it turned out, was thirsty.

This is another good thing about being a balloon salesman. All you have to do to get a cold beer is be thirsty. There is always someone curious enough about the sale of balloons to buy.

"The first thing I want you to do," Hoban said, "is to guarantee that you can run my picture in the paper. My mother has always wondered about whether I'd turn out to be a success in life. I want to send her a picture of me with balloons to show her that I've finally made it.

"She's gone back to Ireland, you know, and I'm sure she'd enjoy it."

Hoban admits his mother doesn't understand his flowing beard. Neither do most policemen who see him peddling his ballons along Rush Street and at Old Town art fairs. I don't understand Hoban's beard, either. It's the fullest beard I've ever encountered.

"Never mind my beard," Hoban said. "I can get away with it. In the first place, I love it dearly. In the second place, I've learned that any man who's carrying balloons can get away with almost anything he wants."

Hoban lifted the stein of dark beer to his lips. In one long draught it was gone.

"Let's have another beer, here," Hoban shouted. "The scribe is buying."

I was, I guess, although I don't remember anyone in the newspaper business being called "scribe" since the days of Horace Greeley.

"I'll tell you my secret," Hoban said, grabbing the new stein in his huge right hand. "I'll tell you how to make a success of selling balloons.

"First of all, you have to have a partner. My partner's name is Marshall Ritchie. He's forty-two. He weighs 110 pounds. He shaves his head and has a goatee. Before Ritchie started selling balloons with me, he won two TV Emmys. I'm not sure whether he won them by himself or for the shows he was associated with.

"But, at any rate, say we're walking south on Rush Street. Well, Ritchie goes on in front, maybe half a block ahead of me.

"Now the kids start walking up to Ritchie, longing for those balloons. They're dying to get one, but by the time their parents realize this, Ritchie is out of the action.

"We know this. That's why I follow a half block behind. By this time the kids are heartbroken and their old man is dying to buy a balloon for them.

"We sell the damn balloons by the hundred. Only trouble we have is dividing the profits. Usually, we go into a saloon and put all the money we have right on the bar.

"Then we start counting. Ritchie gets a five-dollar bill and I get a five-dollar bill. Ritchie gets a one-dollar bill and I get one. Ritchie gets two quarters and I get two quarters.

"Takes a long time that way but at least we know the count's honest."

Hoban, who has a prodigious thirst, had downed another stein by this time. He glanced malevolently toward the end of the bar. Hoban is a man who loves disputes.

"Look at those creeps at the end of the bar, eyeing me," Hoban muttered. "This is the thing I was trying to get across to you in the first place.

"As long as I got those balloons in my hand, I'm all right. Once I go anyplace without them, everybody looks at me like I'm a goddamned hippie."

KOOKY PAUL CARROLL

This column has absolutely no social significance. But I hope you take the time to read it, anyway.

It's about my friend Paul Carroll, a marvelous, tall, kooky man who wears a straw boater and pedals his bicycle from his house on Mohawk Street to his faculty office at the University of Illinois Chicago Circle Campus.

Paul is forty-four years old. Last year his wife presented him with his first son. They called the boy Luke.

"It was March 1970," Paul recalled. "Three weeks after Luke was born, we took him on a trip to the Art Institute.

"As we were walking around this marvelous Brancusi exhibit I found myself talking to Luke, explaining what the sculpture all meant.

"I felt we were at the core of history, of life. It was like being in Plato's 'Paradise,' and that's what I found myself telling Luke."

The rest of us would have let it all drop right there. Not Paul Carroll, however. Paul is a practicing poet and so he went home that night and wrote a poem about the visit.

He called the poem "Ode in a Brancusi Exhibition with Luke Three Weeks Old."

It concludes with the line:

> *Luke, it's lovely here*
> *near the core of the miracle.*

That was the beginning. From that day on, almost every place Paul took little Luke resulted in a poem. They went to the Garfield Park Conservatory, to the Shakespeare Garden at Northwestern University, for walks along Mohawk Street, all over Chicago

By the time Luke was a year old, there were 25 poems, enough for a book.

"There is no message to the poems," Paul says. "All it really shows is that poetry happens on Mohawk Street as well as anywhere else.

"The thing I like about the book most is that it's not pretentious."

But there is great feeling behind the poems.

Take the one Paul calls "On a Line by Rene Char." The line

from the French poet goes, "The oriole enters the capitol at dawn."

From this Paul writes a stanza about watching as Luke lifts his head from his crib for the first time.

> *The song of the wren and sparrow*
> *accumulates*
> *in the dark on Mohawk Street*
> *until gradually cacaphony becomes full-*
> *bodied helping*
> *to celebrate*
> *the resurrection of the skeleton of life.*
> *Luke.*
> *you've taken to attempting to elevate*
> *your head,*
> *sweet periscope.*

The book is called *The Luke Poems.*

Paul wanted to have a cover for the book that would appeal to young people. So he wrote to R. Crumb, one of the most famous underground cartoonists, for permission to use one of his things called "Keep On Truckin," a classic of its kind.

"Crumb wrote back to me telling me that he enjoyed the poems very much. He said that he not only would let me use his cartoon on the cover but that he was particularly happy to do it.

"You see, it turned out that Crumb once lived on Mohawk Street himself."

Paul Carroll is, of course, no stranger to the literary life. He teaches English at the University of Illinois, where he also heads the resident workshop program in creative writing.

He also is a highly respected literary critic whose work has appeared in the *Saturday Review* and the *New Yorker.*

Several years ago he was the editor of *Big Table,* a beatnik magazine that earned the distinction of being temporarily banned from the mails.

That was at a time (1959 to be exact) when the U.S. Post Office was not yet ready for Jack Kerouac and the first ten chapters of William Burroughs' *Naked Lunch,* which Editor Carroll was offering to the public.

But those were different times. Paul Carroll is more contemplative now and quite happy as he says to "celebrate the miracle we call every day."

It's a life so contemplative that he recently came up with a one-line poem describing how it is to be caught in the rain while riding his bike.

The poem is called: "Ode on a Bicycle on Halsted Street in a Sudden Summer Thunderstorm."

The entire poem:

It feels so neat to be a fish again.

This all proves what I said at the start.

Paul Carroll is marvelous, and his presence on the planet assures me the world really won't blow up—in the next few days, anyway.

NEW MEXICO FATS

New Mexico Fats said it first.

As soon as I heard the idea, I knew it was bad news. But Charles O. Finley liked it, and he owned the deciding vote.

Finley is a very big insurance man here, and he is also the owner of the Oakland Athletics baseball team, and he thought the idea was super.

"Here you have this striptease dancer going all around the country," New Mexico Fats said, "and she's leaping onto ballfields, kissing ballplayers, and getting her picture in the national magazines.

"Why don't I just go out tomorrow and get a pants suit and a wig and run out on the field myself and kiss one of your ballplayers? It will blow everyone's mind."

Charlie O. had only one reservation.

"Idea's good," he said, "but why can't we wait until my ball club's on 'Game of the Day'? I'd like to have a national audience."

"Can't do that," New Mexico Fats answered. "I have certain obligations in Chicago and I just can't go running around making free-lance appearances."

New Mexico Fats was certainly right about that. He is, in real life, a very busy man.

So despite the fact that the timing was bad from a publicity standpoint, it was decided to go ahead with the plan.

All Thursday morning, Charlie O. and New Mexico Fats shopped for a gown. It wasn't easy. New Mexico Fats, once a pretty fair tennis player, now weighs in at 260 pounds and stands six foot, two inches tall.

They finally found just what they needed at Lane Bryant. To top the outfit off they purchased a pair of bright yellow flats. The only problem with the shoes was that they were a half size too large and it was necessary to tape them on, the same way sprinters do at track meets.

Once at White Sox park, the two conspirators went to work. They alerted the wire services, all the Chicago newspapers, and the television and radio men.

Even Bob Elson was told about it.

"There's only one thing," they kept saying. "Don't let the Sox managment and Ed Short know about it in advance. He might queer the deal."

Edwin G. Short was the general manager of the White Sox and his job was in jeopardy because the ball club was losing games at a rapid pace. It was a lonely job for him those days because very few people even go to the park to see the inevitable occur.

This is not a condition conducive to promoting a sense of humor, especially since he knows that New Mexico Fats, in real life, is David Condon, sports columnist on the *Tribune*.

Well, at any rate, New Mexico Fats made her appearance in the seventh inning, dashing out from the Oakland Athletics dugout and making right for the club's first baseman, Joe Rudi.

Rudi took one look at the behemoth approaching him in those bright yellow shoes and made for second base.

"Damn it, Rudi," puffed Fats, "stand still. If I have to run all the way to second base, you'll have to carry me back to the dugout."

Rudi halted, dutifully, and Fats grabbed him in the kind of embrace you used to see when people came home after serving thirty-three months in the South Pacific.

"Fats," said Rudi, "if you want me to make it look real good, I'll jump up and you can hold me in your arms."

"You're crazy," Fats said. "If you do that, I'll fall down."

The show lasted less than a minute, and then the Andy Frain ushers moved in and led the 260-pound damsel to the sidelines.

Umpire John Rice rushed over at this point to make sure that law and order was restored. He, too, received a kiss, but only a peck on the cheek.

By this time the ballpark's organist had caught up with the action and swung into a swinging version of "A Pretty Girl Is Like a Melody."

Up in the press box, Ed Short sat, unsmiling.

"My God," Short said, "What's happening to baseball?"

No one answered, but just at this moment, Sox radio announcer Bob Elson came in from the radio booth and tapped Short on the shoulder.

"My God," said Elson, "what's happening to baseball?" Charlie Finley sat there and he looked very happy.

"You have it wrong, gentlemen," he said. "The question you should be asking is, 'What hath God wrought?' "

SAUL ALINSKY

From his desk on the sixteenth floor, Saul Alinsky can lean back in his chair and gaze thoughtfully at the sailboats skittering along Lake Michigan, a quarter mile to the east.

It is doubtful, however, that Saul has ever taken time to indulge himself in this manner. Yacht-gazing is not his passion. Agitating the power structure is the thing he does best, and it has been a full-time thing with Saul ever since he took on Chicago's big meat-packing firms in 1938.

The story of how Saul Alinsky won his battle in the Back of the Yards and his work in Woodlawn, Kenwood, and countless other places around the country is an oft-told and often misunderstood one.

People are not neutral about Alinsky. Some love him, some despise him; and Saul likes it that way. He is a very tough guy who can deliver four-letter words with more striking force than any truck driver you ever met.

He was standing up now behind his desk and firing away, and if you put your hands over your ears it would have been possible to consider him just another intellectual with a doctor's degree from the University of Chicago.

He was well dressed, his hair was cut short, and his black shoes were shined, not too well, but shined.

But there is fire in his eyes and bite to his inflections and he is taking shots at everything that comes to his lightning mind.

"The rhetoric of the Black Panthers hasn't helped matters at all," Saul says. "What has been very unusual is the coolness of the police.

"What I think we're going to see, finally, is black officers in the ghettos and it will happen because the white officers no longer want to go there.

"Know what I think will happen then? The black officers will get shot, too."

Alinsky strode two steps to the side of his desk. He rested one hand on a wall bookshelf.

"The killing will go on until the large elements of the black community have had it as far as crime among themselves is concerned.

"That's when they will clamp down on their own black militant nuts. You see, I happen to believe that white men and black men are equal, and so I see there are as many white nuts as there are black nuts.

"I'll tell you something else. Frankly, the rhetoric of the Panthers is a big pain in the ass."

He went on to tell a story of being interrupted at the start of a speech before a college group recently by a Black Panther in the audience.

"He wanted to make a speech himself and stood up to tell me he was making a point of order. I told him that I had been invited to speak and that parliamentary rules were not in effect. I told him that if he wanted to make a speech he should get his own crowd and go out on the lawn.

"Then I reversed myself and told him I'd give him five minutes to speak on one condition: That he could speak for that length of time without using all that tired rhetoric about white, Fascist, racist pigs.

"But I like the Panthers. I really do. They're nuts, of course, but they're really a fantasy of the senile political paranoid in Washington, J. Edgar Hoover. They haven't got the numbers and they know nothing about revolutionary tactics.

"What kind of revolutionary is it who shouts that all power comes out of the muzzle of a gun when he knows damn well the other side has got all the guns?"

Despite his running battles with the city administration, Alinsky is still turned on by Chicago.

"One day I was flying back here from Detroit," he said. "It was during the riots after King was shot. I could see the smoke rising high in the air.

"I don't know what came over me. I had to go into the men's room and throw up. It was just such a terrible sight.

"I love Chicago and I know Mayor Daley does, too. I know he'll never forgive me for some of the things I've had to do to him, but I still look on him as the last of the old breed of mayors.

"Guys like Cavanagh in Detroit and Lindsay in New York want to use their jobs as a jump-off point. All Daley wants to be is mayor of Chicago and then maybe retire and become Ambassador to Ireland."

Saul halted, as if hesitating about whether to continue with this train of thought. He nodded his head. He would go ahead.

"I've never told this about Daley before," he said, "but it shows you how a twist of fate, a toss of the coin, can change everything for a man.

"On the Monday before the California primary in 1968, Daley was on the phone with Bobby Kennedy. He gave Bobby an unreserved commitment that if Bobby won in California he would back him at the convention against Johnson and Humphrey.

"He assured him that if Kennedy won in California, Daley would make the announcement back here in Chicago on Friday.

"Well, people who were sitting near Daley at Bobby's funeral tell me he was really a stricken man. He was beside himself with grief.

"Daley kept muttering over and over again that a thing like this would never happen in Chicago even if he had to put policemen and soldiers on every corner during the convention.

"Here's how it changes," Alinsky went on. "If the Kennedys are running the show and Abbie Hoffman shows up in Lincoln Park, the Kennedys have the sense to open refreshment stands and let everybody have a good time.

"If the Yippies want to run a pig for President, the Kennedys would have been smart enough to bring in another pig for them and let it be the running mate.

"And this would be the real twist. Daley would have been working for the Kennedys and pulling all his power tactics against Johnson and Humphrey and all the Yippies and radicals would have been cheering Daley on and shouting 'Atta-boy, Dick' at every turn."

We were walking toward the door now; the interview was over.

"But at least it did one thing," Saul said. "It resurrected Tom Hayden and Abbie and Jerry Rubin. They were dead until all that happened.

"That's what a revolutionary learns over and over. You can always depend on the Establishment to do the wrong thing at the right time."

KENOSHA, THE PEDDLER

Kenosha the Peddler is a burly man with a red face, and if you go to watch the Cubs at Wrigley Field very often you've probably passed him dozens of times.

Kenosha sells baseball pennants and those round buttons with ribbons attached and he's been doing this at various ball parks around the country for years.

He's over sixty now and has the gout and so Kenosha doesn't travel much anymore. Now his regular spot is the northwest corner of Clark and Addison, just across the street from the Cubby Bear Lounge.

"The thing is," he was saying the other day, "that you have to get to the corner early to establish that it's yours. Once a peddler has a corner staked out then no one else is likely to move in on it. That kind of thing can cause trouble."

There aren't more than a handful of itinerant peddlers left in Chicago these days, but most of them still work at Wrigley Field.

Ball Park Bennie, for example, and Louie the Louse and The Horsethief are still there.

Peddlers are a breed apart. They don't give their full names, not even to each other. Most of those who work the streets outside Wrigley Field live less than a block away in furnished rooms above stores. They have no telephones. They insert no name cards in their lobby mailboxes.

"In the old days peddling was great," he said. "Now you're out there most of the time hopin' for room rent (which is eight dollars per week in Kenosha's case).

Kenosha and Ball Park Bennie really don't like baseball. The only interest they have in the game is the effect it will have on potential customers.

Kenosha's biggest baseball thrill came the day in 1960 when he made thirty dollars in half an hour selling pennants to Pirate fans in Pittsburgh after the home team won the seventh game of the World Series from the Yankees.

Ball Park Bennie fondly recalls the day Gus Sauer hit three home runs to win a game, 3 to 0, for the Cubs. He remembers it because he sold twenty-five dollars worth of Cubs' pennants in nineteen minutes.

In recent years, however, a new class of baseball fan has developed which comes to the ballpark only when it's too cloudy to go to the beach or when it's ladies day on the golf course or the boat is in drydock or when they find themselves too short in the purse to make it to the track.

And so Kenosha continues to stake out his spot on the sidewalk. So does Ball Park Bennie. They stand out there listening to the cheering inside, hoping the excitement will encourage fans to buy enough pennants to pay the room rent.

STUDS TERKEL

Studs Terkel had been sitting in a hardbacked chair for a little more than five hours. It had been a tough five hours for Studs.

He signed a lot of autographs in copies of his new book. He smiled a lot. He nodded a lot in agreement. He listened a lot.

Maybe the listening was the toughest thing of all for Studs, and this was what made the whole thing so beautiful.

Studs, reputedly the best interviewer in the Western world, doesn't like to listen.

But this was one time Studs had to listen because everyone coming into the Old Town Folklore Center Saturday night came to tell Studs how much he liked the new book, *Hard Times,* all about the Depression.

"You know," Studs was saying, "President Nixon likes to talk about his 'silent majority.' You know what we have here tonight? This is what I call the 'gentle majority.' "

Studs was sitting in a little balcony and down on the main floor in front of him were his fans and even some of the people who are in his book.

There was Hank Oettinger, everybody's favorite demonstrator; Michael Wadleigh, the director of the Woodstock Festival movie; John Crosby, old-time television critic; John the Intellectual Garbage Man; Dynamite Garland, the old stripper, and even Win Stracke, the famous folk singer.

Right now Win was singing on stage, and Steve Telow, the America Firster, who is about as far to the right of Studs and Stracke as you can get, was listening and even trying to sing along with the chorus:

". . . Brother, can you spare a dime?"

The funny thing about this song is that everyone knows those six words but only Win Stracke and Studs know all the others.

Studs was wearing a red checkered shirt which looked like it was made from one of those tablecloths they have in restaurants where the most expensive dish on the menu is ravioli, and you could tell how happy he was without his telling you about it.

"How can I describe this crowd?" Studs asked and then went on to answer his own question—as he most often does:

"It isn't like the kind of autographing parties that writers usually have. These are real people, not the kind of people you'd find in book stores.

"They're people from the neighborhoods in Chicago and they're also from the suburbs. To a lot of them, I think the book and the Depression really meant something.

"Michael Wadleigh, who was really involved in Woodstock, took one look around here and he told me he's never seen anything like it.

"Well, if that's true then it's good, because I think the Depression was the thing which really started the generation gap and now, finally, maybe this kind of book is the thing that can help end it."

Studs's book, of course, is all about the Depression. He put it together by going around the country to interview people who went through it and even people who didn't.

Now that the book has been published he has become the darling of the book sections. He has been covered by *Life, Newsweek,* and appeared on the front page of the *New York Times Book Review.*

He has been around Chicago so long everyone takes him for granted—as the guy who does the interview show on FM radio.

Saturday night at this party everyone showed up to eat beans, drink boilermakers, and listen to just about every entertainer who's ever worked on the Near North Side.

"Studs," a man asked, "what do you think of it all? How does it feel to be a big author?"

Studs looked up and smiled. He doesn't believe it, either, and that's maybe the greatest thing about it all.

"It's crazy," he said. "It's just nutty."

And up on the stage now, Win Stracke was singing it so strong it was bringing tears to the eyes of people who weren't even born in the thirties:

"I dreamed I saw Joe Hill last night, alive as you and me. . . ."

DANNY MCMAHON

This is the way I'll remember Danny McMahon.

We were sitting in Butch McGuire's one afternoon and Danny suddenly announces he must leave to visit a friend in Passavant Hospital. (He always, it seemed, had friends in the hospital and he was always rushing off to see them.)

I'm still at the bar that fronts the window and now Danny is back again. There is that bright smile on his face, the one that shows no inhibitions, and he is writing on the window of the bar with a marking pencil.

But Danny is an artist. He doesn't write the way most people do. He is doing it in inverted style so that we can read it inside. Danny writes: "Princeton Forever."

Then Danny walks back into Butch McGuire's. He takes another look at me. I have just come back from Ireland and I'm wearing a heavy tweed jacket purchased in Dublin.

Danny had looked at me with some skepticism before departing. Now he says:

"You're right, unfortunately. The material in that jacket is really sturdy. I'm afraid . . . it will never wear out."

There was another day, I remember (when I felt I was riding high) that we were together and Danny looked at me with a straight face and said:

"You are writing the most boring column imaginable. I don't understand why anybody continues to read you."

But there was still another day, when I was at a low ebb, when Danny called me and said:

"I just wanted to tell you this. The last two columns you've written have been great. I really liked them."

Danny McMahon knew about people. He knew when you were up and when you were down. Because he was my friend, he knew how far to go and in what direction.

But he wasn't only a friend of mine. Danny had so many friends and they came from so many walks of life.

Danny and I shouldn't have had anything in common. His father made a lot of money and he lived most of his early years in the Drake Hotel. He went to Princeton. He knew a lot of rich people and liked them.

There is nothing in my background that would make me like a guy like Danny McMahon. But I did.

He did such great things. He attracted such fine people, even the rich ones. When Danny walked down the streets, dogs broke away from their masters' leashes to come and be petted by Danny.

Children toddled to Danny and he created marvelous drawings for them.

Middle-aged women and young women headed for him and he told them fantastic stories, some of them true.

The stories. The one-liners. I make a living as a writer and yet Danny's mind was so much faster at these things than mine that I was always secretly glad he decided to be a dress designer.

Danny was a great cook. The last time I was with him he cooked two hot dogs for me in his apartment. He described the process as "special" and refused to tell me how he had done it.

Danny was a man you could not walk down Michigan Avenue with on schedule. He was always being stopped by society matrons, bartenders, waitresses, visiting ballet dancers, dress designers, policemen—everybody knew him.

And he traveled all over the world. And that marvelous sense of humor was always with him.

One day a famous Indian society matron approached.

"When you see her coming," Danny said, "you'd better draw your wagons in a circle."

Another day he told the wife of a prominent Texan who has become a millionaire through his ownership of a restaurant specializing in Mexican food here in Chicago:

"I think you have a wonderful apartment here. The only trouble is that it looks like a room in a Texas motel."

I remember another day that he said of the wife of an oil company executive as she walked into a society party:

"She looks like Rebecca of Sunnybrook Farm. But at least that's an improvement. Last night she looked like Jane Eyre."

Danny's gone now. He died Sunday, alone, in his apartment on North State Parkway. He was 45. He is the first good friend I've ever had who died.

I can't believe he's gone. I know he had been ill but I also know he didn't want to go. We were planning a trip to Florida together in the first week of January and that's all we talked about the other day when we were last together.

I knew Danny so well and yet I didn't. That's the way it is with most friendships. There are so many shadowy corners.

Tuesday night, I read in Danny's notebook this message he had written to himself about the imminent death of his mother just a couple of years ago.

It shows such a different side. So much more serious . . . Danny's thoughtful note reads:

I'm sitting here thinking of you—alone, yet not alone. The haze of age has closed over you—life has gone, yet not gone, and I wonder what is next.

Will you remember all the lovely things? Is it all over? Will the next step be away from us? I'll do anything to make happiness. I'd do anything to bring you back to life again. But where to start?

Danny couldn't find the place to start for his mother. When it came right down to it, he couldn't find the place to start for himself, either.

Danny wanted so little from life for himself and he had so much he wanted to give.

John Weitz, the designer, was one of Danny's friends.

"You never went to lunch with Danny," Weitz said. "You went to a party. Wherever you went with Danny, you were at a party."

Nick Johnson probably said it best. "A really bright light has gone out," he said. "Wherever you met Danny you met interesting, bright people from all walks of life."

Danny, we're all going to miss you . . . so much.

JIM AND MIKE

The other day a number of the closest friends of James S. Tuohy and his lovely wife, Michaela, received the following letter:

You are cordially invited to attend a party at the residences of James S. Tuohy on Saturday from twelve o'clock noon until, perhaps, Monday.

It will be a moving event, both physically and emotionally.

The physical part comes from the fact that the Tuohys are moving from their pleasant, one-story, ranch-style apartment at 2016 North Cleveland, to a more traditional, two-story, early-Chicago-style apartment at 617 West Dickens, two blocks away in the academically oriented Waller High School area.

The emotional part of the move comes from an element of suspense that has been introduced. On Tuesday, April 25, the Littlestone Company obtained an eviction order from the Circuit Court of Cook County against the Tuohys. That should make for an interesting race: who will get the furniture out first, the Tuohys or the Elrods?

One of the reasons for the eviction notice is that the Tuohys did not pay the last month's rent on the Cleveland apartment, preferring, instead, to spend the money on beer, food, and other refreshment for their friends on moving day.

Mrs. Tuohy, the well-known Michaela the Mouth, of *Daily Planet* gossip-column fame, has authorized a guest list of at least fifty of the Tuohys' closest friends. This means that if these good friends show up, no one will have to carry more than an item or two, leaving plenty of time for the most important thing: drinking the rest of the weekend. In fact, since Mrs. Touhy is taking the next week off from work, perhaps there will be drinking well into May.

Well, Saturday was moving day. There were almost fifty persons involved. Since very few of the group were professional movers, a few slip-ups did occur. Four boxes of garbage were moved inadvertently and stacked in an upstairs bedroom of the new manse.

Somehow, the washer and drier were forgotten.

But the move was completed and Sheriff Richard Elrod's eviction crew thwarted.

Michaela Tuohy sat in her new living room Sunday afternoon and looked around. There was a warm glow on her face. Also sitting around the living room were seventy-six empty beer cans and fifty-two cardboard boxes filled with clothing, dishes, and books.

Do not get the idea that Michaela drank all seventy-six of those beers. In truth, she did consume her share. But the bulk of them were drunk by a group of friends that Michaela and Jim had brought from the Oxford Pub when it closed at 5 A.M. Sunday.

Michaela was justifiably pleased that the move came off so well, but she is a little miffed at some of the friends who showed up, but did not work hard enough.

"Karen Conner did nothing," Mike said. "All I ever saw her do was model my old hats. And Jack Lane didn't even show up until he knew most of the work had already been done."

Michaela was also a little put out because some of the furniture was declared to be in such a state of disrepair that no volunteer would move it.

"Oh yes," she said. "We also left the flower box behind. But then I've never felt the same about it since the day Tuohy buried our dead cat in it."

BURTON BROWNE

I finally met a rich man I like. The thing I like about him is that if he were set adrift tomorrow without any money, he'd probably turn around and make it all over again. He's got the system figured.

His name is Burton Browne. He is an amply built man with a white beard who celebrated his sixty-fifth birthday a week ago. He owns both an advertising agency, which bears his name, and a string of spots around the country called the Gaslight Clubs.

I am really at a loss as to how to begin describing Burton Browne to you. The best way perhaps is to remind you of that great line Zero Mostel once delivered in a movie called *The Producers*.

If you saw it you'll never forget Mostel's comment about being rich: "If you got it, baby, flaunt it." That's Burton Browne.

"I love being rich. Doesn't everybody?" Burton is saying now. "As a matter of fact, I grew up thinking everybody was rich. To tell you the truth, my grandfather thought being rich was great fun and so do I."

Burton has just returned from Tahiti where he plans to buy more land and open another Gaslight Club and finish it all up having the biggest ball of his life. That last probably should really be in quotes because they are his words.

"Let me tell you something," Burton says. "There are three people I have really loved: Genghis Khan, John Paul Jones, and Grandpa.

"Grandpa became a multimillionaire. Here's how he did it up in Jackson, Michigan. He'd buy an old house, send a crew in to paint it, put wallpaper on the walls and fresh sod on the lawn, and then on Sunday he'd take his rocking chair out there and sit on the porch and sell it for a good profit.

"Grandpa said there was a secret to being able to sell those houses, though. He always told people how close they were to stores and how nice the neighbors were.

"But the thing that really sold the house was that Grandpa always had the sense to tell them there were two things wrong with the house. He'd always tell them that the kitchen sink had to be replaced and that one of the back stairs had to be repaired.

"He did this, because otherwise they'd be afraid to buy because the whole thing looked too good to be true."

Burton started his Gaslight Clubs seventeen years ago as an offshoot of his advertising agency. The first was a one-room affair leading right from the agency offices called the Sundown Room, and it was a perfect place to entertain clients.

It was so popular, in fact, that after a while Burton couldn't even get into it himself and that's when he decided the thing had bigger possibilities.

"Hefner started the Playboy Club in imitation," Burton says, "and he admits it. I don't mind a bit. The kind of people we attract are top business executives who can pay top dollar. Hefner gets a younger crowd and there's plenty of room for both of us."

There are four Gaslight Clubs around the country now. In addition to Chicago, they are in New York, Washington, and Beverly Hills.

Burton's proud of this, but he's much happier about the money they make and the fun that he has with them.

"Let me tell you about making money," he says now. "Buy business real estate. It's better than stocks and bonds.

"I'll tell you a story about that. Back in 1951 a friend of mine and I were out walking. He pointed to a business property and said to me: 'Burton, just twenty years ago I could have bought that building for $60,000. Now it's just been sold for $280,000.'

"Well, this is what I learned about buying business properties. The same man could very well come back to me in 1980 and tell me that in 1951 he had a chance to buy that building for $280,000 and now it's just sold for one and a quarter million.

"This is the lesson. This country's been going through inflation for three hundred years. Buy business property and there's no way you can lose."

The tall blond waitress-singer who had once been a Sunday School teacher brought Burton another perfect manhattan.

"Are you old enough to remember Sherman Billingsley?" Burton asked. "He used to own the Stork Club in New York. When I opened my Gaslight Club there, he gave me a year. He was sure it would fold.

"What happened was that he folded. He never kept up with the times and people just tired of looking at those old men waiters he had.

"Finally, he closed the place and I figured he'd sell the land and retire to Florida. Know what happened? It turned out he'd been renting all along. A couple of years later I read in the papers that Billingsley had left an estate of fifty-seven dollars."

Burton takes a sip of his perfect manhattan.

"Here's what I've told all my associates. If the concept of the Gaslight Clubs goes out of style, just close 'em down and sell the property. And then just sit back and laugh . . . laugh . . . laugh."

A man sitting at the table asks Burton why he is drinking perfect manhattans when everybody knows that champagne is his favorite drink.

"To tell you the truth I'm on the wagon," Burton says, his whole upper body shaking with laughter.

"For the past two weeks I've been drinking champagne twenty hours a day and now I'm taking it easy.

"Let me leave you with a profound message," he adds. "In the words of Will Rogers, I've never tasted an alcoholic beverage I didn't like."

CHAPTER 4

NORTHERN IRELAND

There is so much tragedy in Northern Ireland that the effect on the mind is numbing. You write about one death today, and tomorrow you go on the streets and there is another death to write about.

Each time you return you must stay in a different hotel because the last one has been bombed shut.

What happens here? A dummy who admired Bernadette Devlin is killed by a soldier whose command he doesn't understand. A Catholic priest is killed trying to help a wounded man. Thirteen people are massacred in 'Derry in the biggest single British mistake so far.

Where do you go for another view? You go on patrol with the British and find out why they're so trigger-happy. You visit the pubs and find that internment doesn't necessarily mean that everyone will rally to your support—even your own brother.

You go to the church of the Reverend Ian Paisley and see how a real spellbinder and hate-monger operates. And when it's all over you go back to Dublin—the last outpost of civilization—and somebody steals your car.

DEATH OF A DUMMY

STRABANE, Northern Ireland—More than an hour before Bernadette Devlin was scheduled to speak from the steps of city hall, Eamon McDivitt, the town's dummy had taken up his vigil.

"He's always been very fond of Bernadette," a bearded young man handling publicity for the speech said. "I don't think he's ever

missed a speech that she's made in this city." McDivitt saw us looking over toward him and waved.

"You wouldn't know it to look at him," the publicity man said,
"but Eamon's twenty-eight years old. He looks much younger.
Known him all my life, I have. Fact is, it seems like everyone in the
city has always known Eamon. You know how it is. He's the man
you always wave to and smile at and yet never really know."

The crowd began moving steadily into the narrow street fronting
city hall and it was easy to forget about Eamon McDivitt. It was especially easy because the publicity man was so anxious to produce
facts and figures about his city.

"It's the ancestral home of Woodrow Wilson for one thing," he
said, "and that print shop right down there was once owned by
John Dunlap, who migrated to the United States and help print the
Declaration of Independence."

He explained at great length how the town had a population of
slightly more than 10,000 and that they were all on a general strike
for the day to protest the British internment policy. The town is
only half a mile from the border of the Irish Free State and fourteen miles southwest of Londonderry.

"Twenty-seven percent of the males in this town are unemployed," he said, "and that's about the highest you'll find in all of
Europe."

Relief from the deluge of statistics was finally granted by the arrival of Miss Devlin, the M.P. for mid-Ulster. Slowly, she made her
way through the cheering crowd to the steps. She is expecting the
birth of her first child soon and not surprisingly she appeared very
tired. But she is only twenty-four years old and there has been not
time for her to become jaded or to lose her charisma from the
speaker's platform.

Once Bernadette took the microphone in her hands she became a
different person. Her eyes sparkled, her arms moved dramatically,
and she kept changing her position on the steps, giving the illusion
to each member of the crowd that she was talking directly for his or
her benefit.

"People of Strabane," Bernadette began, "there is one thing we
have in common with the people of 'Derry and Belfast. The British
army came and dragged off our people, 2,300 of them, our friends,
our relatives, our loved ones. They clapped them into jails without
trial.

"And we are all sick, sore, and tired of being stepped on by the corrupt regime of the Six Counties." This was greeted by a great burst of applause and one of those clapping his hands most vigorously was Eamon McDivitt, the deaf mute.

"Working-class people are not polite people," Bernadette continued. "We do not fly backwards and forwards to London for chats with Mr. Maudling [the British foreign secretary], but without us, the working class, the country doesn't run. What we want now is our freedom.

"We have fought for our survival up in the Bogside at 'Derry and down on the Falls Road in Belfast. And so now we're not asking, we're demanding that internment be ended immediately."

The crowd roared again. Bernadette stood there, her face appearing even more angry and determined than it does in photographs.

"The working class is the one class that has never sold out," she shouted. "We are going to withhold our rents and the payments for all other services until we get what we demand.

"And just remember this. There are more of us than there are of the Royal Ulster Constabulary, the British army, or any other class. We are the people and we are going to win." Bernadette put the microphone down and several men formed a barricade and helped lead her back to the auto parked at the foot of the steps. The crowd moved forward to either shout a greeting or obtain her autograph.

Eamon McDivitt tried to push his way through from the rear of the crowd, too, but he couldn't make it. Bernadette's car had driven off long before he got close.

An hour after Bernadette left town for her home in nearby Cookstown, rioting broke out. First target for the mob was the drapery shop of Gilbert Bruce, a Protestant who had refused to honor the one-day closing of all the town's businesses. Bruce's place was burned to the ground. After this, cars were turned over at a main intersection to form a barricade and then set afire.

The British army moved in then and began firing gas canisters and rubber bullets to disperse the crowd which by this time had taken to pelting firemen with rocks and bottles. Eamon McDivitt followed the mob from place to place, grinning at a form of activity he had never seen before in this normally placid little town.

He was crouched in a doorway when a soldier fired a rubber bullet that hit the wall above his head and bounded away. Eamon ran to retrieve the bullet and brought it back into the doorway with him. He was very pleased to have such a trophy and he waved it high above his head, trying to signal his friends standing in adjacent doorways. A British soldier saw Eamon wave the rubber bullet and thought it was a pistol.

"Drop that weapon and put up your hands," shouted the soldier. Eamon looked at the soldier and smiled. There was no way for him to hear what the soldier was saying and the soldier was too far away for Eamon to read his lips.

Eamon continued to smile at the soldier and waved the rubber bullet at him again. The soldier squeezed the trigger on his rifle. The bullet went through the center of Eamon's forehead.

Eamon was still smiling as he fell to the ground, dead.

PERIL IN THE ARDOYNE

BELFAST, Northern Ireland—My plan was already disintegrating. The idea was to go on a night patrol with a British army unit in the most dangerous section of the city, a place called the Ardoyne.

Shooting incidents take place in this Roman Catholic ghetto every night of the week. Gelignite bombs are often detonated as troops pass by. Nail bombs are tossed at them, too.

Some of the most formidable gunmen in the Irish Republican Army are known to inhabit this half-mile-square area where there are no street lights and where no regular police can enter to enforce the law.

But it had been my thought the patrol would travel in an armored vehicle.

I suspect that Major Peter Wildblood, commander of the First Battalion of the Queen's Lancashire Regiment, knew I was hoping for the easy way out. Why else would he smile that way when he said:

"I'm glad to hear you want to go on patrol. We'll make it a good show for you. We'll get you a full uniform, put the grease on your face, and you can go with the men on foot.

"You'll have an interesting walk. The gunmen are shooting out there already. It will be good for an American pressman to see what the British soldier goes through here."

I nodded and smiled—but I didn't mean it. The idea of walking out there in the dark did not appeal to me one bit. But it was impossible now to back out or even admit I wasn't wildly enthusiastic about the prospect.

Lieutenant Richard Gething stepped up to introduce himself. He was to be commander of the platoon I would accompany. He was smiling, too.

"Here's your uniform," he said. "I think you'll find they all fit. Once you get these on we'll find you a flak jacket and a tube of grease to blacken your face."

I began changing clothes.

Major Wildblood, an eighteen-year veteran, is tiny and trim and his eyes are alert. He began talking of previous campaigns in which he had served.

"I was on Cyprus and Aden when the shooting was going on," he said. "Nasty business, both places. But in many ways I think this campaign is even more difficult."

He smiled, halting as if suppressing a thought. But then he let it out: "You don't mind getting shot at, do you?"

The truth is, of course, that I do. In fact, the whole prospect terrifies me.

"Doesn't bother me a bit," I said. I think he may have even believed me. At times, I can be quite an effective liar, especially when I'm close to panic.

Major Wildblood left the room and Lieutenant Gething began giving me hints on how to behave on patrol.

"When we get shot at," he began, "I won't have time to tell you anything. Stay about eight paces behind me at all times. Do what I do. If anything happens, don't get in front of any of our riflemen. Just freeze.

"Initially, we'll take cover. We'll observe. We'll try to locate the gunman. If we can identify the spot from where the fire came, we'll return fire."

Lieutenant Gething has been in the army five years and plans to make a career of it. He is of medium height and is built like a weight lifter. He is talking about a grim business but he has a sense of humor.

"Generally speaking," he says, "the gunmen don't hit us. It's just a quick burst of fire and he's away. Generally they stand back from a ground-floor window and fire at us as we walk by. Then they duck out the back door, down an alley, and they're gone."

Lieutenant Gething has forgotten one important item and now he gets to it.

"If someone is hit, the man closest will administer first aid until help comes and another man will stand guard over them. That takes three men out of the platoon right away."

My basic training in the British army was over. Lieutenant Gething led me down two flights of stairs and into a courtyard outside the makeshift army post set up in an old factory. As we arrived, one of the soldiers was zeroing in the starlight sight, which is the patrol's most lethal weapon. The sight makes it possible to see in the dark. It costs a lot of money but it works and it frightens away all but truly dedicated IRA snipers.

"All right men," Lieutenant Gething said. "There's been some shooting out there already tonight. The locals seem a bit tense. So just stay alert."

Lieutenant Gething was interrupted by the sound of two rifle shots—less than a block away from where we were standing.

The soldiers looked at each other nervously. Some of them are under twenty. None is over twenty-three. Most of them are married. All come from Lancashire, England, and they have now served two months of a four-month tour in Northern Ireland. When their time is up they will return to Germany where they are stationed permanently. All left their wives there because they will get only two days off during their entire four-month tour here.

"As I said," Lieutenant Gething added, smiling easily, "you can expect some action. Look smart now. Don't go haranguing the locals. Let's go."

Now it was silent.

Quickly, Lieutenant Gething led the way out through the heavy gate and into the pitch-darkness of the street outside the post. He trotted across the street and leaned with his back against the brick wall of a building. After a few minutes, he moved down the street about twenty-five yards and then leaned against the wall again, looking and listening into the dark.

No one made a sound. It took our patrol ten minutes to move a block. By that time I already knew what they felt every night. The dark is their enemy.

They have no way of knowing when the bullet will come for them. Since their arrival in Northern Ireland, forty-seven British soldiers have been killed here and twice as many wounded—many on patrols just like this one.

The soldiers are on duty sixteen hours every day. They almost never leave the confines of the army post. They hold dances inside to which both Protestant and Catholic girls are invited and when there are no dances they watch television and play cards.

Don't think British soldiers do not date Catholic girls. The average number of marriages between them is higher than you might expect.

Lieutenant Gething was concealed in a doorway now, and we waited as the second section of the squad flitted past us while the first section covered all suspected windows and rooftops on the street.

"We've only had a couple of casualties," he said. "I like to think that it's because we're all regulars. Every one of these men has been highly trained in the use of all weapons. They know what they're doing and they're careful."

A car came down the street with its lights on. It was the only thing moving in the empty road, and Lieutenant Gething's body tensed.

We stood there watching as one of the soldiers waved to the driver to turn down his lights. As the soldier waved, four others took aim at the driver with their rifles.

"Anyone in a car is a threat," Lieutenant Gething said. "Anyone who puts lights on you may be ready to kill you. He may have another man in the car with a gun. He may have a gelignite bomb or nail bomb in his hand. He may be just putting the lights on you so someone else can get a good shot at you."

The driver lowered his lights. I heaved a sigh of relief. Incredibly, this thing was getting to me. I had only been wearing the uniform for half an hour and already I was feeling everything in the dark as a threat.

I think my stomach contracted before the sound registered in my brain. It was a shot. Then another. The patrol froze in position. They were peering up at the roofs and into the windows on the darkened street. The soldier carrying the seventeen-pound starlight weapon moved it around carefully, looking for the gunman.

Lieutenant Gething leaned toward me and whispered in the dark: "Almost impossible to tell where the shots come from in a place like this. The buildings distort the sound. Everybody thinks he hears it someplace else.

"You just have to wait. Luckily, as I said, they don't try to fire at you more than once. They're content to hit and run. You see now what I mean about our purpose on these missions. We're here to kill gunmen. There's no half measures."

I could also see something else that Lieutenant Gething wasn't explaining at this point. The gunmen are also out to kill British soldiers.

Tension grew during the remainder of the tour. It did for me, anyway. At times like this, odd thoughts go through your mind.

I really wasn't worried that much about being shot. The thing I was worried about was explaining what I was doing in a British army uniform if I did get shot.

But nothing more happened. It was dark. Several times there were unexplained noises, flicking on and off of lights, and suddenly approaching cars—all considered signs of danger—but nothing more.

It seemed to me that we had been patroling all night. We had been gone a relatively short time. Two hours.

We re-entered the courtyard inside the army post and B Company went past us on their way to pick up the patrol. Lieutenant Gething congratulated the men and told them to go to their quarters and take it easy for two hours until they would go out again.

He led the way upstairs to the officers' mess and poured two cups of coffee for us.

"Believe it or not," he said, "a lot of the people have grown friendly to us since we've been here. A lot of them talk. They don't want anyone to know it, but they talk. They'd talk a lot more but they're terrified of the IRA. This is our big problem. We are fighting an enemy that has the overwhelming support of the people. They leave their doors open so the IRA can use their homes as escape hatches. They warn them. They feed them.

"But still, there are some who want to help us. It's just that they have to be careful how and when they do it."

Lieutenant Gething took a sip of his coffee. He went on:

"To be truthful, it's not half as bad right now as it was before internment. We've lifted all the really dangerous known gunmen. They're all in the internment camps. The area is fairly pacified and . . ."

Lieutenant Gething never finished. He was interrupted by the sound of an explosion so powerful that we both felt the concussion. I could hear men running all over the building. The radio operator down the hall was shouting excitedly.

A captain, tall and with a handlebar mustache, walked swiftly down the hall and stood at the door.

"It was a gelignite bomb," he said. "It got two men in S Company. They were going over the same area you just left. Ambulance is on the way."

"How did it happen?" Lieutenant Gething asked.

"Looks like the bomb was planted in front of a doorway and then tripped from half a block away as the patrol passed," the captain said.

"We think someone in the block flicked a bedroom light as a signal to the bomber."

Lieutenant Gething clenched his fists and cursed.

"Bombers," he said. "I really hate them. Snipers I can understand, but bombers . . . it's all so cowardly."

"WE HAVE SUFFERED EVERYTHING . . ."

Six months later I went back to Corpus Christi Church to find Father Desmond Wilson. They pointed out his house to me. The cab driver, who was a Protestant, refused to drive to it because he saw a group of children loitering about.

"If I bring the car there and they find out I'm a Protestant," he said, "they'll kill me sure."

BELFAST, Northern Ireland—The Reverend Hugh Mullan was a tiny, round man with a bald head. He had an infectious laugh and a great love for children. He could play the guitar and carry a respectable tune.

The children of Corpus Christi Roman Catholic Church in the Ballymurphy Estate here could sense Father Hugh's feelings toward them. He was their favorite priest.

Sunday the children and their parents who inhabit the 650 homes located here at the foot of the Divis Mountain moved quietly into the church to attend mass and pray for Father Mullan's soul.

Father Mullan is dead at thirty-eight. The immediate cause of his death was a rifle bullet fired into his heart last Monday by a British paratrooper as Father Mullan was attempting to give the last rites of the Church to a wounded man.

Contributing causes were two other rifle bullets fired into his leg and side by two other paratroopers who ignored the fact that he was wearing clerical garb and waving a white flag at the time.

Urban guerrilla warfare is a brutal business. There have been so many people killed, wounded, beaten, and brutalized in this one that it becomes almost impossible to convey the impact it is really having.

In a way, the death of Father Mullan drives it home like a spear through the heart.

The Reverend Desmond Wilson realized that on Sunday as he looked out over the crowded pews before beginning his sermon.

"The epistle today," he said, "is from St. Paul to the Corinthians. St. Paul says:

'With God on our side, who can be against us.' "

Father Wilson put down the book from which he was reading.

"We have reached a tragic point in the history of our parish," Father Wilson said. "This past week, six lives have been lost here.

"Father Mullan died an heroic death in the best tradition of the priesthood. Frank Quinn, who raced out into the field to save him, died an equally heroic death."

Father Wilson took a deep breath.

"We have suffered everything that can happen to a people," he said softly "death, tragedy, loss of homes."

As Father Wilson spoke, a company of British soldiers was busy a block away clearing up burned-out cars, felled lampposts, and chunks of concrete that had been used to construct barricades against them by the Ballymurphy residents.

Only half of the soldiers were working. The others had their guns trained on the people of the neighborhood who stood watching silently.

Joseph Fox, the sacristan of the church, wiped tears from his eyes at the close of Father Wilson's sermon.

Fox was one of Father Mullan's best friends. He hasn't been able to think about anything else since he first got news of the shooting.

"I was with Father Mullan right here in the sacristy," Fox said, unbelievingly. "He had just finished saying mass and we walked out together.

"He lived in his own house over in Springfield Park and was heading there. We both knew that there was a lot of trouble and people were very frightened.

"As we walked out the door, a woman said: 'God bless you, Father.'

"He turned and smiled and pointed his finger at her, making believe he had a gun. 'Bang,' he said, 'you're dead.' "

Fox put his hands up to his eyes and squeezed them with the thumb and forefinger of his right hand.

"You know, I can't help but think he knew something all along.

"Just a little while before, a woman had come in and made a request to have a mass said for her dead mother. Father Mullan told her he'd do it Tuesday and then he added: 'That's if I'm still alive.' "

John McKenna and his wife, Pat, live at 43 Springfield Road in a two-story brick house that sits alongside the one in which Father Mullan lived.

Sunday, after mass, they were sitting in the living room and looking out toward the open field in front of their house where their neighbor and friend had been shot to death.

"We all knew it was going to be a day," McKenna said, "when we heard that the internment had begun. This street is right in the middle of two Protestant ones, you know, and as the day went on they began stoning and firing at our homes from both front and back.

"Finally, it got so bad up at the end of the street that they started evacuating and the mothers and children were being taken across that field toward a safe place in a rescue center up the hill.

"Father Mullan was right here with us and so was his friend, Father Felix McGuchan. The rifle fire was something fierce and it was coming not only from the soldiers on the roofs of the flats behind us, but also from members of the Protestant Ulster Volunteer Force."

It was just past supper time when the event that ended Father Mullan's life occurred.

A man was carrying a small child across the weed-grown field when he was struck in the back by a bullet and fell.

Father Mullan, who had been crouched in the McKenna house along with the others, leaped to his feet.

He ran to his car, pulled a stole from a small black bag, and began running across the field to give the wounded man the last rites of the Church.

"I saw Father Mullan trip and go down right after he got into the field and I thought he was a goner," McKenna said. "But he got right up again. He had only tripped.

"He was carrying a white handerchief and waving it over his head and he kept running until he reached the wounded man and knelt down beside him."

"Can you imagine? They let him get all the way there and then they shot him."

Father Mullan appeared to leap in the air and then fall in the field. A few minutes later he was hit by another bullet, and McKenna, his wife and their five children could hear him cry out in pain.

It was at this point that Frank Quinn, another member of Corpus Christi Parish, ran into the field to assist Father Mullan.

Quinn was killed instantly by one rifle bullet that struck him in the back of the head.

Gerald Mooney was at the other end of the field when that happened. Mooney, serving as a volunteer first aid man, was wearing a white helmet and carrying a white first aid bag.

He dashed into the field and made it to Father Mullan's side.

"I lifted the priest and cradled him in my arms," he said. "He was praying to himself and when he realized I was picking him up he shook his head and said: 'Run for it, lad. Save yourself.'

"The soldiers started shooting then and I had to drop him and dive for cover.

"I could see the bullets hitting all around Father Mullan and then he groaned and that must have been the bullet that killed him because he was quiet after that.

"I looked up toward the rooftop where the soldiers were. They must have known they'd got him because two of those paratroopers in the red berets were standing there shaking hands with each other."

Mooney's face turned dark with anger.

"I served two years in the British army myself," Mooney said. "I was in the medical corps. I never thought I'd see the day when the British army would deliberately shoot a priest who was waving a white flag."

Mooney was pinned down in the field for perhaps two hours, he says, and then was able to crawl away when it became too dark for the paratroopers to see him.

Sunday morning, it was quiet in the field where Father Mullan died. There were three crosses set into the weeds, marking the spots where the men had been shot.

Father Mullan and Quinn, his would-be rescuer, died. John Clark, the man to whom Father Mullan wanted to give his last rites, is alive.

And the situation is such here that he has gone underground in fear that the British somehow will find a reason to throw him in prison for his part in an episode that has proved such an embarrassment to them.

The spot where Father Mullan's body was retrieved was covered with a black cross, some freshly picked flowers, and a large piece of cardboard with a crudely printed message:

"This is the place where Father Mullan was shot dead by the British army trying to help people move from their homes."

The sign looks very much as though it had been printed by a child.

I stood there for several minutes looking at the cardboard, then ahead to the top of Divis Mountain.

It was bright green on the mountaintop and the air was crisp and clean. That was the view that Father Mullan used to get every morning from the front window of his home.

He used to tell the McKennas that people in America would pay a fortune to have a house with such a view.

Father Mullan had that view for just over a year, and the price he paid eventually had nothing to do with money.

THE MAN WITH THE ICE-WATER BLUE EYES

The night before Joe Cahill came out from under cover, I met him in a school which had been opened up to house refugees who had been burned out of their homes. I thought he was a carpenter. He certainly looked like one. And he was. But he was also the head of the Provisional branch of the IRA.

BELFAST, Northern Ireland—Joe Cahill is a tiny man of fifty-two with ice-water blue eyes who has spent nearly half his adult life in British prisons.

On Friday morning this father of seven, who wears a winter overcoat and a checkered cap pulled over his forehead even in summer, started the day as the Irish Republican Army's most-wanted man.

Before dark, Cahill, who commands the IRA guerrilla force in the six Northern Counties, had succeeded in making such a laughingstock of the British army leaders here that pride will never allow them to rest until they put him behind bars again.

This is how it happened:

This was the day that Brigadier General Marston Tickell, chief of staff of the British forces in Northern Ireland, decided to hold a press conference and declare that his forces had inflicted a major defeat on the IRA. "We have wiped out the hard core of them," General Tickell said, "and we have probably killed between twenty and thirty and wounded as many more."

At almost the same time Tickell was making his self-congratulatory remarks, Joe Cahill, accompanied by six bodyguards, was walking down a long corridor in St. Pete's school in the Ballymurphy section of Belfast to begin his incredible demonstration of *chutzpah*.

There were more than fifty newsmen from all over Europe and the United States waiting in the school gymnasium for what had been touted as a press conference given by Paddy Kennedy, a member of the Northern Ireland Parliament. But it was Cahill, never deigning to remove his cap or overcoat, who dominated the next hour.

Spotted immediately by British and Irish journalists as the IRA top man, Cahill was asked to evaluate the current situation here.

Despite the fact that British troops were patrolling the streets outside the building, Cahill betrayed no sign of fear.

"Morale is very high at this time," Cahill said. "We have lost thirty men through internment. Two men have been killed by the British army. Eight others have been wounded. But the men they have interned were not ranking officers. They were only volunteers [privates]. The leadership is intact."

Paddy Kennedy, the youngish member of Parliament, broke in to point out that the presence not only of Cahill but of Aohn Kelly, another IRA leader, proved the British were wrong when they boasted they have cowed the IRA leadership.

"Do you think that if the IRA were beaten and demoralized by the British that they would walk right in front of these television cameras and flaunt the British army this way?" Kennedy asked.

Kennedy went on to explain that Cahill and Kelly were doing so only to demonstrate that the battle with the "foreign force" was just beginning.

"The British army has been behaving like the army of Nazi Germany here in Belfast," Kennedy charged. "On Monday, when they interned more than three hundred—most of them civil rights enthusiasts and not members of the IRA at all—they committed all kinds of atrocities."

Kennedy said that those arrested had been forced to run a gauntlet of broken glass and briars in bare feet, had been forced to sing Protestant songs or suffer severe beatings, and some had even been pushed out of army helicopters while they were hovering above the ground.

"This is the occupying force that was sent in here originally to protect us against the Protestant mobs," Kennedy said. "It turns out now that they are the terrorists and gunmen.

"I ask you, who can we turn to in these circumstances?"

Kennedy then did something that will most certainly earn him a stretch in the Crumlin Road jail here as a political prisoner. He made a public appeal to Irishmen in the south to bring guns across the border to help in the fight against the British army and the Protestant Ulster Volunteer Force.

"The situation is desperate," Kennedy said. "We need ammunition right away. We can't hold out forever."

There have been twenty-five persons killed during street fighting this week but there was a lull in the tempo of the battle on Thursday and Friday. Cahill explained why.

"We are tired," he said, "and we need to re-group to decide on new tactics. We're not finished with them by any means. The sniping will continue. We'll all have to remain underground. But we know every move the British are going to make before they make it.

"That's why they won't win."

A British journalist moved in closer to Cahill with his microphone to ask a few questions designed to demonstrate his own loyalty to Britain.

"Do you mean to say that you'll be arrested on sight by the army?" he asked in what must rank as the overkill question of the week here.

"That's right," Cahill answered, not bothering to raise his eyelids. "But don't worry. The British army isn't going to get into this building. My men are all round it."

The British journalist blanched: "Do you mean to say this building is surrounded by armed gunmen who will shoot British soldiers?"

"That's right," Cahill said, smiling for the first time, "That's exactly what I mean. I'm glad you finally understand."

At this point a burly, red-faced man in a black leather overcoat tapped Cahill on the shoulder. The two whispered to each other for a moment.

"Sorry, gentlemen," Cahill said. "It's time to leave." With that, Cahill got up and walked through a side door of a hallway just off the gymnasium.

Cahill trotted down the inclined runway leading to the side of the building opposite from which the soldiers were approaching. He trotted with a very light step for a middle-age man and it was only seconds before he was out of sight.

BRENDAN

BELFAST, Northern Ireland—Brendan McCann had so many things on his mind he thought his head was about to burst.

"Please, love," Brendan groaned to the waitress, "bring me a pint of Guinness, that's a good girl."

Brendan leaned forward, cupping his temples in his two large puffy hands.

"I'm such a lonely man," Brendan said. "There's my old brother James. He's the tower of strength, and he's sittin' up in the Crumlin Road Prison. And what am I doin'? All I'm doin' for him is sittin' here nursing this awful head of mine. It's the drink, you know. It's the drink that's got me feeling this way. If only my head would stop pounding."

A dark-haired young woman came through the door of the pub, heading toward Brendan with a determined step. Attached to each of her hands was a small child, a boy on one hand and a girl on the other.

"Brendan," she said coldly, "Brendan, you're little better than a criminal. What did you do with the money?"

Brendan looked up. He gave the girl a helpless look, spreading his hands in front of him. "Deirdre," he began, "as God is my judge I didn't take any money that wasn't mine. And all I did with it anyway was to buy fruit and newspapers to bring to James and your brother Peter up in the Crumlin."

"Brendan, you're twenty-nine years old. You're a married man with four children and you haven't been home to your wife in two days. You haven't been home since you came to my house and talked my mother into giving you that ten pounds you promised you'd bring up to the prison to give to the boys for fags and things they need."

"Deirdre, love, let's not go on like this about things you don't understand. I went up to the prison and I brought with me all the newspapers and magazines a man could find. I brought fruit and I even brought three bottles of lime juice laced with vodka."

Brendan shrugged his thick shoulders and threw up his hands.

"Wouldn't you know those guards would suspect something from the likes of a McCann? They wouldn't let me leave the lime juice. So what could I do but drink it myself? Deirdre, you understand these things, don't you, love?"

Deirdre sat there across from Brendan, glaring. The waitress came to the table again. Brendan's face brightened.

"There's a good girl," he said to the waitress. "Bring Deirdre a vodka and peppermint. I'll have another Guinness, too. I do believe my head is beginning to feel a little better."

The waitress departed.

Now the two children, Tara, three, and Sean, four, were crawling on the floor on their stomachs.

"Bang, bang," shouted Tara, her arms cradling a make-believe rifle.

Sean, who was crawling a little to the rear, looked very intense. But he was making no sound.

"Sean makes a much better sniper, don't you think?" Deirdre said. "Tara's just like a woman. Too much talk. Not enough action."

The waitress returned with the drinks.

"Well, Brendan," Deirdre said, "what are you going to do? Both of our brothers are up there in that rotten dungeon and they're waiting for you to help."

"I know, I know, love," Brendan said, his face looking as though it were about to crumble under the weight of his own follies. "But what can I do? Most of the money's gone now, and I don't really want to face my brother and tell him that. And now I've been away from home so long I don't want to face the wife, either. I feel like a ruined soul."

The television set, which had been playing softly in the rear of the pub, was suddenly turned up. Brendan winced, both at the noise and at the distinctly British accent of the BBC announcer.

"And stay with us for the next hour when we'll bring you, live from Aintree, the running of the historic Grand National," the announcer was saying. "Stay with us for all the thrills and spills as a field of thirty-eight outstanding horses runs the course and attempts the thirty exacting jumps over the fences. . . ."

As the announcer continued to rattle on about the horse race, Brendan's face began to lose its dour look. Now he was smiling. Suddenly, he seemed relaxed, without a care in the world.

"Deirdre," he said, "My troubles are at an end. Sit right where you are a wee moment. I'll be right back."

Brendan got to his feet, hurrying toward the door. Deirdre cried out: "Wait a minute. Where do you think you're takin' yourself?"

"Deirdre," Brendan shouted, "it's to the turf accountant around the corner that I'm going. I'm putting all I have left on a horse called Lord Jim. And then we'll sit here together right in this pub and cheer him to victory on the television."

Brendan went through the door. Suddenly, however, he turned round and poked his head back inside the pub.

"Deirdre," he shouted, "Don't ever think that I've forgotten our brothers up in that jail. Think how proud they'll be when they find out how I raised all this money for them."

PAISLEY

BELFAST, Northern Ireland—For more than an hour, they had been shuffling slowly into the Reverend Ian Paisley's Martyrs Memorial Church. It is a large, impressive new church fronting on a vast stretch of park. The Union Jack flies from the pole on the front lawn.

By 7:30 P.M., when Mr. Paisley walked majestically up a short flight of stairs to the pulpit, there wasn't an empty seat. A rough guess would be that more than 2,000 persons were there waiting to hear the word from one of Northern Ireland's most famous men.

In addition to being pastor of this church as well as twelve others in Northern Ireland, Mr. Paisley is a member of the Ulster Parliament and the foremost spokesman for anti-Catholicism in the Six Counties.

"We'll begin our service tonight with a beautiful hymn," Mr. Paisley said in a deep baritone voice that carried beautifully. "Open your hymn books to Number 202. Together now, we'll sing that fine hymn that carries a message for us all today, 'Love Lifted Me.' "

At a signal from Mr. Paisley the congregation rose and the organ began to play. As the congregation moved into the spirit of the hymn with more and more fervor, Mr. Paisley stood very erect in the pulpit, arms setting the pace, his voice booming over all through the speakers set in every corner of the church.

They call him "the big fellow" here, and it is easy to see why. He is a huge man and almost as broad as he is tall. Mr. Paisley's appearance is really quite uncommon. In fact, he doesn't look like anyone you've ever seen in modern times. The only place you meet a face with as much definition is on the heads of ancient coins. He has a prominent nose and large lips set close to his face. His eyes, though small, have a piercing quality.

"All right now," Mr. Paisley said after three verses of the hymn had been sung. "You are doing just fine but I know that you can do even better. I say service each Sunday morning in the Crumlin Road Prison and this is the favorite hymn of the men who are confined there. Let's try that chorus once again and this time let's hold that word 'love' for a full octave when I give the signal."

Obediently, they went through the chorus again, booming their voices for what would be the grand finale. Then, at a signal from Mr. Paisley, their voices echoed against the church walls in one resounding blast:

> *Love lifted me . . .*
> *When nothing else could help,*
> *Love lifted me.*

It was over. Mr. Paisley looked down upon his congregation with a warm smile and bade them to be seated.

"We are here today," he began, "to speak about a common

ground. I'm going to tell you about a common ground on which all men of Ulster, of Northern Ireland, can be united and settle their differences.

"But, before that I want to tell you of an experience I had the other day as I drove my car to the Parliament building. I was halted at a roadblock by soldiers and they searched my car. One of them even got down on his knees and looked underneath to see if I was transporting guns."

Mr. Paisley looked down on his congregation, chuckling at the memory of the search.

"But after they were finished," he continued, "I told the soldiers they had missed the most important thing. I told them they didn't realize it but I was carrying a sword in my glove compartment."

Laughter from the congregation filled the hall.

"I told them I was carrying a Bible in there and that the Bible is a sword that will conquer all. Yes, my dear brethren, I told them the Bible will conquer all and told them the truth."

Scattered shouts of "Amen" interrupted Mr. Paisley. He looked down at a sheet of figures on the lectern in front of him, waiting for the enthusiastic response to pass.

"This morning," Mr. Paisley said, "at our 11:30 service we were able to collect 587 pounds for our church building fund. I trust that you here tonight will be able to better that mark."

(Roughly translated into American dollars, that would be slightly more than $1,400 for the morning collection, certainly a generous amount considering the economic climate in this city where so many are unemployed.)

Mr. Paisley, who received his doctoral degree from Bob Jones University in South Carolina, is probably the most successful churchman in all of Ireland.

The chief reason for his success, aside from his talents as a speaker, comes from his outspoken approach to the continuing battle here between Protestants and Roman Catholics.

When he founded his Free Presbyterian Church little more than ten years ago, Mr. Paisley could count one thousand members. Now his church has numerous branches and this newly constructed building on Ravenhill Road cost in excess of $500,000.

"I am glad that we have some visitors here today from Dublin and from the United States," Mr. Paisley said now. "The only thing

I am sorry about is that they will have to find out that I do not actually have horns."

There was genuine laughter in the hall and it rolled around for several minutes until Mr. Paisley raised his right hand as a signal for it to stop.

At this point he went into his political message for the week, explaining to the congregation why he was opposed to the recent election of Brian Faulkner as Prime Minister.

"This man has said the most evil things about Protestants," Mr. Paisley said. "He spoke so insultingly at a speech in East Belfast, in fact, that he was stoned by the good people there."

It didn't matter to either Mr. Paisley or his followers that the man he was talking about is also a Protestant. Here in Northern Ireland these things don't matter. The slightest deviation from Mr. Paisley's hard-line philosophy is enough to bring down serious wrath.

Mr. Paisley, who opposes the attempt by Prime Minister Faulkner to form a moderate government, closed his political section by predicting that the new government would not last long.

Then he went on to a thundering attack upon the fall of the regular Protestant and Roman Catholic churches brought about by what Mr. Paisley believes is their rejection of the truths contained in the Bible.

"I'd like to go to Armagh and shout in the Papist cardinal's ear," Mr. Paisley shouted, "to tell him that he is a sinner.

"I'd like to go to Rome to shout it at the Pope."

" 'You have all sinned. You have all sinned,' " Mr. Paisley shouted he would shout.

"And then I'd go to the Protestant bishops and shout it in their ears, too," Mr. Paisley shouted.

"I'd tell them that all men are sinners and nothing but fuel for Hell. The only way men can be saved, I'd tell them, is by going back to the truth of the Holy Bible. And that is how we could find a common ground for our political differences here in Ulster, too."

Mr. Paisley had his hymn book out again. He raised his arm, indicating it was a time for more song.

"This is a grand old hymn," Mr. Paisley said, "and I want you all to stand and sing and throw your hearts and minds into it with all your spirit."

The organ music flowed over the congregation and the voices began to boom out:

> I love to tell the story,
>   'twill be my theme in glory,
> to tell the old, old story
>   Of Jesus and his love.

The service was at an end. Slowly, the huge congregation began shuffling out of the hall and into the night.

'DERRY MASSACRE

I was in Chicago when I heard about the 'Derry massacre. As soon as I heard it, I knew that I had to get on a plane as quickly as possible and get over there again.

LONDONDERRY, Northern Ireland—The cab was taking us down William Street. In a few minutes we would be under the great stone walls of the city, in the heart of the Bogside area where thirteen civil rights marchers were shot to death by British paratroopers.

It was shortly after 4 o'clock Monday afternoon. Barry Liddy, who has emerged as a sort of hero of Bloody Sunday, was sitting in the back seat of the cab. Beads of perspiration were standing on his forehead.

"It was just about this time of day Sunday a week that it all happened," Liddy said. "This is my first time back to the area. I said I wanted to come back to look it over but now I know it's a mistake. I really don't want to see it again. I want to forget it. But how can I? It was the worst day of my life. I won't forget it until the day God calls me."

For more than two blocks the cab had been trailing a British armored carrier. It was after noticing the soldiers that Liddy started to sweat. The armored carrier swerved off William Street and over the sidewalk into a vacant lot where perhaps a dozen grammar-school-age kids were playing. As soon as the kids saw the armored carrier, they began throwing rocks at it. The soldiers retaliated by firing six canisters of CS gas in the general direction of the kids. It scattered the kids and shrouded the area in sickening haze. The armored carrier turned a sharp circle and sped away from the area.

Liddy's face took on a look of cold fury.

"I was in the British army six years," he said. "I served in Palestine and in Korea. But I don't like to mention it now. I don't class myself the same as them."

We waited a few minutes until the gas cleared and then moved into the scene of the Sunday shooting.

Thirteen persons died. They were all males. They ranged in age from seventeen to forty-one. None of them was found to be carrying a weapon. The majority were shot in the back while trying to flee. All had been taking part in the civil rights march that had been borken up half a block away when the soldiers barricaded the street and began shooting gas canisters and rubber bullets into the crowd of several thousand.

Liddy was out of the taxi now and limping over to the wall of a two-story brick apartment building. He stood with his back against the wall and his eyes were taking on a look of fear, as though he were back to that awful day once again.

"I stood right here," he said, "and there was a priest, Father Bradley is his name, standing next to me. The paratroopers had just jumped out of their Saracens [light armored vehicles] and they were spraying the area with fire from their semi-automatic rifles. There were four other young lads with us and I shouted to them to stay with me up against the wall. 'Stay right here,' I warned them. 'If you try to run for it, they'll kill you.'"

Liddy is a short man with slicked-down hair. He is forty-five and he has bad teeth. He doesn't look heroic, but he was on that day. You could understand that even though the terror was in his eyes as he looked out into the center of the street where a makeshift barricade against the soldiers still stands. He pointed to the three black flags on the barricade.

"I could see that one boy had been badly shot," he said. "That was Billy Nash. Father Bradley tried to get out there to give him the last rites.

"The paras saw Father Bradley's collar but they fired a blast at him to drive him back. I pulled a handkerchief out of my pocket and tried to go out under it.

"Couple of bullets tore the white flag right out of my hand. I can't understand how I wasn't hit. A girl was standing out there and I rushed out anyway and pulled her back behind the wall. She was too hysterical to move. We stood there against the wall then, wondering what would happen and whether any of us would get out alive."

As Liddy watched in horror, he saw seventeen-year-old Michael McDaid, wearing a freshly pressed tweed sportcoat, walk toward the soldiers. He was killed with a single bullet that went through his cheek and down into his chest. Hugh Gilmore, also seventeen, was trying to avoid being hit by crawling along the pavement, close to the nine-story apartment building across the street.

Liddy watched young Gilmore crawling for the entry door and safety. The soldiers kept firing as he crawled. They missed him three times, Liddy recalls. Gilmore made it to the door and began crawling in when the fatal bullet struck him in the neck.

Someone ran up to Liddy at this point to tell him his brother, John, had been shot.

"I ran around the other side of the building," Liddy said. "He was on the ground. But he hadn't been shot with a lead bullet. They had only hit him under the heart with a rubber bullet and knocked him out."

He helped carry his brother to safety. By the time he was back against the building wall, he saw another seventeen-year-old stumble and fall after being shot while trying to run away. He died instantly. This turned out to be Michael Kelly, Liddy's nephew.

"The paras were advancing toward us now," Liddy said, "firing as they came and they were approaching from both sides of the building we were hiding behind.

"The four lads still standing with me were terrified. I told them to just sit down and put their hands over their heads in a gesture of surrender. They did it for a while, but now one paratrooper came around the corner, firing as he walked. Three of them panicked and ran. All three, James Wray, Joseph Friel, and Gerry Donaghy, were shot. Wray and Donaghy died. They must have fired a hundred shots. It didn't last long but the firing was murderous.

"After it was over they took some of us to the barracks for questioning. That's when I got hurt. They beat me with their batons."

Liddy couldn't believe it was all happening to him. He had worked as a barman in a British army post here for quite a while. He knows many of the soldiers. But he didn't know the paratroopers because they had been brought in especially to control the crowd during this march.

"They beat me for what seemed like hours. Later, it turned out that they held me for only six hours. But I haven't been able to walk until today. I'm black and blue all over my body."

He pointed down toward the middle of the block, and it was as if he were seeing the nightmare all over again.

"They jumped out of those Saracens and they had no riot shields in their hands. They had no batons with them for riot control. They came in shooting because they thought they had trapped the leaders of the IRA.

"All the time they were running me through gauntlets or putting me up against the wall and knocking my feet out from under me, they kept shouting, 'Where's your IRA now? Why don't they come to help you?' "

The nightmare passed, Liddy relaxed. His head dropped. He stood there staring down at three black flags in the street barricade marking where some of the dead had fallen.

Then, unexpectedly, he smiled.

"But I don't have to worry about serving them drinks anymore," he said. "I got word the other day that I've been sacked from my job because of all this. They told me not to worry about coming back. They told me they'd just send me what they owe me in the mail."

IRA GRAVEDIGGER

BELFAST, Northern Ireland—He has been digging graves in Milltown Cemetery for many years, but he had never seen so many people in one funeral procession.

James McCrea, lean and weatherbeaten, dropped his shovel to the ground as he saw the men of the Irish Republican Army and their families bearing the coffin to the grave he had just finished digging.

"There must be thousands of them coming." McCrea said.

McCrea looked down at his black knee-high rubber boots and remained silent for a few moments. It was almost as though he felt he had said something wrong.

Then he looked up again, squinting slightly as he peered toward the group that was carrying IRA man Tony Henderson up to a grave in the plot that contains more than fifty other of his comrades. Henderson, who lived less than a mile away from the cemetery, had been killed by a single bullet fired into his temple. It happened, the IRA announced, during a training exercise outside Dublin.

Many of Henderson's IRA comrades were risking immediate arrest by appearing at the cemetery. They were wearing black berets, marching in military style, and wearing Easter lillies.

The coffin was draped in the green, white, and orange tricolor that is banned in the north of Ireland. The men marching along with Tony Henderson's body were risking a minimum of six months on each offense every step of the way. They were staring into the faces of the heavily armed British soldiers.

"I've dug the graves for the last five IRA men to die," McCrea said. "I've dug graves for a lot more of them, too, but I've never seen so many people turn out."

It wasn't hard to figure why so many turned out for the funeral of Tony Henderson. With the British army conducting nightly searches of homes and the Easter marching season only days away, this city is ready to explode.

McCrea, who lives in the Catholic Ballymurphy area, considered by the army as the city's most volatile ghetto, knows this all too well.

"Do you know," he said, "that despite all the shooting and the bombings, I haven't even had a broken window yet. But I'd better not talk that way. Easter is still coming, isn't it?"

When the Irish get onto a topic they feel is too dangerous for discussion they quite often just change the subject suddenly. They are talking to you about something wildly different, but they carry it off well. They tell you these new unsolicited facts as though it were something you had come upon them especially to ask about.

"Now take this grave right here," McCrea said, "This will be the third coffin in it. Each portion of the grave can take four coffins, one on top of the other."

McCrea halted. His face showed alarm.

"Oh, I don't want you to think we strip the dirt right down to the coffin. We leave four inches of dirt in between. Actually there's no difficulty telling when you've dug down far enough. The spade always hits the coffin below. You can tell right smart enough. The smell is always there."

A little while later a Roman Catholic priest in black vestments had finished his prayers over the coffin of Tony Henderson. McCrea and three assistants hurriedly covered the grave with dirt. As I stood there watching them, I couldn't help remember what McCrea had said a few moments before about this particular grave.

"It's really good dirt to work with, you know," he said. "Some of the other graves around here have heavy clay. It sticks to your spade. This is almost like sand."

The grave was covered over in less than ten minutes. Then, over a loudspeaker, Malachy McNally, one of the IRA leaders in charge of the funeral, delivered an oration. McNally, short and stout, wearing a leather overcoat, bears an amazing resemblance to Jackie Gleason.

"We do not grudge, O Lord, that the flower of your youth has been placed here in the last eighteen months," McNally began. "But we regard it as a tragedy that in this day and age that a young man has to lay down his life in the cause of Irish freedom."

McNally spoke for a few minutes more in a soft and saddened voice as the huge crowd of mourners circled around the area. And then McNally concluded, his voice breaking as he did so:

"Farewell, comrade, angels guard thee."

COME GATHER ROUND ME PARNELLITES

But there is one thing that stands out in my mind about Ireland. If you're in Dublin, "The Trouble" is a hundred miles and a thousand light-years away.

It certainly doesn't bother the men in Madigan's Long Bar.

DUBLIN—Professor Thomas Joseph Benedict Kiely was standing to the left of the double door leading into the premises of James Madigan and Son, spirit merchants on North Earl Street. Ben Kiely, the name his friends know him by, had just ordered another glass of Jameson's. "I have sold another story to *The New Yorker,* a magazine," Ben said, "and this time they paid me the magnificent sum of 1,300 pounds." Now 1,300 pounds figure out to something like $3,000—an amount that was not lost on Ben's companions.

"That's a marvelous sum, Ben," Tony Riordan said. "And it's

even more marvelous if it's true. But it would be even more marvelous if you would buy a drink, Ben. The last time I saw you buy a drink was back in 1961 and I'm beginning to think I'll have to live out the rest of my life without seeing it happen again."

Now in most American bars that I know Tony Riordan's challenge to buy a drink and its implication would have been considered cause for an abrupt end to a friendship.

Not so in Dublin, called "the last outpost of civilization" by its inhabitants.

Ben merely looked over the top of his glasses at Tony, the taller of the two.

"When you wish to speak to me, Tony, will you kindly address me as Professor Kiely? I think that would be a more fitting manner of behavior for a civil servant standing in the presence of a man who is perhaps Ireland's best living writer."

"I'll call you professor or anything you like, Ben, if only you'll buy a drink. For the love of God, Ben, let us see you buy a drink . . . for the first time since 1961."

"Oh, you are a bloody man, Tony Riordan. You are truly bollocks and I would see you in Hell before I would add to your wickedness by buying you another drink."

Kiely, who has served as writer-in-residence at perhaps half a dozen American universities, including Kenyon College in Ohio, Emory University in Atlanta, and the Universities of Oregon and Buffalo, then began reciting a poem by Yeats.

> *Come gather round me Parnellites and praise our*
> *chosen man: Stand upright on your legs*
> *awhile, stand upright while you can. . . .*

At the start of Ben's poetic reading of the fall of Irish political figure Charles Stewart Parnell, a nineteenth-century Irish nationalist, Tony turned to signal the barman. Tony was buying the round of drinks. As he handed the glass to Ben, Tony joined in with the recitation:

> *. . . For soon we lie where he is laid, and he is*
> *underground:*
> *Come fill up all those glasses and pass the bottle round.*

At the sound of Ben and Tony reciting Yeats, the whole end of the bar fell into respectful silence. Moving in to join them came

Tony's brother, Dominic, a poet, and Brian Fallon, the feature editor of the *Irish Times*. In almost perfect unison all four men went through the next twenty-four lines of the poem as easily as an American group reciting the members of the Chicago Cubs infield.

> . . . *For Parnell was a proud man, no prouder trod*
> *the ground.*
> *And a proud man's a lovely man, so pass the bottle*
> *round. . . .*

It was at this point that Ben raised his right hand as a signal to the barman that he was going to stand the next round after all.

As the glasses were placed on the bar in front of them, four old friends had reached the ending which goes:

> *But stories that live the longest are sung above the*
> *glass,*
> *and Parnell loved his country, and Parnell loved his*
> *lass.*

Perhaps the Dubliners are right, maybe this really is the last outpost of civilization.

CHAPTER 5

THE BREAKS

The piece on Patti Counts drew as much reaction as any I've done. Two assistant city editors thought it too long and that she wasn't important enough to rate the space.

Let's face it: That's what assistant city editors are for; to keep readable stories out and make sure all the details of the latest proposed real-estate project are set down.

Who else is here? Tom Erhart, who used to do the Schlitz beer commercials, and Pete Ristich, a small-time hoodlum, who died in a gun battle.

There's Henry Baumann, who died defending his money in a battle with muggers.

And there's Jammed Prince, a favorite who lost it all.

THE REDHEAD

Maybe Laura Patricia Counts, all five foot, eight inches of her, was the most flamboyant thing ever to hit Chicago's Rush Street. Everyone on the street knew her as Patti Counts, the redhead, and almost everyone went for her, especially the swingers and the characters, because they could see right away that Patti was both without even trying.

Patti was a natural, just like Rick Casares, John Wayne, Joe DiMaggio, Red Skelton, and Milton Caniff are naturals in their lines of business. They were Patti's friends, too. But then so were the panhandlers she never passed by, the newsboys for whom she bought winter coats, and the various characters she kept lending money, knowing it never would be returned.

That's why nobody could understand what happened and why someone who had such an obvious zest for life would end it all by putting a gun to her head at thirty-five. This was a girl who came to Chicago from Radford, Virginia, in 1952 and got her first job as a waitress in the London House and fought her way up the ladder to hostess, then public-relations consultant, and finally the successful owner of a club called The Redhead.

On the way she became a familiar name to Chicago newspaper readers because she made the gossip columns more than her clients did. She even gained brief national fame when that late eccentric, Mayor Paul Egan of Aurora, appointed Patti as his police chief for a day back in 1958.

Iris Paul, Patti's best friend, summed her up pretty well. "If she liked you there wasn't anything she wouldn't do for you," Iris said. "But she had a tremendous temper. If you crossed her, you were in for a battle because she wasn't afraid of anybody who ever lived."

In the end, however, all the fight had gone out of Patti.

"I can't say I was as surprised as everyone else," Iris said. "I think that life just finally wore her down."

But maybe it was life on Rush Street that wore Patti down more than anything. Patti wasn't the first beautiful girl to arrive in a big city, dominate it for a time by the sheer force of her drive and personality—and she won't be the last. Patti had been captain of the girls' basketball team at Radford High School and the chief promoter and star of the school's theatrical presentations.

"She was always after me to bring home poster paper," her father recalls, "because she had a real talent for drawing, and she loved to see that all the school's athletic events got maximum advance publicity."

Even then Patti loved to dance and sing, but she wanted to get out of small-town life. She came to Chicago to get a job as an airline stewardess. But the airlines didn't hire her because she was too tall and so she took a job as a waitress in the London House.

"When Patti first started working, she was just an ungainly kid," George Marienthal, co-owner of the London House recalled. "But she learned so fast."

She went into business for herself as a public-relations consultant. By then she was becoming such a big name on the street that Mayor Egan named her his chief of police. Her appointment was a bombshell. It drew national attention, even stunning George Halas, the owner and coach of the Bears, who was sitting in a hotel room in California when he saw Patti's picture on television.

"Isn't that the girl who's dating Rick Casares?" Halas said to Pat Joyce, the Bears' publicity man. "Isn't she something?"

Halas had reason to know Patti well, too, because it was around that time he was forced to fine his entire team because of an incident involving Patti's dog, Little Sam. Fullback Casares had given the dog to Patti as a present. One day, while Patti was driving Rick to practice, the dog disappeared. The entire squad was recruited to find Little Sam, and when the Bears trouped in late for practice after accomplishing their mission, Halas read the riot act to them.

Those were the happy days when Patti was in the news all the time.

Her beautician's fiancé was in the army in Hawaii, and the beautician didn't have the money to make the trip. Patti began a drive to raise enough money for the air fare and a week's hotel stay by collecting Green Stamps. They poured in from all over, even from Holland and Scotland, where the stamps are pink instead of green. The hairdresser went to Hawaii.

Bob Rasmussen, owner of The Store, wanted to start a girls' softball team that could win the Rush Street championship. He contacted Patti. She became the captain and pitcher and they won the title.

Another happy time.

But Patti never really wanted or expected a great deal out of life, her mother, June, recalls:

"The thing she wanted was to have a little club of her own which would be high class. She always could sing, you know, and when she got older her voice got hoarse and she could sing a few tunes, and create the same effect that Marlene Dietrich used to. Songs like 'Red Roses for a Blue Lady' and 'Am I Blue?' "

Patti's mother remembers much more than that about Patti. For example, the time Patti footed all the bills to bring her parents from their home in West Palm Beach, Florida, to celebrate their twenty-fifth wedding anniversary with a weekend at the fashionable Ambassador East Hotel.

"Patti never did anything second class," Mrs. Counts recalls. "The highlight was a big cocktail party in our honor, and there were more than a hundred people there. I remember one of them was Joe DiMaggio."

One day Mrs. Counts's doctor told her she was suffering from cancer and would need extensive treatment and hospital care.

"I didn't know what to do because we didn't have the money," she says. "But my husband called Patti. Within an hour my doctor was on the phone telling me my hospital room had been arranged for. I'd no sooner hung up the phone and it was Western Union. Patti had sent five hundred dollars for my room deposit and she paid all the rest of the bills, too."

Patti finally opened the little place she had always wanted in the summer of 1965. The Redhead—on Chicago just east of Michigan —was a smash.

But it didn't last. One night a man who has been described by at least five people who were there as a "big political figure" walked into The Redhead and proceeded to get loaded and abusive.

Patti never had learned to back off from anybody and so she went for him, ordering him to clean up his language or get out. He threatened Patti then that he would find a way to get her place shut down.

Not long after, the vice squad raided the place and arrested everyone working there, including Patti. When the case came up in court, the judge threw out the charges against Patti, but a girl who had been hired as a part-time singer was convicted. That was enough to close the place, and from that time on, Patti knew nothing but heartaches.

She tried to open another place on Walton Street, to be called The Carrot Top, but the word was out that she would never be able to open another place in Chicago.

About a year after The Redhead closed down, Billy Day, who was one of Patti's great friends and a bartender in The Redhead, shot himself in the head. He lingered for months in the hospital before he died. Patti went to see him every day, watching him die by inches.

Then one of her dogs, Little Sam, the one given to her by Rick Casares, died. Patti went to Atlanta then, hoping to open another Redhead Club there. But negotiations dragged on. Every time it seemed she was making a step forward, she would learn she actually was two steps further behind. Then, one night, Patti called a friend in Atlanta, Willard Allgood.

"I was shaving at the time," Allgood recalls, "so I asked her if I could call her back. She said all right. About ten minutes later I called.

" 'I'm glad you called back,' Patti said. 'I left two notes. One's for you and the other is to tell you what to do with my dog.' "

The next thing Allgood heard was the crack of the pistol.

"Maybe it's because she was just too good-hearted," Iris Paul says. "Patti gave everything she had and she couldn't understand it when people turned out not to feel the same way about her."

Patti's real name was Laura. Remember the classic motion picture? In the end Gene Tierney walked through the front door and she wasn't dead at all. She had just been on vacation. That's the way Patti's friends would like it, too. They'd like nothing better than to see her walking into The Surrey or some other North Side spot, her wild red hair flowing, wearing a tight-fitting green knit suit to match her green eyes, and that magnificent charm bracelet on her wrist.

Then maybe she'd sit on the piano and they'd put the spotlight on her and turn out all the other lights, and in that husky Southern drawl, just one more time, she'd sing for them, so they'd remember it forever, her favorite song:

"Give me some red roses for a blue lady."

"YOU ONLY GO AROUND ONCE IN LIFE . . ."

Tom Erhart braked his bicycle to a halt on Lincoln Avenue at the door of Oxford's Pub. Erhart, tall and slim, a look-alike for actor Tony Perkins, opened the door and wheeled the bike inside.

People at the bar were applauding and patting each other on the back as Tom walked inside. They had all been watching the Cubs game on television in which Jim Hickman, the first baseman, had just hit his second home run of the day.

Erhart shook his head at the sight of grown men sitting in a saloon and watching baseball.

"I don't even have a television set in my house," Erhart said. "I think it's all a bunch of shit."

The baseball game broke now for a commercial. Erhart smiled.

"There I am," he said, "this is what I do for a living."

Everyone in Oxford's Pub was watching closely, too. On the TV screen, men on a ship were performing heroic deeds, all part of the skillfully produced color commercial.

"Listen," Erhart said, "that's my voice."

Sure enough, it was. Coming out of the television set, however, it sounded so much more important.

"You only go around once in life," Erhart said via TV. "You gotta grab for all the gusto you can, even in the beer you drink. Why settle for less? When you're out of Schlitz, you're out of beer."

The commercial is beautiful. So is Erhart's voice, and now he was explaining about that.

"I had such a hangover the day I cut those commercials," Erhart said. "It was so bad I could hardly read. I've always had a whisky voice and that day it all came out just right."

There are some things you should know about Tom Erhart. First of all, he doesn't drink beer. In fact, he particularly dislikes Schlitz. In a time when so many of us are hauling down our flags and selling out, Tom Erhart is still challenging the Establishment at every opportunity.

"Look," he said, now settled safely at a table, "two years ago I filed income tax on $6,000. Last year I got lucky and made some commercials on the West Coast and I filed on $43,000. What is it now, August? Well, already I've topped the $43,000 by a lot. I don't know how high it will go this year."

Erhart sat there smiling, staring at the green bike he had parked in the vestibule of Oxford's Pub. A man with a beard, whom everyone on the street calls Dirty George, approached Erhart.

"I got a generator for your bike," Dirty George said. "I'm broke."

"How much?" asked Erhart

"Four bucks."

"No thanks," Erhart answered. "I've been goin' home loaded every night in the dark. I don't suddenly need a light."

"Tom," Dirty George said, "I'm broke. Besides, I took this from a broad who had just bought it for fifteen bucks. I got the tools. I can put it on right now."

Erhart smiled, relenting.

"Here's the dough," he said.

Erhart handed the money over. But it was no big deal to him.

"I'm a guy who's been around a long time," Erhart said. "I'm forty-one years old. I've been married three times and all my ex-wives are good friends. I've been kept out of trouble by friends . . . bailed out. Now that I've got money I don't intend to save it. I intend to circulate it, put it back into the community. What else do you expect? I'm in the 50 percent bracket. Right away Uncle gets half. My agent gets another 10 percent.

"I don't intend to save any money. Hell, last year, I bounced a $4,500 check for my income tax. Right now, all I wanna do is do something good with the money while I have it."

We were sitting, as I said before, in Oxford's Pub. But a few blocks away, in a place called O'Rourke's, there are several large photographs on the wall.

George Bernard Shaw, Sean O'Casey, Brendan Behan. The only other photograph you can make out of the small ones is of Tom Erhart. I can see nothing wrong with this selection.

The Cubs had scored another run in their game with the San Diego team, and Jack Brickhouse, who announces the games, was shouting enthusiastically. Erhart grimaced.

"The only thing I hate about getting rich," he said, "is that I have to be on the same show with Brickhouse. I can't stand him."

At this point, Brickhouse's voice faded and the beer commercial began all over again.

"You only go around once in life," Erhart's voice rang out all over Oxford's Pub. "You gotta grab for all the gusto you can. . . ."

Erhart smiled, leaned back, and relaxed. It was a pleasant way to spend the afternoon. If somebody would pay me all that dough, I'd team up with Brickhouse, too. Maybe.

NOBODY CRIED WHEN PETE DIED

Nobody cried when Pete Ristich died. And none of Pete's friends around Central and Madison went to his funeral, either. But then they never had a chance to because Pete was buried just hours after his body had been identified in the Cook County morgue and removed to a funeral home.

But the way Pete Ristich died is haunting. He died in a gun battle with police which he brought on himself and from which he had no chance of escaping alive. Some of his friends think he just went crazy. Others think it was Pete's way of committing suicide. There's no way any of them will ever know which theory is the right one.

Pete Ristich was an ex-convict who had spent twenty-seven of his fifty-seven years behind prison walls. He was a loner with fringe syndicate connections who worked out of the Machinery Movers union hall. Never married, he lived alone in an eighty-eight-dollar-a-month walkup a block away from the taverns in which he spent his spare time.

Given his past prison record, and the fact that he served time not only for burglary but armed robbery as well, how do you figure Pete Ristich to spend all day on the street and then walk into Joe Fiala's tavern in his own neighborhood and pull a gun on Joe?

"He wasn't drunk," Joe insists, "and as soon as I saw the gun, there was no way I was gonna die protecting the lousy forty bucks I had in the register. So I gave it to him. Believe me, if I knew how it was gonna end up that way, I would never of called the cops."

It ended up less than half an hour later in the Parkside Lounge a block away with Pete stepping out of the men's room and firing point-blank at Patrolman Samuel Greco. The policeman was hit three times but he kept pumping his own pistol at the same time and so did his partner, Patrolman Earl Leib.

When it was over Pete was dead and Greco was critically wounded and he'll always carry the bullet scars on his chest, jaw, and wrist, and he'll never forget how close to death he came.

And Earl Leib will never forget how it felt to see a man die right before his eyes.

It was 7 A.M. that day when Pete walked into the Old Lennon's Tavern and ordered a Canadian Club and water from Russell Nemitz, the bartender.

Nemitz is a man who has been around. He has an instinct that tells him which of his customers can hold their liquor.

Pete Ristich was a man who could hold his liquor but even Nemitz thought it strange that Pete would come into his place every morning. Especially after what had happened there four years ago.

That was when Pete Ristich fell in love for the only time in his life and it ended so badly. In September 1965, the police nabbed Pete after a young woman testified Pete had shot and killed Pat Lennon, the owner, and had tried to kill her, too.

Lennon had offered to give the girl a ride home, she testified in court. But Pete saw them together and, according to her testimony, shot Lennon and killed him.

Pete's connections with the syndicate helped him here. Sam De-Stefano's lawyer, Robert McDonnell, took over the case and won an acquittal because the police never could find the murder weapon.

"Funny, isn't it," Nemitz said, "that Pete would just keep right on coming in the place, just like nothin' had ever happened."

The Lennon shooting was the one break Pete ever got in his numerous scrapes with the law. The thing about Pete that you have to remember is that although he was a criminal, he was not a skilled criminal. The good ones don't end up behind bars as often as Pete did.

The burglary that earned him a life sentence as a habitual criminal back in the 1930s is typical. That time he broke into the home of a police sergeant who was on vacation.

But while Pete was in the apartment he made the mistake of placing a long-distance call to the Pontiac Reformatory to talk to some of his old buddies. When the phone bill came back, it was a simple matter to check the call and find out who made it.

"How could you trace the call?" Pete asked in disbelief when they nabbed him. "I was very careful. I even pulled the phone out of the wall after I made it."

Two years after Pete entered Stateville, he was named as a ringleader in what was called one of the most desperate attempts ever made at breaking out from that prison.

Pete was first over the wall in a group of five. He climed a rope that was hanging dead center between two machine guns and made it to the top. And then, in what was to become a continuing pattern in his unsuccessful career, Pete dropped to the ground, sprained his ankle, and was quickly recaptured.

A couple of years later Pete's sentence was reduced and he became eligible for parole in 1953. Within months of his parole, Pete was hooked up with what the headline writers called "The Friday Gang."

It was nothing more than a collection of small-time heist guys who hit on the idea that Friday afternoon would be a good time to stick up savings and loan companies.

They did pretty well for a while, but it ended up with Pete being captured and sent back to prison. This time he did eleven years, coming out in 1964.

It was less than a year after getting out for the last time that Pete got involved in the tavern shooting. Since then, however, there had been no serious trouble.

He worked steadily. He kept to himself. His habits were so regimented that you could look at your clock and tell where Pete Ris-

tich was. It was either in the old Lennon place or a little farther
west at Glad's Place.

"Pete liked to sit in here in the evenings," recalls Mrs. Gladys
Harrell, the owner. "He was a gentle man. At least around here he
was. He'd come in and pick up a broom and sweep the place out
for me. He was always willing to do favors.

"He was sensitive, too. I remember awhile back when my husband died that Pete was very upset. 'Glad,' he told me, 'you didn't
ask me to be a pallbearer. My feelings are really hurt.'

"'Pete,' I told him, 'you don't even have a suit. How could you
have done it?'"

"That's right," Pete said. "Here I am, fifty-seven years old, and I
don't even have a suit."

On the last day of his life, Pete stayed for little more than an
hour in the old Lennon place. He apparently went home then and
got some clothes to take to the cleaners and from there went up to
Glad's and sat around for several hours.

"I left the place for lunch," Glad says, "and I swear that Pete
was fine. He hadn't had too much to drink and he had plenty of
money with him, so he certainly didn't pull that holdup because he
was broke."

Less than an hour after Glad left, however, Pete was in Joe Fiala's and the way he moved to the bar with the pistol in his hand
was enough to make the three men at the end of the bar move
away.

Fiala handed Pete the money and Pete reached along the bar to
pick up the few more dollars in change that was in front of the
other customers.

Slowly, almost like a man walking to church, he ambled the
length of the long bar to the front door. As he opened the door,
Pete turned to another bartender, E. C. Bruce, and said:

"Okay, now you can call the cops."

About fifteen minutes later Pete had reached the end of the line.
Ironically, the Parkside is just across the street from Lennon's old
place.

Nemitz, who figures himself something of a philosopher, thinks
about the little ironies in the story a lot these days as he stands behind the bar in Lennon's.

"Just think," he says, "if Lennon were still alive, he could have
stood right here and looked across the street and seen them carry

Pete's body out. Feet first, they took him out. I never knew before that they take your shoes off when you're dead."

That's the way the story ends, and the nagging thing about it is that it's so unsatisfying. The character of Pete Ristich remains in the shadows.

Not even his older sister, Mary, would help.

"Why would I want to talk about Pete?" she said. "He's gone now. It's over. I'm heartbroken. But there's no sensational story. What difference does it make to anyone but me now?"

"Forget about it," says Nemitz, shuffling a deck of cards. "Pete's time was up and that's all there really is to it."

ELEGY FOR A NEWSIE

Henry Bauman wasn't the nicest guy who ever sold newspapers at the corner of North and Clark. But still he didn't deserve to die the way he did.

Henry, who was pushing seventy-five, died of a heart attack after he had been beaten and robbed by four men as he made his nightly rounds of the North Avenue and Wells Street bars to sell papers at 25 to 50 cents apiece.

He had been selling papers in the neighborhood nearly forty years, and there wasn't an amateur mugger around who didn't know Henry was always carrying money with him as well as that stack of newspapers.

Within the last few years he had been mugged four times and beaten on every try. You see, Henry was never a man to back down and he was in the game for money. He never willingly turned it over, even when threatened.

"I'm not gonna be run out of this neighborhood by punks on the street," he used to say as he walked into a saloon at 3 A.M. or so with his head bandaged.

Once he fought three attackers, one of whom finally decked him with an aerosol can, the end of which had been cut off with a can opener. The blow left a perfect circular scar on Henry's head and the attackers made off with 25 cents and a bottle of aspirin.

This last time, it was four muggers who attacked him. One of them grabbed Henry around the neck and choked the breath out of him until the old man collapsed on the sidewalk. They got away with $50 and the police took Henry to Augustana Hospital.

"Damn near choked me to death," Henry told Herman Fleming, who runs the North and Clark newsstand during the daytime. "But I'm not gonna stop walking the streets. That's where I make the money. And besides that, if I just stood there in a newsstand all night long, I'd never get a chance to visit my go-go girls."

In an area that abounds with colorful characters like John the Garbage Man, the Balloon Man, Eddie the one-armed Spanish Civil War vet, Willie the White Rat, and Funnie Herbie, Henry was much too straight to command attention.

But he will be missed. The same people who used to battle with him nightly when Henry attempted to charge them 50 cents a paper that should cost only a dime will be complaining there is now no place to get a paper. They will sit around and recall when George Lincoln Rockwell was shot to death and remember what Henry had said while hawking papers that night.

"Why did they have to shoot him?" Henry shouted. "He never did nothing to nobody."

Henry used the same approach the night that Bobby Kennedy was shot, too, and from this you can perhaps get a hint that Henry had no deep political feelings. In fact his only real feeling, so far as anyone can recall, was for money, a commodity which he never succeeded in collecting in vast amounts. If you offered him a dime for a paper, Henry would sneer at you and growl that he was in business to make money, not to provide a public service.

Try to explain to Henry that you only wanted to pay the price asked for on the front page of the paper and Henry would get angry and answer: "You don't bother me and I won't bother you."

Each time Henry would show up in O'Rourke's on North Avenue with a bandage on his head, Hank Oettinger, everybody's favorite demonstrator, would beg Henry not to battle the muggers anymore.

But Henry was too old. He was too set in his ways. And he liked money too much. He never quit battling. So Henry had his last fight. He lost fifty dollars, and although his friends say he had plenty of money stashed away, it seemed to take the fight out of him.

A couple of days after the fight, Henry suffered a heart attack and he told Herman Fleming that he never felt so sick and old in his life.

"But I think I'll make it out of here, Herman," Henry said. "I think I'll make it home." Herman sensed differently, however.

"I just took one good look at him and figured he was a goner," Herman said. "Hell, he told everybody he was only sixty-eight, and yet I know he was older than I am and I'm seventy-three."

Herman was right. Henry died the next day and now there'll be nobody around in those saloons early in the morning to haggle over newspaper prices. And perhaps the saddest thing about it is that all those people who have argued with old Henry over the years will find out his last name for the first time when they read this piece.

MISSING THE BOAT

These were three of the most delightful men I've met in years. I met them in a place called June's Printcraft, a place where people with ties are looked upon with suspicion. John Lenahan, one of the best photogs in the business, came to take their pictures. You guessed it, the man named Big Bad John was so ugly, Lenahan won a prize. All I got was a hangover.

"There was nothing else a true Scotsman could do," Big Bad John Craig was saying now. "Here was this beautiful Russian bride and not a man in the place who could kiss the way she deserved to be kissed on this the greatest day of her life."

Big Bad John was sitting in a Grand Avenue tavern sipping beer with two shipmates from the Scottish freighter *Roonagh Head* and telling them of this day that became so very important in his life.

"So I gave her a hug and a kiss," he said now, "and the next thing you know the whole Red Guard is swooping down on me. They have no sense of humor over there at all, you know, and by the time I caught my breath I was serving eighteen months in a Leningrad prison."

Jimmy Hartness, tiny and round, chuckled at that.

"When you've been around the world twenty times like I have, John," said Jimmy, "Then you'll learn when it's a time for kissing the girls and time to be running the other way."

"That's right, lad," said Alec Forbes, his other companion. "Damn foolish thing you did. I'm sorry that they clapped you in but it was damn foolish."

"Listen to the man, will ya?" said Big Bad John now. "Listen to the pair of them. Here's a man right here, Jimmy Hartness, who is

one of the well-known sheep stealers in all of Glasgow, and he's tellin' me about kissin' the girls.

"Hartness, do you remember what Robby Burn's said? 'There's
death in the cup, so beware.' That's what Robby Burns said and
it'd serve you well to remember it when talkin' to the likes of me."

Jimmy Hartness was unimpressed.

"John Craig," he said, "I have seven sons and five daughters
back in Glasgow and when we get back home all seven of me sons
will be there waitin' for you and teach you what it is to have respect."

"Respect—it is that you're askin' for, is it?" said John. "You're a
man with a price on his head for stealin' sheep. You deserve to be
preached to death by wild curates."

Alec Forbes laughed for the first time.

"He's right about that Jimmy," Alex said. "When I first met
you, you were a good Celtic man [Roman Catholic] and now I
don't know when it was that you went to a church last."

"Coming from a Ranger man [a Protestant] that's a hard thing
to take," Jimmy answered. "Do you remember when we were sank
together on the Murmansk run? Don't you remember we've been
sailing together for more than thirty years now?"

Forbes's eyes misted over. He put out his right hand toward
Jimmy Hartness.

"Sure and I do," Forbes said. "Give me your hand on it, mon.
Give me your hand."

The two old shipmates shook hands then, and now there were
tears streaming down their cheeks.

Even Big Bad John was affected by the display of their affection
for one another.

"Shipmates," he said. "Friends. That's the way we should always
be. Give me the hand of both of ya."

"Tell you what I'm going to do," said Jimmy Hartness, pulling a
purse from his pocket. "I'm going to buy a glass for us all. We'll
drink to each other like true Scotsmen."

The waiter came with the drinks. Jimmy Hartness looked up at
the clock on the wall.

It was 3:15 in the afternoon. The three friends nodded knowingly.

"The *Roonagh Head* has already left for Milwaukee," said
Jimmy, smiling happily now, "and the captain, that fine gentleman,
is no doubt wondering where we are.

"Let's think up a good excuse, lads. We'll have a night on the town in Chicago and tomorrow it's the bus for Milwaukee and a showdown with the captain."

BOB GIBSON

Here's a classic case of a guy who had the game won. They sent him down and he's been fighting to get back ever since. He's still great, too, but it just doesn't seem to get him back on top.

It was late in the afternoon. In the darkness in the Earl of Old Town pub, less than two dozen people sat blinking into the flickering candles placed at the center of each tiny table.

Up on the stage one folk singer after another took a turn playing a set. After four or five songs, a new singer would step to the microphone. It went this way for a long time. It was all very calm, relaxed, unhurried.

Over in a corner, Bob Gibson was taking it all in, applauding enthusiastically for each song and talking about some of the things the music business has meant to him.

Now in his forties, Gibson, with long hair and a dashiki, looks as though he had once been in charge of all the wine barrels in King Arthur's court and made away with them. His face is a beautiful ruin.

Less than ten years ago he was the hottest thing to emerge from the folk music scene and then he grew tired of it all and went away. Now he's working at putting it back together.

"I don't know about the comeback thing," Gibson was saying. "I don't think it's really that. I split. I went to hide out. It was really a weird time.

"Let's just say that I've stopped my sabbatical, my hiatus. I had to pause to get it together again."

The story of Gibson's effort to get it all straightened out is pretty much public knowledge. Gibson has made no secret of the fact that at the point when he was making an annual income of $40,000 plus, he was badly hooked on drugs.

It wasn't easy for Gibson to beat it, and now that he is on the road back, the drug scene seemed like very heavy conversation for a

Sunday which is a day when even the busybodies should stop prob-
ing.

And anyway, Gibson was in good spirits. For the next three
weeks he will be playing in Chicago on Monday and Tuesday
nights in the Earl of Old Town. After that he is going to the West
Coast to do some things with Roy Silver, the money manager who
turned everything into dollar bills for Bill Cosby and Tiny Tim.

"Maybe it's that it always came easy for me. Maybe that's why I
never wanted to go through changes that people have to go
through.

"I guess I was pretty lucky but I always figured that all it took
to make fifty grand was to have some talent and to pay your dues."

Gibson made the money all right. He was magic in the clubs.
Wherever he went, the name Gibson was a big draw. But it isn't that
big a draw anymore, and he is aware of it all and is fighting to get
back.

Little more than ten years ago the big news in the entertainment
sections was that Bob Gibson was opening at the Gate of Horn,
that a singer named Tony Martin was coming into the Chez Paree,
and that Lenny Bruce would be at Mr. Kelly's.

The Gate of Horn is gone. So is the Chez Paree. Where is Tony
Martin? He's Mr. Cyd Charisse. Lenny Bruce? Lenny Bruce is dead.

"I worked in so many places with Lenny Bruce," Gibson was saying now as another guitar player stepped to the microphone.

"I remember him working in the Blue Angel in New York.
They'd have a complete turnover in the audience within a single
show. That's how many people he'd manage to insult.

"But the clubowners didn't mind. The people would leave and
others were waiting in line to take their place. They'd get double
the cover charge out of every show.

"You had to be incredibly narrow and shallow to think of him
as a dirty comic. One night I remember in Minneapolis, I was the
banjo-playing folk singer on between shows.

"He came back after walking the streets for forty minutes looking for a place to buy a piece of pumpkin pie and a cup of coffee
and did a whole routine on it.

"It was hilarious and I never heard him use another line of it
again. He just brought it right off the top of his head. I can't believe the pressure he put himself under to do that."

Gibson's past and his big years are all intertwined with the big names in the folk singing field. He got into it all after meeting Pete Seeger and then, for a time, played for five dollars a night at the College of Complexes as a second act to Big Bill Broonzy.

It was Gibson who helped Joan Baez, then an unknown, by inviting her up onto the stage to sing with him at the Newport Folk Festival.

"That was contrary to orders," Gibson said, his ample stomach bobbing up and down as he laughed. "They warned me just before I did it that if we all brought our friends up on the stage that we'd never get the show over with.

"She's real people, Joan is. I think one of the things that made her is that she's always been a little weird.

"The coffee shop thing was under way when she was coming on strong and when people would ask her to sing, Joan would tell them she didn't want to.

"Well, people who run things like this can't take it when you tell them you don't want to perform. They turn right around and offer you a whole lot more money. Joan's strong point was that for a long time she really didn't want to be a singer.

"And the longer she kept saying that the more money people wanted to pay her to sing. I remember one time in Boston with her. There she'd be with a full house and she'd sing maybe twenty minutes and quit. Then she'd go out in the alley and sing to a couple of friends for a whole hour."

It was quiet in the place again and Bob Gibson said that even though he wouldn't make any dough for it, he'd like to play a few tunes.

As he walked toward the stage and stepped up on the platform there was a spontaneous burst of applause.

Gibson smiled and the sound of his guitar was warm and rich in the semi-darkness. He began to sing then and all his talent was still there.

> *Snow drifts rise outside my window,*
> *Sit and wonder where did spring go . . .*

He sang several more songs, some sad, some happy. And when he stepped away from the microphone and walked back to the table, the applause followed Bob Gibson all the way to his chair.

THE LAST RACE OF JAMMED PRINCE

I have everything about this minute clear in my mind. I'll never be able to wipe it out.

I've been involved in so many things I had no right to walk away from, but this time I know I'm right. I'm walking away from stall Number 14 in Barn 27 at Arlington Park race track because I don't want to be there when a horse named Jammed Prince is finally put to death.

Just minutes ago, Jammed Prince stood up to the restraining ropes in front of his stall and pushed his head toward me.

"Don't worry," said Bob Hicks, his trainer, "he's pretty sedated. It used to be that he'd lunge at people who passed by the stable but he won't do that anymore."

Hicks, who is thirty-one and a native of New Orleans, walked into the stable and pointed to a spot on the left front leg of Jammed Prince.

Hicks looked back out of the barn and began talking like a man giving a lecture at a veterinary school.

"They call this the proximal sesamoid," Hicks said. "It's just gone, all fractured. Without it, he'll never be able to do anything more than hobble around on three legs.

"He'll have to be destroyed. It's the only fair thing for him."

While Hicks talked of Jammed Prince's imminent death, the seven-year-old gelding, his brown coat still shining from the prerace grooming, stood eating a mixture of oats and bran.

"That's what we usually feed all the horses after a race," Hicks said. "He's used to it, so he might as well have his meal until the man comes and puts him away. Don't you think?"

Jammed Prince had come out of the chute in the first race a 5-to-2 favorite. He was right up with the leaders, seconds after the start, when his leg went out.

Oscar Sanchez, his jockey, knew right away that Jammed Prince was in trouble. He maneuvered the horse to the center of the track and reined him to a halt.

"That's the only thing to do," Sanchez said. "Once a horse pulls up lame you've got to get out of the pack. You try to stay inside and you're liable to get killed."

It took only minutes for the track's emergency squad to reach the scene to give Jammed Prince a tranquilizer to kill the pain in his left front leg.

By that time, no one in the crowd other than those who had bet on Jammed Prince was watching. They were all standing and cheering about the finish of a close race in which the favorite was no longer competing.

That had happened at 2 P.M. Now it was nearly three hours later and Jammed Prince was still standing in his stall waiting to be put to death.

"We can't do it until we get permission from his owner," Hicks said. "He's been a good horse. You never do something like this until you get the owner's permission and he's in Detroit."

"How long will it take?" I asked.

"It could be any minute," Hicks said.

Dr. James Lamar, the vet handling the case, walked quickly along the front of the stall and ducked into the stall next to Jammed Prince.

He jammed an injection of painkiller into the left side of Jammed Prince's neck.

"There you are," he said to Jammed Prince, "there you are. You'll feel better now."

Dr. Lamar walked back out of the stall.

"How will you do it?" I asked.

He understood my meaning.

"We don't shoot them anymore," he said. "All we do is go in and give them an overdose. It's painless. We just give them a shot and they don't wake up."

The doctor walked away.

"We don't usually do it here right in the barn," Hicks said, "unless there's no other way to move them. We usually just walk them out to an open area where they can fall down and where a truck with a winch can pick them up."

I don't know what I was thinking but I do remember that Jammed Prince seemed to be staring at me with what appeared to be blue eyes.

I'm not sentimental about anything and I certainly don't believe horses can communicate with people. But Jammed Prince was looking at me, wondering what I was doing there.

And I knew more than he did. I knew he was going to die.

"How do you think he'll take it?" I asked.

"He'll take it just like all the others," Hicks said. "He'll either rear up a time or two and fall down or he'll go right down on his front legs, make a few noises, and die."

Hicks did not look happy about it.

"You're perfectly welcome to stay and watch," Hicks said. "It won't be long now."

"No, thanks," I said, "I don't want to watch."

And that brings me back to where I started: walking away from Barn Number 27.

Chapter 6

JUSTICE IN CHICAGO

The Black Panther Raid was one of the biggest running stories in Chicago for a couple of years. Fred Hampton and Mark Clark, the Panthers, were shot to death.

State's Attorney Edward Hanrahan was indicted and then unslated for re-election by the Democrats because of all the heat.

Incredibly, Hanrahan ran as an Independent in the primary and beat the Democratic machine's candidate.

We start out now with Bobby Rush, just a few days after the raid.

FRED HAMPTON: "A DEAD MAN CAN'T SAY THANKS"

The sign on the front lawn said the Church of the Epiphany had been built in 1885. But that wasn't why the entire floor of the building was vibrating.

Perhaps three thousand men and women had squirmed their way inside the church on a Saturday evening in December 1969 to attend a three-hour Black Panther rally in memory of the slain Fred Hampton. They were stomping their feet and shouting "Right on!" to the speakers.

They filled every aisle, the altar, and the entire back portion of the building. Those who couldn't find seats sat on the floor. At least 30 percent of the crowd was made up of middle-class whites who had never had anything to do with the Black Panthers before.

As Bobby Rush, twenty-two, the likely successor to Hampton, spoke, the crowd frequently halted him with the floor-shaking foot-stomping.

Rush, who had been freed on bond little more than an hour before, was the final speaker.

His appearance was unexpected, and when he strode through a side door, wearing a black fur cap, dark sunglasses, suede jacket, and green slacks, the effect on the crowd was electric.

Rush walked slowly to the microphone at the altar and made it evident from the start that he hadn't come to speak of peace or reconciliation with the police—whom he held responsibile for the deaths of Hampton and Mark Clark of Peoria earlier in the week.

"This crowd here tonight," he said, "is a message to the pigs in the power structure who are bent on killing black people.

"Fred's murder the other morning set the precedent for genocidal plots against the entire black colony."

The crowd began stomping its feet once more, and Rush held up a hand to silence them.

"Fred told me that before this fight was all over we would all see terrors that would terrify us," Rush went on. "We've seen it happen now.

"Those pigs came the other night armed with shotguns and machine guns and they came with the idea of murdering everyone in their beds.

"But their intelligence was wrong. They thought I was in there too."

Rush halted again and the shouts came from all over: "Right on! Right on! All power to the people!"

"After the massacre of Fred and the others," Rush said, "I had to decide what to do.

"Now I've decided. I'm not gonna relinquish the struggle. What we're gonna do is intensify our struggle."

Once again the crowd went wild in a state of near frenzy as the meeting came to a close.

Earlier, they had approached the same state while listening to William Hampton, Fred's older brother.

He is a tall man with flashing eyes and he was obviously angry as he talked.

"It's nice of all you people to come around now," he said, "but it doesn't do Fred any good because a dead man can't say thanks.

"But there's one thing. Anyone here who doesn't know enough to pick up a gun and get to the business at hand with the pigs is a damn fool.

"My brother died when he was twenty-one years old. I only want to say that it doesn't matter how long you live but what you do while you live that counts."

Hampton then brought his dead brother's fiancée, Debra Johnson, to the microphone.

Miss Johnson had been in the house with Fred Hampton and the other members of the Black Panther Party when the predawn raid by state's attorney's police took place.

Miss Johnson, nineteen, was wearing a tan polo coat and a green dress. She was eight months' pregnant.

She spoke briefly but not softly.

"Pick up your guns and be men!" she shouted into the microphone. "Sisters, you pick up your guns and fight the pigs, too.

"If you don't, they're gonna kill you all for sure."

BOBBY RUSH BATTLES ON

Bobby Rush dropped out of sight after giving this speech. It wasn't until two years later that I saw him again. He called and said he wanted to talk. He was calm. He was a totally different man.

"Are you happy, Bobby?" I asked.

Bobby answered with a sad smile.

"No," he said, "I'm not too happy."

He was now the head of the Black Panther Party in Chicago and Illinois, and he began talking about where he and the Black Panthers were going.

Bobby Rush has lived in Chicago since his mother moved the family here from Sylvester, Georgia, when Bobby was seven.

He is more than six feet tall and weighs nearly two hundred pounds, but he is not overweight. He was wearing tinted glasses, an orange shirt, and bell-bottom slacks. His black boots were shined to a high gloss.

Bobby Rush was the Minister of Defense for the Panthers on December 4, 1969, the morning Hampton and Mark Clark were killed in the raid that is still the subject of court action.

That was a night he'll never forget.

"I still think about it a lot," he said. "I went to the morgue, along with Skip Andrew, our attorney, to identify his [Hampton's] body.

"I still think that the biggest tragedy was not his murder but the fact that he would have been such a great black leader if he had lived. He was only twenty-one when he died.

"Fred was an articulate and powerful speaker and within three years he would have emerged into something great. Most people don't know yet what potential Fred Hampton had."

Bobby sat there silently for an instant, as though thinking over what Fred Hampton might have become.

"What are the Panthers doing now?" I asked. "It seems almost as though you've all gone underground."

"No," he said, "we haven't gone underground. We're more together now than we've ever been. It's just that the Establishment press doesn't think the Panthers are doing anything unless we're having a confrontation with the police.

"I'll tell you a few things we're doing. Last month, for example, on December 4, the anniversary of Fred's death, we passed out 5,000 food baskets and nearly 2,500 pairs of shoes. We're still running our breakfast program for school kids in five centers around the city. We serve nearly 2,000 breakfasts each week.

"We still have our medical center, and during the last year we administered nearly 10,000 tests for sickle-cell anemia."

Bobby was also interested in talking about the newest Panther project on the boards.

"We're conducting a voter-registration drive among young blacks," he said. "We want all the young people, eighteen and up, to get registered to vote.

"We want to gain the power to throw the corrupticians out," he said.

"The Daley machine is in power because of the votes of the black people, and yet it has clearly shown it's not responsive to the needs of black people.

"The murder of Fred and Mark Clark and the complete callousness of the machine toward it has shown people in the black community that it is in their interest to stand up, to come together. That's why we're going after them with this voter-education plan.

"Going after the voters will show the Daley machine we've learned to go after them where it counts."

"But don't you feel that making statements like this will only increase any level of harassment you're now experiencing?" I asked. "Wouldn't it be better to be quiet or even to split town?"

Bobby shook his head. His face did not change expression.

"Within the next six or seven months, I'll either be in jail or dead," he said. His voice was flat. "I'll either be railroaded to jail or killed.

"But if I go down struggling, then my people will begin to see . . . it will become crystal clear to them what their opportunities are."

He then said a surprising thing.

"You know, in a way, Daley is the same as us. He started with the Hamburgs, which was nothin' but a street gang. He understands the energy and the determination of people who are oppressed because he's Irish and he was oppressed, too, when he was young."

The only light in the room was pouring at us from one of those desk lamps that throw a narrow beam. Bobby sat silently now, his face silhouetted.

There was nothing more to say except good-by. Then we headed back to our separate worlds.

HANRAHAN INDICTED

Finally, there came the day that the indictments were opened and Hanrahan was officially indicted.

Edward Vincent Hanrahan stood ramrod straight, directly in the center of the sunlight from a window to the left of Chief Criminal Court Judge Joseph A. Power's bench.

The Tuesday afternoon sun was at Hanrahan's back. The light brown shade had been pulled all the way down to cut the glare in the courtroom, but the heat was still on Hanrahan's back. Little beads of perspiration sat on his temples.

There was nothing about his facial expression that would give a clue to what thoughts were taking shape in his mind.

With the harsh light beaming over both his shoulders, the fifty-year-old state's attorney of Cook County appeared no more than a silhouette to anyone more than five feet away in the crowded courtroom.

Verna Sadock, an artist for NBC News, was standing only a few feet from Hanrahan. At precisely 1:57 P.M., a silence fell over the courtroom. All eyes sought out the door leading from the judge's chambers through which Power would enter to ascend to the bench.

Hanrahan had been staring straight ahead, but now he turned to his right as he heard Miss Sadock's pencil scratching on the surface of her pad.

He turned to face her head on. Hanrahan folded both his arms in front of him and peeked over the top of Miss Sadock's pad.

He smiled at her as she looked up with a startled expression.

"Listen," Hanrahan said, "when you get finished with that, would you send a copy to my office?"

Before Miss Sadock could answer, he continued.

"Say," he said, "make the nose less aquiline, will you?"

Hanrahan's light blue eyes almost twinkled with amusement as Miss Sadock's mouth opened and remained that way for a moment.

"Say, what newspaper are you with, anyway?" Hanrahan asked.

"Oh, I'm not with a paper," Miss Sadock answered. "I'm sketching you for NBC television."

Hanrahan's eyes stopped twinkling and suddenly turned cold blue.

"Well, you know how I feel about your station," Hanrahan said, his voice revealing anger.

"You people don't check out your news. You don't care what you put on the air."

It was a performance typical of Hanrahan. If Miss Sadock had said she were with any of the other television channels, radio stations, or newspapers in the city, his reaction would have been the same.

Hanrahan maintains that every uncomplimentary story written about him has been inaccurate and that the only competent reporters are those who have written puff pieces about him.

Miss Sadock's face registered the shock she was feeling at Hanrahan's reaction. She smiled and made an attempt at small talk the way people do when they wish to avoid an argument.

"Mr. Hanrahan," she said, "I met your brother the other day when I was upstairs sketching the Cabrini–Green trial."

Hanrahan glowered. He looked around the crowded room and then back to Miss Sadock.

"It would be better if everybody went to the Cabrini–Green trial today, too," he said.

Hanrahan turned away from Miss Sadock then and toward the bench. Judge Power had just walked through his chamber door and everyone in the room stood up.

It seemed almost as though the entire scene were something taking place in a movie flashback. There was absolutely no sound in the court as Judge Power opened the sealed indictment he had been holding for months.

Judge Power tore open the envelope at one end and then pulled out the indictment.

Power began talking with the lawyers in front of the bench in a low tone. Hanrahan, unable to hear, moved six steps forward until he was standing right behind the staff of Special Prosecutor Barnabas F. Sears.

Then Judge Power mentioned the name of Edward V. Hanrahan. The state's attorney's expression did not change. He turned and walked back toward the window.

As Hanrahan reached the window he stopped for just an instant. The stoic expression disappeared and now only the misery inside him was in his eyes.

It was for only an instant, though. And then Hanrahan turned around to face the court. Once again, his face was like a map without roads. There was nothing to read.

BATTLING BARNEY SEARS

The man who emerged from the case as a hero to many of us was the special prosecutor, Barney Sears. This piece explains why.

We're all going to remember Barney Sears long after this business has been concluded.

This will be no sad song for Barney. He doesn't need one. Years from now, those of us who were lucky enough to see him operate in the courtroom of Chief Justice Joseph A. Power will remember what happened.

By that time some of the details will no doubt be blurred. We may even forget who the three famous lawyers were who were his adversaries in the hearing at which they questioned Barney's work as special prosecutor for the grand jury investigating the Black Panther case.

Editorial writers and reporters who wear ties five days a week always refer to him as Barnabas F. Sears. They describe him as being silver-haired and sixty-eight years old.

They report that he smokes a pipe and that his manners are courtly. That is all correct.

But in the court, Barney Sears displayed a toughness, a magnificent roughhewn courage against odds, that you had to admire.

He battled Judge Power. He battled his adversaries, attorneys Thomas P. Sullivan and George J. Cotsirilos.

Repeatedly, he stood up to Judge Power, telling the judge he would soon explain the law on this or that matter to the jurist.

And when it was over and Judge Power had departed from the bench, Barney delivered a short but pointed lecture to his adversary attorneys as to what he thought of their performance as lawyers.

It is always kind of magnificent to see a strong man battle against superior fire and that's what Barney was doing.

"I will be as brief as I can," Barney said, "which will be a surprise to a great many people."

Then Barney moved on to a legal precedent cited by his adversaries in asking that the grand jury be questioned in private by Judge Power.

Barney explained to Judge Power that the case cited did not apply and that it was like a word taken out of context.

Without batting an eye, he quoted Justice Oliver Wendell Homes:

"A word is not a crystal, transparent and unchanged. It is the skin of a living thought that gathers meaning only in the context of its utterance."

Barney then explained to Judge Power that he was not there to defend his own conduct before the grand jury.

"If it needs defending," he added, "there are people more capable than I who will be enlisted to do that."

Then Barney, who lectures frequently before bar association groups, trial judges, and law school students, moved in close to the bench for a lecture on what a grand jury is. He explained that it is a last bastion of civic decency in free societies and that it has been in existence since 1167.

"It is the essence of the rule of the people," Barney added, and pointed out that no man can interfere with a grand jury without injuring the free society as we know it.

"The power of the grand jury is not dependent on the court,"

Barney said, "and it need only answer to the general body of citizens."

Barney went on like that for more than an hour. He cited Judge Learned Hand and spoke of the Stuart and Tudor kings and Star Chamber justice.

And he concluded, finally removing his spectacles and looking Judge Power right in the eye:

"It is not your job to supervise the grand jury nor to inquire about what is going on inside its minds before the jury reports. That has been the law."

Barney turned and headed for his seat.

Then he wheeled halfway around and said in parting:

"And I thank Your Honor for his attention."

THE MURDER OF FRED HAMPTON

And then there was Mike Gray, the Chicagoan who had the temerity to make a movie and called it The Murder of Fred Hampton.

And you can imagine how happy the Democrats were when he showed up in the Sherman House on slate-making day and asked them to come and take a look at it.

Mike Gray came through with flying colors. He didn't win or lose. He didn't even get a draw. But Mike Gray spent the entire day doing something to which he feels morally committed and any time any of us carries that off, it's a good day—win, lose, or draw.

Gray, thirty-six, is a slightly built man with a full mustache who often looks like the late comedian Ernie Kovacs. There are times, in fact, when Gray displays a sense of humor that fits this image. But Monday was not a funny day in his life.

Gray, you see, is the filmmaker responsible for the production of *The Murder of Fred Hampton.*

It is a film that many people talk about but few have seen because no major U.S. distributor will touch it.

The film consists of a record of the last year in the life of the former head of the Illinois Black Panther Party as well as a compilation of the events surrounding his death. Hampton and Mark

Clark were killed during a raid by state's attorneys police on December 4, 1969—state's Attorney Edward Hanrahan is now under indictment for conspiracy to obstruct justice in connection with an investigation of the raid.

Hanrahan was attempting to gain reslating by the Cook County Democratic Party despite the fact he was under indictment.

Gray believes Hanrahan should not be re-slated, and he put himself on the line in an attempt to dissuade the slate-makers from doing so.

This is what Gray did. He rented a room in the Sherman House, where the slate-makers were meeting, and arranged to hold continuous screenings of the movie for all fifty slate-makers and anyone else who wanted to see it. Telegrams were sent to the offices of Mayor Daley and Hanrahan himself, inviting them to attend. Invitations were printed for all sixty members of the slate-making committee and handed out by Gray and his associates.

To make sure he would be able to make contact with the slate-makers, Gray checked into the Sherman House at 7:30 A.M. and was waiting in the hall outside the Emerald Room when they arrived.

It was fascinating to watch the reactions of the slate-makers as they accepted the envelopes. Without exception, they appeared anxious to flee the scene as far away from the man with the envelopes as possible.

Gray waited until 5 P.M. No slate-maker appeared to take advantage of the opportunity to see *The Murder of Fred Hampton*. Gray packed up his equipment and headed for home. In the elevator he met County Board President George W. Dunne, and this is what happened next, as Gray recalled it:

Dunne was fascinated by the movie equipment.

"What have you been doing?" he said.

"Well," Gray answered, "as a matter of fact we've been showing a film called *The Murder of Fred Hampton*. I know you're a busy man, Mr. Dunne, but I'd certainly like the opportunity to show it to you at any time and any place, at your convenience."

"That's very interesting," Dunne said.

"Well," Gray said, "when would be a convenient time and place for you?"

Dunne shook his head from side to side.

"No," Dunne said, "I guess I really don't want to see it. This thing . . . it's been such a shame the whole thing ever happened."

Mike Gray got out of the elevator then and the hollow feeling of defeat that had been sitting in his stomach lifted. As he walked through the lobby, he realized he really hadn't lost after all.

HANRAHAN: "I DID IT MY WAY"

But Hanrahan is nothing if not resilient. His idea of defense is to come out to center ring and start swinging from the floor. Here he is, just a month after being knocked off the Democratic slate.

The sound of Frank Sinatra's voice was coming over the jukebox in a place called Alfie's on Rush. It was one of Sinatra's best, a tune called "My Way."

In it, Sinatra sings about doing everything his own way. He has a few regrets but really too few to mention.

"And more, much more than that," Sinatra concludes, "I did it my way."

Just as the Sinatra record was ending, State's Attorney Edward Hanrahan walked through the front door. He blinked a few times, getting his eyes accustomed to the darkness, and then began shaking hands on his way to the bandstand.

This was how it was in January as Hanrahan made a campaign appearance before the Milline Club to talk about his run for re-election.

Hanrahan made his way to the bandstand. Once there, he was presented with a silver-plated bowl by the club president.

"Mr. Hanrahan," the president said, "we are presenting this to you as a token of our appreciation because you came here today to shoot the bull."

Hanrahan smiled as he took the microphone.

He began with a facetious remark about the state's attorney's "happy and unharried life." Then he added:

"I wish I had someone with a G-string sitting here next to me to be sure that you all would be happier."

There was laughter from the small audience of advertising and public-relations men who make up the club's membership.

"I hope there are some registered voters here," Hanrahan said, "who have the courage to go out on election day and vote your conscience and not be intimidated by what these television lights here and a few people with pencils represent."

Once again, Hanrahan was conducting a frontal assault on media coverage of his conduct as state's attorney. It is obvious he believes press coverage of the December 4, 1969, raid on the Fred Hampton apartment finally led to his indictment and subsequent dumping by the Democrats as their candidate.

For nearly an hour Hanrahan spoke of his term in office and his belief that his story hasn't been fairly told in the press. He also referred several times to a civil rights leader on the South Side who he said never has come forth to help Hanrahan in the fight against street gangs.

Then the meeting was opened for questions.

"Mr. Hanrahan," one man began and was quickly interrupted by the state's attorney.

"Wait a minute," Hanrahan said. "Are you a member or a reporter?"

"I'm a member," the man replied. "I hate to bring this up about your indictment, but it seems to us that everyone in the state from top to bottom is under indictment.

"We have the ex-governor under indictment. We have all of these things about the former secretary of state and the state's attorney.

"What can we do as citizens if all the corruption is at the top?"

Hanrahan looked out sternly at his listeners.

"Have you ever been to a meeting of the County Board?" Hanrahan asked. "Have you ever volunteered your services to the PTA at your local school?

"Officeholders must be responsive to voters. I certainly know that," he added.

Another member asked Hanrahan a question.

"What happened on Monroe Street?" he asked. "Were those deaths really justified?"

"That's a moral question," Hanrahan shot back. "I'm not responsible for moral questions. Two successive grand juries have said no crime was committed, that no one was murdered, contrary to the wild charges that were made."

"But how can you say that when you come through the front door and kill me . . ." another member asked, but was interrupted from all sides before he could finish.

"Don't try him here," one man shouted.

"Never mind," Hanrahan said, "that's all right. I'll get back to that question."

"But where do we go for help?" another member asked. "You seem to be against the press and against the courts. You find fault with so many people."

"Well," Hanrahan said, "I read about my being indicted when I was on my way to church on Sunday. How would you like to look in the Sunday paper and see that you were indicted?

"Then I read about how the special prosecutor had exhorted the grand jury to indict me. You've got to realize something about an indictment. It is only a charge against me. It hasn't been proved and won't be."

There was time for only one more question.

"Mr. Hanrahan," a man asked. "You have pointed out how much you have done for the black people in fighting street gangs. How do you think you will do in the black wards?"

Hanrahan smiled.

"I predict we'll have vast support and that we'll carry all the South and West Side wards," he said and then waved his hand good-by to the Milline Club members.

"Thanks," he said. "I'll be back to see you all again sometime after the election."

Minutes after Hanrahan left, the jukebox was playing again. You guessed it. Once more, Frank Sinatra was singing about doing things his own way.

And Hanrahan did it, too—his way.

DICK DALEY STRAIGHTENS THE RECORD

Just when we all thought the police could be wrong at times, Dick Daley stood up on his hind legs to tell us all how wrong we were.

Mayor Daley had finished his speech. Now he looked down at the text to make sure of his closing line. He looked up again and said:

"And remember, it is better for all of us to light one candle than to curse the dark."

At this point several hundred of Daley's aldermen, city department heads, and heavies from the Chicago business world rose to give the mayor a standing ovation. The ovation lasted until almost everyone in the City Council chamber had risen to pay tribute.

I was happy to hear that it is a fine thing to light candles because that was the only new thing I learned from the mayor at this session supposedly called to iron out differences between the police department and the people of this city. It was left to Police Superintendent James B. Conlisk, Jr., to come forward with whatever substance there was to the meeting.

I heard Mayor Daley charge once again that newspapers and television had distorted the news during what he now refers to as the "great convention riots of 1968."

I heard Mayor Daley charge that television camera crews had placed bricks in the hands of people posing for pictures during the early hours of the West Side riots.

I heard him complain because he had heard of an incident in which citizens refused to sign a complaint after being held up and say that this showed once again that the citizens of Chicago are not cooperating with the police.

I heard him say that policemen have feelings and faults and that none of us is perfect! "They are just as human as you and I," Daley said. "It is like a football team when the quarterback gives the signal and sometimes the halfback doesn't follow it."

I heard him say that policemen don't like being called pigs and brutes and SOBs and that they don't like to be spit upon or have "human manure" thrown at them and have their mothers insulted.

I heard him give a remarkable impromptu peroration in which he asserted that the editors of this city's newspapers are responsible for the "saddest desecration and abuse of the news media" for putting what the mayor believes to be rumors in the paper.

"They put it on the wire and it's out, and those machines up there do the same thing," Daley said, pointing to the bank of television cameras.

He thinks news about all minorities is slanted. He put it this way:

"Whether it's about a Jew, a Spaniard, a German, or even a turkey . . . if you ask for the facts, you'll never get them."

I heard the mayor say all these things. But I had gone to the meeting expecting to hear something about a positive plan to assure black people that they will no longer be beaten up by overeager policemen.

Instead, I heard only from the mayor that the police were attacked in 1968 and that the news media are responsible for playing all these incidents out of proportion.

Where has Mayor Daley been recently? When was the last time he spent a real effort in seeing the ghettos himself rather than having it done for him by front men like Alderman Claude W. B. Holman?

And it must be more than thirty years since Irish were referred to as "turkeys." Can Mayor Daley be that far behind the times?

I am told the guest list for Wednesday's meeting was compiled by the mayor's press secretary, Earl Bush. I wonder, too, how much in touch Bush is with the ghetto and its problems. If Bush is, he must spend a lot of time on the road. He thinks Chicago is such a swell and safe place to be that he lives in Skokie.

Opposition aldermen are always willing to give views contradicting the mayor and I don't usually seek them out for that because it's too easy—like shooting lifeboats.

But I ran into Alderman Leon M. Despres outside the press room and we stopped to talk. He wasn't even trying to make a statement for publication.

"I'm just sad," Despres said. "The mayor is just out of touch with the community."

Alderman William S. Singer was like a ballplayer who had been called out on strikes after only two pitches had been thrown.

"I'm appalled," Singer said. "We were called here for a meeting to discuss the police department's problems. People still wanted to speak and the mayor just arbitrarily stops it.

"The issue is not the conspiracy against the police. The police department is in trouble. There are corruption and indictments. There are allegations of brutality. None of these things was discussed."

Alderman Singer left the press room and in came Alderman Vito Marzullo, one of the mayor's staunchest supporters. He had the administration line down pat.

"The public should pay attention," Marzullo said. "They should cooperate with the police."

I asked Marzullo if the real issue wasn't the complaint that cops are brutalizing people in the ghetto.

Marzullo thought a second. "Only when they have to," he said, "only when their backs are against the wall."

I came away from the meeting feeling that it could be dismissed in one paragraph or that a lengthy piece could be written detailing all the ludicrous side events that took place.

But one picture sticks in my mind and if I were a cartoonist I'd draw it this way.

Late in the meeting, Daley sat back in his chair and knocked over his water glass. It fell to the floor and shattered. Daley sat there looking straight ahead as though the incident had never happened.

Conlisk, sitting next to Daley, bent over and began picking up the pieces. He wasn't lighting a candle, but at least he'd go home without a stubbed toe.

WAR IN THE STREET

This is what it's like for a cop in Chicago. It isn't easy. I don't know why anyone in his right mind ever takes the job.

The police squad car pulled to a halt on Larrabee just south of Division. The crowd in front of the doorway of the Cabrini–Green project building had been waiting and now they started to jeer.

It was shortly after 10 o'clock on Friday night, a time when policemen assigned to the Eighteenth District have grown to expect the snipers to start firing.

Patrolman Ed Hoover, thirty-three, was first out of the car. Patrolman Dennis Brucato, thirty, the driver, was next. Hoover is black. Brucato is white. The men and boys in front of the door were black.

"Here come Mayor Daley's kissin' cousins," a big guy in a red beret shouted as they approached the door.

Policemen have a way of handling hecklers. They don't pay attention to them. They never let on they are apprehensive. They act as if nothing out of the ordinary is happening.

Hoover, a slim black man with a mustache, grew up in the neighborhood and played basketball at Wells High. He knows his way around. The taunts don't faze him.

"What's the trouble?" he asked a man in the crowd.

He was answered by a whooping chorus of voices. The disturbance, it turned out, was over a naked man lying unconscious in the first-floor elevator.

They entered the building, elbowing their way through the crowd jamming the corridor. The black man was unconscious and he didn't have any clothes on. He was shivering badly in the cold.

Someone threw a pair of trousers, ripped in the knee, over the crowd and into the elevator. Hoover, who led the way, began pulling them onto the man's inert form.

"Call for a wagon," he shouted to Brucato. Brucato, who had carried a walkie-talkie into the building, tried to do so but the signal didn't penetrate the building walls to the dispatcher.

By then there was so much shouting in the dark and narrow corridor that it was impossible to understand what anyone was saying. But everyone was having a grand time. Many of them had been drinking.

"He came stumblin' in here awhile back," a middle-aged woman with a gold tooth in the front of her mouth said. "He was drunk. But when he got on that elevator he had clothes, at least. Now he's naked as a jaybird."

Hoover was not spending any time listening to gossip. By then, with the assistance of two other project residents, he was carrying the man through the hallway to the squad car.

Brucato was back now. "I got through," he said, "but they don't have a wagon to send. Let's take him with us to Henrotin."

At Henrotin Hospital, Brucato and Hoover made a few checks and found that the unconscious man was an eighteen-year-old runaway from Chicago State Hospital.

About an hour before they had picked up a fourteen-year-old white boy who had also escaped from Chicago State with a black friend named Willie early in the day. The fourteen-year-old boy, also unconscious, had been taken in by a Puerto Rican family in the 700 block of Schiller after they found him on the street.

"I call you right away," the Puerto Rican mother had told Brucato as he entered her frame house.

"If we leave him on the street, he'll be killed."

"Who gave you the whisky?" Brucato said, shaking the boy to consciousness.

"My friend Willie," the boy said. "Willie got it for us. I told him I had never been drunk before."

The boy passed out again. Within two hours he would be back at Chicago State, where he had been an inmate nearly four years.

The Eighteenth Police District is one of the highest crime-rate areas in the city. The most dangerous part of it for a policeman is the four-block-square area called the Cabrini-Green Housing Project.

In its thirty-five acres, 25,000 people are jammed into seven-, ten-, and nineteen-story buildings. Police report sniper fire from them almost nightly. The only way for a policeman to move when approaching the projects is quickly. Policemen who walk slowly make too tempting a target.

Often calls for help are made from the projects merely to lure squad cars within shooting range. Policemen who get inside the building face the danger of being trapped in elevators. Those who climb the stairs face the danger of being shot at from darkened corridors.

Friday night, Hoover and Brucato spent eight hours in the area, much of it cruising in and around the project. It was eight hours of tension in which every call presented the potential of turning into a fatal gunfight.

And even when they were not breaking up brawls in crowded taverns or preventing husbands and wives from murdering each other, there was the constant threat of attack from riflemen poised in the high-rise windows.

The most dangerous building in the district, policemen will tell you, is 1150–1160 North Sedgwick, in the project, and now Hoover and Brucato were on their way there.

"Here we go," said Brucato. "Man armed with a shotgun threatening a woman. That's great. I thought this was going to be a quiet night."

By the time their cruiser moved into the parking lot, another, driven by Patrolman Bill Dunn, was parked and waiting. A third car, driven by Sergeant Ray Peddie, pulled up seconds later.

Delores Hill was standing by the elevator with tears in her eyes. She was still very frightened.

"He had a shotgun," she said, "and a scarf over his face. He pointed the gun at me and told me to throw my purse on the floor. I didn't have much money in it, just some change.

"But this stuff's gotta stop. My God, it's gotta stop. Hurry, they say they saw him on the tenth floor."

Brucato pushed the button on the elevator. It wasn't working.

The art of halting elevators is something that every petty hood-lum living in the projects has long mastered.

Last fall, someone lured three policemen into an elevator in one of the buildings, stopped it, and then tossed a Molotov cocktail at them. The policemen barely escaped being burned to death.

"Let's take the stairs," said Sergeant Peddie.

"Wait a minute," he said to a fourth patrolman who had arrived with a shotgun cradled in his arms. "You go first. Do you have a round in the chamber?"

The officer nodded, grim-faced. All four policemen began walk-ing up the stairs, searching each floor. They had no idea in what darkened corridor the man with the shotgun was waiting.

The only officer to remain behind was Ed Hoover, who was fill-ing out a report in the squad car.

It was a long climb in the dark to the tenth floor. By the time the four policemen reached it, they were puffing.

The man with the shotgun wasn't there.

One of the policemen stood at the grated railing catching his breath and looking out over the city. It was a clear night. He could see the glowing lights ringing the top of the John Hancock Build-ing. In the other direction he could see the Wrigley Building bathed in spotlights.

He was looking at the face of Chicago which appears in the four-color magazine advertisements. But he was standing in a spot that is terrifying in its reality.

"They all talk about how we're losing the war in Vietnam," the policeman said. "They don't even know about this war. What's worse, by God, is that we're really losing this war and no one seems to care."

A shotgun blast rang out and then echoed.

Patrolman Dunn walked over to the railing. "Let's just say that was a firecracker," he said, smiling. "Firecracker, my foot. It's start-ing now. They'll be going all night.

"See that building over there," he said, pointing to another part of the project. "A couple of weeks ago the snipers were on all top six floors at one time. Boy, that was a night."

"All right," Sergeant Peddie said, "we can't do any more here. Let's go back down the stairs. For God's sake, be careful. Keep look-ing."

The walk back down the stairs was easier.

Patrolman Hoover was waiting in the hallway, his gun drawn.

"What's wrong?" asked Sergeant Peddie.

"Think somebody took a shot at me," Hoover said. "Blasted the window out of the squad car. I just rolled right out the other side of the car and made for here."

Sergeant Peddie shook his head from side to side.

"Well, let's beat it for now. Head for the cars and don't take your time about it. We don't even have a chance this way."

The policemen moved out into the parking lot and got into their cruisers. But they didn't run. They didn't even seem frightened. Perhaps they figure that you can't outrun a bullet anyway.

The window on the driver's side of Hoover's and Brucato's squad car was shattered. The front seat was covered with broken glass.

Brucato was driving now, heading back into the Chicago Avenue station where a report would be made on the shattered window.

Neither patrolman spoke for several minutes as the car drove away from the Cabrini–Green project.

Hoover spoke first.

"You know," he said, "havin' a thing like that happen just shakes the hell out of you."

CHAPTER 7

STAR LIGHT, STAR BRIGHT

Who the hell does John Wayne think he is anyway? He has had lackeys running around and doing his bidding for so long he really believes he's all of those heroic figures he portrays in the movies. Well, why shouldn't he believe them? We made him a millionaire because of them, didn't we?

I don't know whether the piece about Dick Gregory really works or not. But I like him and I like to jog so it was easy to put the two together.

JOHN WAYNE'S COMMANDMENTS

Trail boss John (Duke) Wayne dies in his film *The Cowboys.* Wayne dies—heroically, of course—after being shot in both arms, one leg, and twice in the back by the leader of an outlaw gang.

In true John Wayne style, the Duke takes all five of the bullets in the back rather than turn around and let the outlaw have the satisfaction of seeing the Duke's face while he dies.

Several scenes later, the eleven youngsters, ranging in age from nine to seventeen, who make up Wayne's entire trail gang in the film, gather around the Duke's grave while Roscoe Lee Browne, playing a black trail cook, delivers a eulogy.

"He's not alone," Browne says as the youngsters break into tears. "There are many of his kind resting here. The prairie is like a mother to him."

You get the picture, I'm sure. It is typical John Wayne. As usual, he is big and gruff and he likes to drink whisky neat. He has *machismo* and he is marvelous with his fists, with women, and with kids.

He shoots straight and he has a heart of gold. If only there were more like him, our country would be in a lot better shape than it is today.

This is a character Wayne has been playing in the movies ever since we can remember. It is a character largely created for him by screenwriters and directors. But one now suspects that the screen John Wayne has memorized so many of these scripts and taken so much direction that there no longer is any other John Wayne, if indeed there ever was.

You couldn't help but think this as Wayne stood on the stage of the Bismark Theater here and spoke to four hundred student editors from all over the country who had just viewed a preview of *The Cowboys.*

They greeted him with a standing ovation, and it seemed for a while that everyone in the theater had brought his own camera and flash-bulb attachment to capture this picture of the Duke in his dark, single-breasted suit and his horn-rimmed glasses.

"They told me to come out here on stage and do what I do in the movies," Wayne chuckled, "but I didn't want to shoot you all."

There was laughter from the audience.

"All kiddin' aside," the Duke said, "weren't those youngsters in the film wonderful? You see, this is a wonderful story of how boys grew up the hard way in the old West."

There was more applause from the student editors.

In order to appreciate the point Wayne was making, you should know something of the plot of *The Cowboys.*

In it, Wayne, playing the trail boss, hires eleven youngsters to run his herd of cattle to market. They are set upon by rustlers. Wayne is killed.

But the youngsters have learned well their lessons from Wayne. They break out their guns and go after the rustlers for revenge.

In as bloody a ten minutes as you're likely to encounter in the movies, they kill all thirteen rustlers. One is stabbed in the stomach by a boy actor who can't be more than nine.

Another is killed by having his head crushed by three youngsters wielding rifle butts. Another rustler has his neck broken.

All of the others are shot except the chief rustler. His fate is special. He is the one who killed Wayne.

We see him groveling in pain under a horse for several minutes, screaming that his leg is broken. The youngsters stand around looking impassive. Then one youngster cuts the horse loose so it can get on its feet. Another fires a pistol to stampede the horse.

The rustler with the broken leg is dragged screaming into the sunset. The process of growing up has been completed for the youngsters.

"Growing up is not meant to be easy," Wayne said from the stage, "but it's easier if you pick your values along the way."

Wayne was reading from a prepared text but with sincerity.

"Love your parents and your flag and your God," he said. "Learn the Lord's Prayer and carry its meaning with you. That's the first thing.

"The country is the second thing. You know, this country was started a couple hundred years ago by a boatload of pilgrims. Maybe we grew too fast and maybe we made some mistakes. But that's no reason to throw stones and tear up the best flag that God ever made."

The Duke was interrupted by applause.

"Well, you kids," Wayne continued, "someday you may have to leave this country to fight a war and give it everything you got. If it's threatened, you may have to give it more than you've got."

The Duke knows about giving his life for his country. He did this in *Sands of Iwo Jima* and *The Fighting Seabees*.

Wayne's voice broke slightly and it wasn't certain whether he was out of breath or choking back the tears.

"You're America's tomorrow," he said. "You're all that guys my age have going for us. You have obligations to this country. Pay your way. Live by the Golden Rule.

"Don't kick a man when he's down."

The Duke removed his glasses and looked over the lectern and down into the audience. He is a tall man with a ruddy face and he is very broad, both in the shoulders and around the middle.

But you couldn't mistake him for anyone else in the world. He owns one of the world's most famous faces. He gave the audience that wry smile he always turns on at the end of the picture, just before riding off.

"Shucks," he said. "I didn't mean to do all this preachin'. Just bein' with you today has brightened my life, now and always."

The Duke walked off the stage then, his head high, in that unmistakable movie walk, as the audience rose to applaud.

DICK GREGORY BY DEGREES

A light rain was falling. The cinder path that runs around Washington Park was dotted with puddles.

But Dick Gregory didn't mind. He already had been jogging for twenty minutes, tiptoeing around the water in his red, white, and blue track shoes and tailor-made blue sweatsuit.

It was late Tuesday afternoon. In less than two hours Dick would be walking into Peoples Church of the Epiphany on Ashland to accept an honorary doctor's degree from Malcolm X College.

"Man," he was saying now, "this is really cool. Here I am, a dude that never even finished college myself, and I'm gonna become a doctor.

"Hell, this'll be a great thing for me. I'm gonna go right out tomorrow and start accepting patients."

He started laughing at himself then, obviously having a good time.

"Hell, by the time anybody finds out I'm not a real doctor I'll probably have cured about thirty-seven people of what ails them."

Dick, who speaks at a different college virtually every day of the year, had cancelled a speaking date Tuesday so he could attend the Malcolm X commencement.

"Man, I really feel good about this one," he said, "because I really had so much admiration for Malcolm. You know, kids come up to me all the time and they tell me they want to be like Malcolm.

"I tell them I think that's fine, but they really should know what they're about. Malcolm wouldn't be an easy guy to be like because he probably was the most moral man I ever met.

"When he got into his thing he didn't smoke, he didn't drink, and he didn't mess around with women. That's why they had to kill him. There was no way they were gonna be able to discredit him and they knew it because he was just too strong for them.

"So the only way they could stop him was to kill him, and that's exactly what they did."

Dick dodged a wire that was hanging from a tree branch.

"No matter how many times I come through here," he said, "I always jump when I see that wire. It always comes up on me when I don't expect it and I always think that it must be hot."

Dick was smiling again now, his large white teeth made ever more pronounced by the contrast with his full black beard which now has a tiny patch of gray on the right side.

"Man," he said, "if I had been a nigger who played within the system I probably would have been one of those Junior Chamber of Commerce dudes and tonight I might be getting an honorary degree from Loyola and people would be paying twenty-five dollars a plate to come to see me.

"But I like it much better this way. Imagine a thousand years from now when the archeologists come digging around my bones and they find that degree from Malcolm X.

" 'Hey,' they'll say, 'dig this cool cat with the degree from Malcolm X College. We'll have to go into this one further. There really must be some story here.' "

There certainly is some story behind Dick Gregory. A college track star at Southern Illinois University, he has a younger brother who was captain of the track team at Notre Dame.

And for the last ten years, every time there has been a civil rights demonstration, Dick Gregory has been in the front line of the march, sacrificing a career as a nightclub comic that could have earned him more than $100,000 a year.

Now he is into a whole new thing with his lectures on college campuses, which he figures bring him into contact with more than a million students a year.

"Those kids are really turned on," he said now. "I knew all along that Kent State was a hotbed. A lot of people thought they were just farmers down there, but they've been into it for a long time.

"I'll tell you something else. The five most radical campuses in the country are the University of Buffalo, Miami University in Florida, Iowa, Arizona, and, hold on for this one, South Carolina.

"Buffalo is just outta' sight. I went up there and gave a talk that should have lasted an hour and it seemed like I was on stage for seven hours.

"All you have to do is scratch your nose and you get a standing ovation. I'm not sure I even have the strength to ever go back there again."

Dick had finished his three-mile stint for the day and started back for his station wagon.

"You know," he said, "things are so much better for us today.

The young people who are coming up are just so strong. And they've got so many models they can go for.

"There's Malcolm and Martin Luther King and, yes, Stokely and Rap Brown.

"They have so much strength and determination that all us old dudes have to do is sit around and give advice."

I don't think anyone would believe for a minute that Dick Gregory thinks of himself as just some "old dude." Certainly the policeman that Dick met in the dry cleaner's a few minutes later didn't think that.

"Say," Dick said, loud enough for the policeman to hear, "know what all us black folks are laughin' about today?

"We're all talking about Mayor Daley askin' for Governor Ogilvie's resignation. As long as he's asking for resignations, why doesn't he ask his pal Hanrahan to resign, too?"

Chapter 8

"IS THAT ALL THERE IS?"

Strange, the things that come to mind when you look pieces over after not seeing them for a while. I went out to see Janis at Ravinia and it was only a short time before she died. But what sticks in my mind is Jack Lane, the photographer, nudging me and saying:

"Do you know who that guy in the cowboy suit is?"

"Yes," I said, "He's Janis's manager."

"Yeah," Lane said. "and he's also Alistair Cooke's son."

Looking at the Peggy Lee piece I think of the time I went to the Empire Room to do an interview with Tony Bennett. It was a disaster. He had nothing to say. But what I really think about is the night I went there with Jimmy Breslin and Bennett dedicated a song to Breslin.

As soon as Bennett began to sing, a fight broke out between people at two ringside tables. The house lights went up and Breslin waded into the fray.

"Goddamn," he said, "let's stop these mothers. This is the first time in my life anybody ever dedicated a song to me."

JANIS'S SOUTHERN COMFORT

"It's like I told Mike Wallace before I went on his show: 'Don't ask me those dumb questions or I'm going to start screamin' . . . for all your million listeners.' "

Janis Joplin, twenty-seven, the pride of Port Arthur, Texas, and Haight-Ashbury, sat in her dressing room in Ravinia waiting to go on stage.

Joplin wore blue silk slacks and a purple see-through blouse. She had matched them with oversized blue sunglasses and purple ostrich feathers that reached up in the air a foot above her head.

"All right, man," Joplin said, "you're here to ask some intelligent questions. Go ahead, say somethin'."

A look of crafty understanding appeared in Joplin's eyes.

"No, no," she shouted at a photographer. "Keep the two bottles of Southern Comfort out of the pictures. My manager says my national image is bad enough already."

Joplin snorted. Nervous laughter in the small room. Incredible. Everyone is afraid of her. She is so big in her little world, this girl with the double chin and pockmarked face, that everyone is really afraid.

"Damn," Joplin shouted. "Where's the goddamned tea? Somebody get me a pot of tea."

"Right away, Janis," a man called in a frightened voice from outside the door. "It's on the way. It's just that there are so many people outside." (An estimated 18,000 fans, including Senator Charles H. Percy, attended the show.)

"Does it make you tired when people ask you about the derivation of your style? When they ask about Bessie Smith and Otis Redding?"

"Naw!" Joplin said, "naw, that doesn't bother me. That's just irrelevant."

"Well, what does bug you?"

"People who come in and ask me questions about Otis Redding," she replied with a triumphant snort.

The three young men in the cowboy hats and handlebar mustaches—who were there to ask for jobs—broke into laughter, competing with one another to see who could provide the most genuine laugh.

The tea arrived. Cheers all around.

Another Joplin assistant in a cowboy hat moved in.

He grabbed the Southern Comfort bottle and filled a paper cup to the halfway mark.

In goes the tea bag. Then the hot water.

"For the throat, baby," Joplin said. "Sometimes I don't think it's gonna last another day."

"How is it with you now that you've made it?" a man asked.

"Made it? It's been so long, baby, I don't know. . . ."

Then Joplin comes down off the put-on.

"It's more complicated," she said. "It's harder to make friends

. . . harder to figure out what everyone's after. . . . You're travelin'
a lot and you don't see the people you want to see . . .

"Yet when you get on the stage, there ain't nothin' like it.

"When I weigh that rush they give me on stage and the feelin' it
gives me against waitin' for some insurance-salesman husband to
come home . . ."

Joplin had talked in the past of something she calls the "Saturday night swindle."

Everybody has experienced it in one way or another. When they
were kids and watched their parents get dressed up on Saturday to
go out for a good time.

"It was a swindle," Joplin said, "because when I got old enough
to go out on Saturday night I found out nobody was really havin' a
good time.

That's the Saturday night swindle."

"Okay, Janis," she was asked, 'how has success really been for
you? Has that been a Saturday night swindle, too?"

Joplin laughed a deep, throaty laugh.

"Naw," she said, "not that way, it hasn't. Everything lets you
down, man. You know that.

"But once you know it, you're okay. 'Member, couple o' years
ago I had what I called the Kozmic Blues?

"Now, it's not that way. Once you know you're gonna get let
down, there's nothing to do but laugh.

"Once you know it's all ridiculous, it's all fine. . . ."

Joplin was pleased with herself now. She smiled as if she was
about to say something as eloquently as Albert Schweitzer.

"Why not sit back and enjoy it as long as you know you're
gonna crap out in the end, anyway."

PEGGY LEE AT FIFTY

Norma Engstrom is fifty years old now and she's been a star for
almost thirty of them. You would think she long ago would have
learned how to coast.

But there she was Tuesday afternoon in the Empire Room of
the Palmer House, sitting in a straight-backed chair and listening to
the orchestra as it ran through the numbers for her opening-night
performance.

The bus boys and waiters were shuffling tables around and rattling silver in the background, but apparently they had no effect on her concentration.

Her platinum hair was hanging down over the shoulders of her black pants suit. She had a Coke in one hand and a cigarette in the other. She was catching every sound that was coming from the twenty-three musicians in front of her.

Nobody has called Peggy Lee by her real name for a long time.

But the story of how she pawned her graduation watch, borrowed her father's railroad pass, and took eighteen dollars with her on a train from Jamestown, North Dakota, to Hollywood has become a legend to every girl who ever wanted to become a big-time singer.

The trouble is that there hasn't been any room at the top for so long.

It must seem to every kid who could carry a tune that Peggy Lee and Ella Fitzgerald have always been up there barring the path.

"There's one chord in the introduction that bothers me," she said through the mike in a voice that is husky and yet so distinctive it is difficult to describe.

"Turn up the mike, a little, will you?" she asked her manager.

The band started running again through a tune called "Come Back to Me" and she called a halt.

"Drummer, roll into that part," she said. "Maybe you can do something on the cymbals . . . and make it just a little bit slower."

The orchestra, which was being led by her personal musical conductor, Lou Levy, started over.

This time Peggy Lee began singing along, still seated so she faced the band.

At first she sang softly. After a while she apologized to them.

"My voice hasn't opened at all yet," she said. "But it'll be all right. I'm gonna do a lot more singing before the afternoon is over."

By the time the orchestra was running through the next song, one of those sad bits about fated lovers that she always does so well, Peggy Lee was on her feet at the mike. Now she was facing the waiters who were still moving tables and bringing out fresh tablecloths.

". . . And tomorrow if you ask me for the world, somehow I'd get it. I would give my very soul and not regret it . . ."

A few of the waiters began to applaud. This is the way it has always been with Peggy Lee. She never has been known to give a bad performance.

The orchestra took a five-minute break. While they were drinking coffee, Peggy Lee called three of four guitar players in the band to one side and ran through a single chord with them over and over that she didn't feel they had right.

"It's not funky enough," she said. "Try starting a little higher on that note. Listen to me sing. I think you'll get what I mean."

Over and over they tried. Finally, they had it.

"Thanks, fellas," she said.

By this time the other musicians were back and ready to go into the third hour of rehearsal.

The last hour was the best. This was the full-scale rehearsal with the lights out and the band playing as loud as it would during the regular performance.

Nobody else in the business works this hard the day they're opening.

She sang songs like "You'll Remember Me" and "One More Ride on the Merry-Go-Round" that have both humor and a hint of sadness, and others like "I Was Born in Love with You" and "Is That All There Is?" and "Goodbye" that can tear your heart out.

Peggy Lee had been working for more than three hours when the band finished the finale and they turned the house lights up.

"What time is it?" she asked her manager, who had been taping the final run for timing.

"It's 6:15."

"Good," she said. "Plenty of time to get my hair set, get dressed, and get back here to do the show."

THE JEFFERSON AIRPLANE

It may seem to you that every time we get more than a thousand people together in one place in Chicago we have a riot. That's not always so. This was one of those times.

There were more than 50,000 cheering and chanting rock fans standing with their arms raised in tribute one Monday evening as

Grace Slick, lead singer of the Jefferson Airplane, stepped to the mike.

The crowd, which had begun forming in Grant Park in substantial numbers at noon, extended as far back to the south as the statue of Christopher Columbus, and as Grace Slick stood there, she could see they were jammed on the rooftops of the refreshment stands to her left and right and balancing precariously atop the light towers, too.

"Since this concert is for free," she told her audience, "you ought to take the five dollars you would have had to pay for the ticket and go get some acid for yourself." The concert was free because the Jefferson Airplane felt like donating its time.

The crowd roared its approval as the Jefferson Airplane, which is the leading exponent of the San Francisco school of rock music, began blasting away at the eardrums of everyone within a hundred yards.

If you have never seen the Jefferson Airplane perform, the thing you have to know is that it is made up of four instruments and two singers who shout and moan as the instruments are played at the highest decibel level.

Among the cognoscenti this is called hard rock, electronic rock, or acid rock. Sometimes, too, it is called love rock because most of its songs have lines like "Reach over and touch somebody."

The crowd, which easily walked through a line of Andy Frain ushers to stand right on the stage with the music group, was made up of the widest possible range.

There were, for example, hundreds who had been in Grant Park the August of the Democratic National Convention.

There was Dave Paten a Loyola student who boasted he had been on the tail of General Logan's horse when the police made their charge.

"Maybe we'll be going back there before it's all over," he said. "You can see I'm ready, can't you?"

Paten, one of the more colorfully dressed in the crowd, was wearing an old tablecloth and his feet were bare.

"It's my war blanket," he said proudly.

He was among the happiest when Miss Slick, a former model who once studied at fashionable Finch College, urged everybody to start dancing.

"You're all sitting there like you're in a classroom," she said, "or, even worse, at a Democratic Convention."

It was a day for colorful clothing and the Jefferson Airplane themselves wear outfits that defy description. Miss Slick, the only female, has the shortest hair of all.

The crowd enjoyed every minute of the two-hour performance which went off without any major difficulties.

There were no policemen visible until the show was well under way and then no more than a dozen ever appeared on the scene.

The move to keep the policemen away was a shrewd one because those that did show up were shown that the events of the convention hadn't been forgotten.

"Look at that gun" one young long-haired man said to a policeman. "Just look down there and take a look at it. It's ugly, man, and you're ugly for wearing it."

But the crowd wasn't made up entirely of political activists. It couldn't be. There aren't that many of them around.

On the fringes were men with attaché cases, mothers with babies and picnic baskets, black-leather-jacketed members of a motorcycle gang allied with the Hell's Angels, and teen-agers Mark and Debbie Schultz from Lombard who brought their afghan, Creme, along with them.

Miss Slick has to be the star of the outfit because she's the only one anybody can understand.

Music critics say she sounds like a cross between Dinah Washington and Mick Jagger. That may be. But it all comes on a little too strong when she sings a song like "Somebody to Love."

There she was, belting out the song, and at least 10,000 of her listeners are going through these wild arm-waving, hip-swinging gyrations that are enough in themselves to shut out all sound.

There was only one close moment when the crowd surged toward the bandstand and it appeared that some people in front would be crushed against the stage.

"Please move back," asked Miss Slick, "Everyone up front is being squished."

Marty Balin, the other lead vocalist of the group, saved the evening at this point, however.

"Listen out there," he said, "there's a big pit under this stage and it's full of alligators. If you don't move back we'll open it up and they'll come out and eat you."

It was a hell of a night for alligators.

CHAPTER 9

RUNNERS WHOM RENOWN OUTRAN

The athlete-hero lives in a world of make-believe. On top, he is invincible. The glory can never end. But end it always must. The day the cheering stops, the silence strikes like a blow to the heart. Now life must start at the beginning . . . but this time on vastly different terms.

If your name is Johnny Morris or Paul Hornung and you have a certain amount of natural charm, you can get a job as a television sports announcer. If you have the drive of a Clint Frank you can become an advertising agency president. But there are only so many jobs in television and even fewer presidencies of advertising agencies.

Suppose your name is Lou Novikoff who once was supposed to be another Babe Ruth for the Chicago Cubs and you never went past the eighth grade. . . . Or Minnie Minoso who dazzled White Sox fans for years with your startling play and then found there was nothing left. . . . Or Barney Ross, who had it all and never even realized until the last moments that it had slipped away.

LOU NOVIKOFF AND MR. RAFT

I learned a lot about big-hearted baseball people doing this piece. I was traveling with the Chicago White Sox at the time I tracked down Lou Novikoff. Howie Roberts, the Sox publicity man, was delighted to hear I was going to see Novikoff.

"When I covered the Cubs years ago, Novikoff and his wife had me out to dinner many times," Roberts said. "Give him my best."

The next day I came back with more than my best. I had two

137

dozen tickets for a benefit they were holding for Novikoff, who was broke and out of work. Would the White Sox or Roberts like to buy any? "Hell, no," Roberts said. "He played for the Cubs, not the Sox."

So much for all those dinners Roberts had enjoyed years before.

Lou Novikoff, baseball's Mad Russian of the 1940s, lives now on the outskirts of Los Angeles a few blocks from the Watts district. He's in his late fifties now, but he still wears the blue baseball cap of the Chicago Cubs at all times—even in his house. It took three days to find him. None of the young men in his neighborhood had any idea that Louis, the funny old guy in the baseball cap who shouted incoherently in the saloon every day, had once been touted as the next Babe Ruth. And then didn't believe it when told.

They had no way of knowing that fans in Wrigley Field used to stand up and cheer when the name Novikoff came over the loudspeaker.

The doorbell rang for a long time before a heavy-set woman answered. Her jet black hair was tied into a bun at the back and she was wearing an apron over her dress.

"Yes," she said. "Lou is here. Won't you come into the kitchen to see him?"

By this time a balding, barrel-chested man with a two-day growth of beard was making his way to the door, too. He was moving with that peculiar rolling gait common among circus bears and professional football linemen.

"And so?" Lou Novikoff inquired in a basso profundo rendered even more impressive by his Russian accent. (It was almost as though Akim Tamiroff were playing a cameo role. "And so what do you wa-a-ant with me?"

Novikoff turned and signaled me to follow him into the kitchen. "Why are you here?" he asked. "Don't you know that what is past is past? I am dead and only waiting to be buried. I am ready for the grave. Are you? You had better be if you cross me."

From her position near the sink, Esther, his wife, clucked her teeth. "Louis," she said, "be nice, Louis."

Louis thought about that. Then he raised a glass of wine to his lips and polished it off. Suddenly, he got up from the chair and walked back into the living room. When he returned he was carry-

ing a softball bat and a ball. He was one of the all-time great softball players, too, and it was only after making the switch from that
sport that he became a $100,000 baseball property.

"Do you see that ball?" he said. "Take it out of the box and look
at it. Do you see who signed it? That is the President of the United
States, Lyndon B. Johnson. I got that when they put me into the
Softball Hall of Fame. They wanted me to send my shoes to them,
but I wouldn't do it. I had no shoelaces for them. It would have
been a disgrace. I sent them my glove instead."

Novikoff sat there now, staring at the softball which had been
handed back to him. His expression became contorted by the effort
to hold back the tears that had appeared so unexpectedly on his
cheeks.

"They are holding a benefit for me soon in Long Beach," he
said. "They are holding it for me, the Mad Russian, the man who
made them. They are holding it for me . . . and it makes me so
ashamed."

He looked up at his wife, still standing near the sink. There
were tears in her eyes now, too.

"Yes, Momma, that is right. I am ashamed. I am a man and this
is what I have come to. All I have left now is pride."

The mood of depression vanished as quickly as it had appeared.
Like a character out of Dostoevski or Gogol, Novikoff was on his
way back up.

"I am still a strong man," he said. "This is my family in this
house and they are what I care about. We have much love here and
because of that we are strong. What do I care about the rest? Next
week we go to the benefit game and they will present me with my
trophy. It will be a great day for us, and we will walk with our
heads up. Isn't that right, Momma? Isn't that right?"

Mrs. Novikoff nodded nervously and managed a little smile
while biting her lower lip.

"Yes, Louis," she said, "it will be wonderful . . . just like the old
days with the Cubs."

Novikoff's eyes flashed again at that.

"What does anyone remember about the old days with the
Cubs?" he said, almost shouting. "What does Leo Durocher know?
But I know and I don't need Leo Durocher. You know who are my
friends? George Raft is my friend. Joe E. Brown is my friend. With
them as friends I do not need all these other people. 'Be proud,

Lou,' George Raft told me. 'Be proud and never bend your knees to any man.' "

"But Louie," his wife said softly. "You haven't seen Mr. Raft since you played with the Cubs, and that was more than twenty-five years ago. And Mr. Brown is dead."

"That's right, Momma," Louis replied with a wily grin. "But I remember it. If I ever really need a friend, George Raft will be there."

MINNIE RIDES THE BUSES

Minnie Minoso is still remembered as one of the most colorful performers ever to wear the uniform of the Chicago White Sox and Cleveland Indians. When baseball decided he was over the hill, Minnie refused to agree. He wouldn't quit. So he endured the long bus rides of the minors and continued to play in the Mexican league rather than leave the game that had given him fame.

I met Minnie one day in his room in Chicago's Southmoor Hotel, where he was staying for a few days before leaving for Guadalajara to join his team, Charros de Jalisco. After fourteen seasons as a major-league star, he was going back to the bushes. Only this time Minnie was admitting to being forty-two or forty-three years old. Why did he do it?

"This is the one profession God gave me," Minnie said as he leaned forward in his chair. "I'm going to do it until He tells me I can't do it any more. I slow down sure, maybe one foot, no more. My eyes are the same. I hit .300. I keep playing because I want to find out for myself if I can do these things without hurting myself —without getting on the rubbing table every day."

Minnie smiled as he recalled the reaction of Mexican fans to his brand of play, which has often been described as eccentric but never demeaned as being dull.

"Every city in Mexico I go to," he said, "writers and radiomen come to me. They ask me, 'Minnie, how come you are here? You can still play in the big leagues.' Sometimes they even ask: 'Did you do something wrong that you must be here?' I tell them that I did nothing wrong except to run into a wall for a fly ball or to get hit on the head with a pitch."

Minnie sat quietly, fingering a World Series ring on his left hand. Minnie never played in a World Series game, but the ring was given to him as a gesture of friendship by Bill Veeck after the White Sox won the pennant in 1959. Minnie was with the Cleveland Indians in 1959 but was traded to the White Sox for the 1960 season.

"I know I can still play in the major leagues," he said, "but I guess they want young men who have years to play. Maybe I have one year. The only future I have is to hang up my glove. I have great respect for my profession and for the fans who come to see me play. I would not want to play if I would make the fans ashamed because I would not do a bad thing . . . not be able to do the things I did before."

Veeck is still one of Minnie's greatest admirers. Once he advised Minnie to go to a big-league camp without a contract and ask for a tryout. Minnie, his eyes flashing, recalled his answer:

" 'Veeck,' I told him, 'I'm just like you. I believe I die before I go down on my knees to beg. I have pride. Perhaps it is too much pride. But that is the way I am.' "

Minnie stopped talking then. He stared straight ahead at a picture on the wall through shining eyes. He swallowed hard several times but there were no more words to come.

BARNEY ROSS: A CHAMP GOES OUT ON HIS FEET

Before seeing Barney Ross, the former welterweight and light-weight champion, I talked to his old manager, Art Winch. Barney was dying of cancer at the time, and everyone, including Barney, knew it.

"You know," Winch said, "a fighter never knows when he's finished. That's the way Barney was, too. The night he lost the title to Henry Armstrong he was taking a terrible beating and I wanted to stop the fight. 'Why get hurt, Barney?' I said. 'Let me stop the fight.'

" 'No,' Barney said. 'Don't stop it. I'm the champ. I want to go out on my feet.' "

Winch paused.

"So Barney took a good pasting that night, but he went out on his feet. It's just like a race horse with class. Put them in a stake race, and they'll show you class every time they go to the post."

Barney Ross was sitting in an overstuffed chair in a Chicago health club when I saw him. It was only days before the cancer in his throat killed him.

He was wearing a blue knit sports shirt and blue slacks. His hair was gray. But there was still the same hunter's look around the eyes that you see in photographs taken during the days when he was champ, fighting more than eighty-two professional fights and earning more than a million dollars.

"I feel fine," he said, trying to smile. "I feel a little tired, that's all. I think I'm gonna beat this thing yet. Only thing gets me down yet is that I can't seem to gain weight."

Barney didn't talk about the constant pain that kept him from eating anything but ice cream or ice water nor the operation on his throat nor the cobalt treatments he had been taking. Pain was something he had learned to live with on Guadalcanal as a Marine hero in the Second World War.

He was fifty-six. All the money he had made was gone. The rent for the apartment in which he was living was being paid by his friend, Ira Colitz, who came out of Chicago's West Side with Barney and learned as much about money as Barney did about left hooks.

Barney had once been Ira's sponsor in the days of the street fights that were so much a part of their growing up. Now Ira was Barney's sponsor. And you could see the part about the money hurt Barney. He talked about it.

"Where have I been for thirty years?" Barney asked. "Have I been sleeping or something? Here I am ready to cash in, and there's not even enough dough for the kid [his wife]."

There were plans to hold a benefit for Barney in New York at the time and the only reason Barney let them go through was because he wanted to make sure there was some money left "for the kid" when he was gone.

He was getting tired, almost dozing in the chair, but he roused himself. He tried to smile again.

"I got a lot of friends," he said. "I got a lot of good memories. That's plenty for one man to have in a lifetime."

Barney Ross's eyes closed then. His head nodded forward. He was asleep. Just like that. The only sound in the room now came from the television set where a man named Dennis James was conducting an afternoon panel show. I took one last look at Barney before leaving. He looked like a small boy who had been kept up past his bedtime.

No one is immune to change. Not athletes, not actors, not artists, not politicians.

There's a point in a man's life when everything is heading upward and the work is hard but exhilarating. It isn't until after the corner has been turned and he is struggling desperately to hang on that the realization sets in that the first part was the easiest.

"Show me a hero," F. Scott Fitzgerald once wrote, *"and I will write you a tragedy."*

CHAPTER 10

FREE AND DIFFICULT

You keep getting into trouble every time you write about women. The only piece in this chapter that didn't cause trouble was the one about Carrie Snodgress. The Jane Fonda piece was a public-relations disaster. Everybody who had liked the stuff I wrote about the conspiracy trial suddenly decided I was a fascist. There is one thing you must know about ultra-liberals. They write irate letters. And they don't write them just to you. They go right to the top.

There is a certain irony, too. I met Jane Fonda several times after this piece ran. Either she changed or I did, because I liked her.

JANE FONDA, THE PUMP ROOM RADICAL

Duchess Gold forced her way through the cocktail party radicals packed into the living room and made it to the enclosed porch.

Duchess Gold is something else. She is fearless. The Duchess is spectacular at marches, rallies, and as a partisan spectator at political trials.

But this is a cocktail party in Wilmette for Jane Fonda, and the Duchess is here only because her husband wanted to see Jane Fonda "in person."

Right now, in the sunken living room, Jane Fonda, the famous actress, daughter of Henry who makes the camera commercials on television and sister of Peter, the "easy rider," is standing amid a gaggle of suburban radicals.

Jane is nodding and smiling politely as the tweedy men and be-jeweled women tell her what a heroic figure she is to them.

144

The Duchess, who says she has never been to such a fancy party before, has other worries.

"I'm worried about my pants," the Duchess is shouting so that she can be heard above the clatter.

"See how low-slung they are. Got them in a unisex shop and I keep thinking they're falling off me.

"But I love them," the Duchess says, looking down at the maroon corduroy slacks. "If you buy them in a unisex shop they're stronger. It used to be that I'd flex my thigh muscles and my slacks would rip. Not these, though. These are great."

Inside, Jane Fonda, who has just arrived and must leave very quickly because she must be at the Ambassador East by 5:15 P.M., is giving everyone the benefit of her political wisdom.

The party is at a standstill. There are more than two hundred people jammed into three rooms and all of them have come there to pay five dollars to see Jane Fonda rip the war in Vietnam and the Nixon Administration.

They have paid five dollars at the door and the sponsors of the affair say that all the money is going to end repression in Cook County.

It is an interesting group and I'm glad I had a chance to see them all in the flesh. I had wondered, for one thing, where all those super-liberals who had voted for the late Adlai Stevenson for president in 1952 had gone.

There they were, mingling with all the other people who think that all they have to do is let their hair grow long and wear old clothes to pass as radicals.

And Jane Fonda was just what they needed.

"It's becoming more and more apparent that Nixon has no intention of ending the war," Jane says. "We have to make the peace treaty ourselves."

Jane explained that a group of students has now set off for North Vietnam to learn the enemy peace demands. The students are going to bring the demands back to the campuses and to spread them around to church groups and the hard hats as well so "the American people themselves can end the war there."

"American servicemen are not John Wayne freaks any more," Jane said. "What we have over there is a virtual soldier mutiny. They don't want to fight any more. What they're doing now is going out on patrols and smoking pot."

Jane, who is now paid $400,000 for each movie she makes, was asked if she would make a movie with John Wayne for a million.

"Certainly not if it were *The Green Berets!*" Jane said. "But I would if it were some innocuous Western and it was plain that I would use the money to free all the people in jail."

"Who would you free from jail?" a man asked.

Jane didn't have to think that one over.

"I'd free Angela Davis, Erika Huggins, the Los Angeles 18, the New York 21, David Harris, the Berrigan Brothers, the Pontiac 4, the Peoria 4, the people in Detroit. I'd free all the political prisoners."

"What about the Indianapolis 500?" a man asked.

"What about the American 200 million?" Jane shot back as her fans nodded approval, dazzled by her erudition.

Stan Dale, a former disk jockey who has become a political talk-show pundit (on FM radio, that is), then explained to Jane that there is a serious situation in Cook County as well.

Before Dale could finish, another man in an Afro was shouting into Jane's other ear about how the "pigs from Portugal are trying to rip off Guinea."

Jane didn't have a chance to answer that either.

Now a very sincere type squirmed through the crowd and stationed himself in front of Jane as though he were a small boy and she were a department store Santa Claus.

"I admire you so much," he said, looking down at the floor.

"I just wanted to ask you one thing and I hope you won't mind. I read in a gossip column that your husband, Roger Vadim, was a reactionary. That's not true, is it?"

Jane assured the fellow that Vadim, indeed, was all right, and moved through the crowd herself.

It went this way for more than an hour with Jane talking about the need for a real revolution, her great admiration for North Vietnam, and the necessity for a general strike in which radicals would shut down the country.

"Nixon and Agnew and Laird are war criminals," she said at one point, "and to try Lieutenant Calley without trying them is like trying Corporal Schultz without trying Goering and Himmler."

There were cheers from the crowd at this, all of them so pleased to be in the presence of a real radical and movie star and sex symbol all rolled into one.

Then it was time for Jane to leave. After all, being a radical is one thing, keeping a date in the Pump Room is quite another. Right on, Jane. I hope you can keep fooling 'em.

CARRIE SNODGRESS RETURNS

Carrie Snodgress, suddenly a famous actress, was on her way.

Right now, in the lobby outside the Goodman Theater, about fifty kids who used to know her just two years ago when Carrie was a student in the school of drama, were waiting to greet her.

At the foot of the steps that lead down from the front door stood John Reich, producing director of the theater, and Charles McGaw, dean of the school of drama.

"I taught her to be herself," Reich was saying in his clipped actor's voice. "I was very hard on her, very demanding. I insisted that she not conform to external standards because she has the strength, the talent, and personality to set her own."

McGaw recalled how Carrie Snodgress had been awarded the Sarah Siddons Scholarship as the most promising actress in the school and he remembered something else, too.

"When we ran *Othello* here," he said, "Carrie didn't have a part and so she memorized the part of every woman in the cast. She was ready to go as an understudy at any moment. She works very hard."

Workmen were painting the ceiling of the lobby, and Reich moved away from the center of the lobby to get out of their way.

"You are asking about the school," he said. "I am the head of the whole works here. Everyone else is under me."

I nodded. Once that was understood, Reich continued.

"We have had some great talents here," he said, "Geraldine Page, Shelley Berman, Karl Malden, José Quintero. . . .

"But Carrie is a new type of actress. Her success is based on the fact that she's not what people expect of a Hollywood star. She's not beautiful, but she's absolutely brilliant.

"In fact, when you see her, you'll see she doesn't really look very well." Reich sighed. "She's not getting enough sleep on this tour, I guess."

The workmen were moving their equipment again. Once more, Reich shifted his position to accommodate them.

"Most actresses who make it in Hollywood," he said, "have

beauty and talent. Carrie has talent and brains. But she is also very slim and she has high cheekbones and a very thin face. These faces always show up well on camera."

"Here she comes!" a girl in the crowded lobby shouted. "Here she comes!"

Reich halted his dissertation to meet his famous student. And Carrie Snodgress, at twenty-four the star of a much-heralded film called *Diary of a Mad Housewife,* came walking down the stairs.

Carrie Snodgress is very skinny and her straw-colored hair lacks sheen. Despite the fact her pink-flowered dress with the red sash had been designed by Edith Head, it looked dowdy. If Miss Snodgress had been walking down the main street of Park Ridge where she grew up, she might have been mistaken for an apprentice librarian.

Within minutes, they had escorted her to the Goodman's stage where Miss Snodgress sat on the apron and listened as the applause for her filled the theater and she looked wistfully up into the lights with her eyes brimming the way Judy Garland used to do at the Palace.

"This is a very special moment," she said, her voice tremulous and husky. "I've been away so long. Everything that's come to me has come out of this room, you know, from people like Dr. McGaw."

Miss Snodgress halted briefly to wave and shout to old friends in the audience. "Hi, Frank! Hi, Patrick! How ya' doin'?"

She raised both her arms toward the ceiling as though she were in the last act of *Medea.*

"Say," she said. "I realized a dream. I really don't have any advice that's so great. I'm healthy in the head and I have the theater in my heart.

"My dream is where I'm sitting. When I got up on this stage is when it happened. I really wanna tell you guys because this is where I came from. This is what I love. Oh, you just gotta love this building. . . ."

As Miss Snodgress went on, it was obvious she had reached her audience. There were tears brimming in many of their eyes, too. But the theater is a bitchy place to make a success, and once she opened the thing to questions, this became obvious.

"Do you really have a Rolls-Royce?" asked one student.

"No. I'm still driving a three-year-old car. But I'm not takin' a down trip here," said Miss Snodgress. "I did that picture for only $8,000 and I got the part over Jane Fonda, Barbra Streisand, and Natalie Wood. You know Natalie makes $400,000 a picture?"

There was momentary silence. Then another question:

"Is your brother still freaking out in Wisconsin?"

"My brother has settled down," she said. "He's married and now he has a farm and a kennel and he's raising dogs. He's very happy."

"Is it worth it?" asked a young lady at the rear of the theater, demonstrating her own diction. "Is it worth it to give up your life for your career?"

"No," she said, "I'm not giving my life away. I was being paid seven hundred dollars a week by my studio and I've just given that up to do a play for $125 a week on the Coast."

Miss Snodgress stopped smiling.

"Now because I'm doing that I don't have enough money to make my car payments and I'm gonna take a second job working with preschool children in addition to the play.

"But you see, I have an ambition . . . a dream . . . I think everything can be mine now and I have the discipline to do it."

After Miss Snodgress left, there was a private showing of *Diary of a Mad Housewife* for the students.

In commercial terms, the showing was a disaster. Because of technical difficulty, the sound was almost unintelligible for nearly half the film.

But what came through of the dowdy, skinny girl from Park Ridge with the nodes on her throat was something else.

Critics have been calling her the new Bette Davis and the best actress to come from Goodman since Geraldine Page.

She just may be, this Miss Snodgress. She just may be.

SHIRLEY THE ACTRESS

"George McGovern is cool," the redheaded actress was saying. "He's introverted and shy and not theatrical at all. But he's extremely intelligent and it's a shock to the system to have a man who could be President who's honest."

The Actress is very hip about politics. She has already been elected to the Democratic National Convention as a McGovern delegate. In 1968, she had come to Chicago after being elected as a delegate pledged to Bobby Kennedy.

The Actress is serious about politics and as a big name she can be extremely useful in a political campaign. Her appearance in a big city virtually assures full press coverage and the drawing of large gatherings wherever she goes.

On Monday The Actress held a press conference at McGovern headquarters in the morning—early enough for both the afternoon newspapers and the early evening news.

After that she made it to the student rally at Loyola at 3 P.M. and this was good enough for the morning newspapers and the 10 o'clock TV news. On top of that, she also appeared at two fund-raising cocktail parties on the Near North Side.

I watched The Actress go through her political thing both at the morning press conference and at the student rally for McGovern at Loyola. All the time I kept watching and listening to her talk I kept thinking how good she was in movies like *Irma La Douce,* and *Some Came Running* in which she appeared with Frank Sinatra, who is now supporting the Republicans.

"What about Frank Sinatra?" she was asked. "How come he's switched?"

The Actress had the answer.

"Something must happen to men when they reach their middle fifties," The Actress said. "One tends to gather one's forces so he can feel secure. It usually projects one into a conservative point of view.

"Swift-changing movements are for the young. The old like to take the safe way."

The Actress hesitated as she considered the Sinatra case.

"I'm still astonished," she said. "But I know the man and so I guess I'll have to conclude that I'm only half astonished."

Another listener brought up the arch-conservative of the film colony, John Wayne.

"I never felt the world was my adversary in any of my movies," The Actress said. "But Wayne has always been battling the enemy. His values are absolute. He always had to hate the other side in his roles and so it's not surprising that in *The Cowboys* he turns nine kids into killers and calls it defense."

The Actress delivered her assessments of Sinatra and the Duke at her morning press conference. She saved her blast at McGovern's rival for the youth vote for the rally at Loyola, a somnolent affair which provoked precious little laughter and no applause. It was what theater folk call a dead house.

"Gene McCarthy is an eloquent cynic," The Actress said. "He is brilliantly sarcastic and poetically arrogant."

If this line had been delivered at the right moment in a film, it might conceivably have brought down the house. At Loyola it dropped like a stone into the sea, never to be retrieved.

It was too bad. It was one of her best of the day. The other good one concerned New York Mayor John Lindsay.

"Lindsay blitzes everybody," The Actress said. "Down in Florida last week he announced he was going to investigate underwater pollution by jumping off a bridge in a scuba-diving suit.

"At the last minute an aide told him there were sharks in the area and handed him a knife. He made all the papers. If he's so interested in underwater pollution why didn't he ever jump in the Hudson River?

"He eighty-sixes the issues. Believe me, New York is his Chappaquiddick and he's going to have a tough time living down what happened to New York while he's been mayor."

I thought that now since she had Lindsay down for the count that The Actress would let it go. But she had one more deadly barb to hurl, this one delivered with all the venom at her command:

"He's a movie star," Shirley MacLaine said.

GLORIA TURNS THEM ON

Burt Reynolds, the *Cosmopolitan* Playmate-of-the-Month, was out in the lobby of the Arlington Park Towers talking to the bellboys. He was, he said, too busy to attend a meeting of young women to hear Gloria Steinem do her thing about feminism.

Inside, Gloria was up at the lectern talking to several hundred members of the Intercollegiate Association of Women Students in the Jimmy Durante Room.

Gloria looked fine, as usual. I'm sorry if that can be interpreted as a sexist observation. She was wearing wine-colored cords with bell bottoms and a plum-colored body shirt. Her hair was long and she was wearing the aviator glasses that have become as much her trademark as the cigar is Groucho Marx's.

When Gloria comes to talk she doesn't fool around. In fact, she is deadly serious.

She had been talking and answering questions for more than ninety minutes when a coed from either Kansas State or the University of Arkansas rose to ask about Burt Reynolds and his spread in *Cosmopolitan*.

"I haven't even seen it yet," said Gloria, who broke into the national-magazine-writing field herself by posing as a Playboy bunny for two weeks.

"And I understand he chickened out. I know what he'll look like, though. They no doubt air-brushed the picture so he looks incredibly good and all the men are going to feel just as bad as we women do when we see those air-brushed photographs of the Playmates every month."

Gloria brought herself up short.

"But we shouldn't be in here talking about men. When they have their meetings, they don't talk about us."

Another coed stood up to a microphone in the middle of the room. She said she was from Michigan State.

"I notice," the coed said, "that a lot of women who are into the movement are having more and more trouble relating to men. They're turning to bisexuality as an alternative."

Gloria agreed that there might indeed be difficult days ahead until the right balance was struck between men and women so they can share the world together again.

"It used to be that women went home and cried if someone at a party called them lesbians," Gloria said. "But imagine what that did to a real lesbian. We must realize that our lesbian sister has even more difficult civil rights problems than the rest of us.

"Lesbians have always been the cutting edge of women's liberation because for so long they were the only ones who tried to live an alternative life-style.

"They're fighters. They've been forced to live without protection. We have to help them because they'll strike at them first, then at promiscuous women, then at divorced women, unfit mothers, and finally at all the rest of us. They'll divide and conquer."

The audience of college girls was extremely attentive, hanging on every one of Gloria's words throughout the meeting as she told them it was time to quit serving as cheap labor. "It's time to do away with all those ancient white men in state legislatures who now have the right to control the reproductive systems of women," she said.

She complained about modern history books that mention women only when they are the mothers of famous men, marry Presidents, sew flags, or carry pitchers of water in famous battles.

"We're a second-class group doing work that no one else wants to do," she said and then told her most telling anecdote of the day.

"A friend of mine told me she had made a date to go to the movies with a very intelligent woman whose company she enjoyed," Gloria said.

"At the last minute a man called and invited her to go to the movies with him. He was four feet two and had terminal acne. On top of that, he had no redeeming features. She went with him like a shot because she had been trained all her life that we're nothing without a man standing next to us."

And then Gloria added slyly:

"Of course, if men only understood that it doesn't particularly matter to us which man it was standing next to us, they might be shocked."

The coeds in the audience laughed for the first time. It was good to see that they could.

MY GOD, JULIE NIXON

I had thought that when our President arranged that special college commencement exercise in the White House for his son-in-law, David Eisenhower, and brought in Bebe Rebozo in an academic gown to give the commencement address, that a new low in political nonevents had been struck.

It turns out I was wrong.

Sunday, David, grandson of the former President, and his wife, Julie, Mr. Nixon's daughter, appeared as the star attractions at a rally for Joseph I. Woods.

Joseph I. Woods is the same man that you see on television every day, courtesy of multimillionaire Clem Stone, asserting that if you elect him president of the Cook County Board he'll tow all those abandoned cars away.

The event, which was held in the Conrad Hilton's International Ballroom on the second floor, was by invitation only. It was so exclusive, in fact, that only 3,000 invitations were sent out.

There was an orchestra, a platoon of Secret Service men, several Chicago firemen, and nearly a hundred of the Woods young people decked out in straw hats.

It really began when Stone stepped to the microphone to introduce David, twenty-two, who in real life bears an amazing resemblance to Alfred E. Neuman of *Mad* magazine fame.

"He is an American youth as we understand American youth to be," Stone shouted into the microphone. "He has a terrific future ahead of him.

"I don't have to tell you about his background. You know well what it is."

I liked that about David Eisenhower being a typical American youth. All of us can certainly understand that.

After all, didn't we all go to Phillips Exeter Academy and didn't we all have Dwight Eisenhower drop in at the campus in the Presidential helicopter to see us from time to time?

And the beautiful thing about it all is that young David really does identify with the young people in this country.

He identifies with them so well, in fact, that at Amherst College, which he attended for four years, the other students used to paste his picture on the bathroom walls.

David is so into the youth movement that he backed the Cambodian incursion and also wrote a long paper defending Mr. Nixon in his embracing of Southern racist Strom Thurmond.

There was a rousing burst of applause as David stepped to the microphone.

"I have just received a great honor," he began. "I received an autographed picture from one of my favorite Americans, Mr. Ernie Banks of the Chicago Cubs."

David, who threw out the first ball of the American League baseball season this year as a substitute for his father-in-law, then expressed hopes that the Cubs would win in 1971.

He went on to explain how Mr. Nixon hoped that Joe Woods would win in his current campaign against George W. Dunne.

"Joe Wood understands the problems of urban America," David said. "We need people like him in office in this country if the Nixon program is to succeed."

David then confided to the happy crowd that Republican Senator Ralph T. Smith of Illinois has been a valuable addition to the Nixon team.

"I don't know much about the fellow he's running against," David said, "but I do know that the Stevensons lose the big ones."

More cheers.

"The Nixon family wants Joe Woods to win," David concluded. "We like him and we respect him."

At this, more than a thousand balloons dropped from baskets in the ceiling and Joe Woods stepped to the microphone and the band began to play.

Joe Woods stood there for more than a minute sopping up the applause and the cheering. He has an open face and a warm manner, and I'm sure many voters must be very impressed by him.

"These are two such beautiful young people," Woods began. "Julie says that I helped her father in '68 and one of the reasons I want to get elected is so that I can help him again when he runs for re-election."

I think it's fine that Joe Woods wants to help Mr. Nixon. He should. Joe's sister, Rose Mary Woods, is Mr. Nixon's personal secretary and the personal relationship is so close that Joe wears Mr. Nixon's old suits.

"I know I'm gonna win," Joe added, "because I've talked to the chief salesman of PMA [positive mental attitude], Clem Stone, who is now my campaign manager.

"And now I've prevailed on these beautiful young people to walk through you and shake your hands. We're going to prove right now that we are the democratic party with a small 'd.'

"Go on out there, Julie and David, and meet the people."

For the next twenty minutes Julie and David battled their way through the crowd, surrounded by Secret Service men, shaking hands and saying hello over and over again to people they had never seen before and never will see again.

Finally, the crush around the pair became so bad that even Clem Stone's positive mental attitude was shattered.

A hurried announcement was made over the loudspeaker, urging everyone to form a reception line. But nobody told anyone where the line was supposed to form. Chaos reigned.

The Secret Service men, apparently deciding that even professional Republicans in a body are weak on the law and order issue, escorted the young couple out of the room.

There must be a way that George Dunne, Woods's opponent for

the Cook County Board presidency, can counteract Woods's Sunday coup.

In fact, I know of a way and I will give him the tip right now. He can get his son Murphy, who arranged the Grant Park rock concerts, to set up another date for Sly and the Family Stone.

CHAPTER 11

FRANK THE BANK

PORTRAIT OF THE WORLD'S BIGGEST CHEAPSKATE

I always admire a man who refuses to change his spots. Frank The Bank comes out of this piece looking like the world's biggest tightwad. Some people predicted he would sue. Instead, he requested a hundred copies to send to his closest friends. He made the request to a Sun-Times *driver who got them for nothing. Right on, Frank!*

Despite sub-freezing air and a biting wind, Frank The Bank wears only a dark business suit and smile as he stands on the sidewalk, his right hand grasping the outer door handle of his saloon, the Boul Mich Lounge. It's a few minutes after 5 o'clock on a Friday afternoon, the most critical hour of Frank The Bank's week. It's payday for most of his customers, and by now most of his customers owe Frank money again.

If Frank can last out here in the cold for the better part of an hour, he'll be able to nail almost all of them as they turn the corner at Kroch's & Brentano's on Michigan Avenue heading west to the concrete steps leading to the lower level and Grand Avenue.

"Hello, Denny!" Frank The Bank shouts happily as one of his regulars approaches. "Come in! Get out of the cold!"

Frank, smiling brightly now, opens the door so Denny may enter.

"Got to cash my check," Denny mutters as he walks through the door.

"See me in a little while," Frank answers. "I'll take care of you. You got a little tab, you know. You wanna settle?"

This, of course, is the strategy behind Frank The Bank's trolling in the cold for customers. Those who have forgotten they owe him money will remember when they see him standing at the door. Those who remember but hope to stall him are not likely to have the stomach to ignore his transparent invitation to join him.

"Hello, stranger!" Frank shouts now to a customer who has been missing for all of three days. "I thought maybe you were sick or something. Where's the rest of your gang?"

Poor Frank. The place must be empty. But the customer finds people lined up two deep at the bar with three bartenders and two waitresses scurrying madly around with drinks. For this is the house that Frank built, thanks to his special array of services. He cashes pay checks and personal checks, lends money, and allows customers who run short during an afternoon or evening of good fellowship to run up tabs to be settled on payday.

Frank The Bank's real name is Frank Friefeld. Now in his late sixties, his bald head is fringed with gray but he still walks with a spring in his step. And despite the fact his success as a saloon-keeper-banker long ago allowed him to move to a posh Lake Shore Drive address, his accent is still pure Chicago West Side. Frank calls his wife Dorothy "Dougherty," and vodka is "wodka." People who write for a living are "oughtas." Frank's partner in the business is his first cousin, Sam Beer, also in his late sixties and portly, who likes to recall getting started in the saloon business in 1928 with a five-hundred-dollar stake from Al Capone.

Frank The Bank (his credo is: "I never do anything illegal") was a notions salesman during this period. He joined Sam in running a place called The Three Deuces after Repeal.

The partners opened the Boul Mich in 1940 in a one-story wood frame building on Michigan Avenue. At first it was a package liquor store.

"We had $10,000 in the store and we couldn't make a dime," Sam recalls. "Frank and I were sharing a single room across the street in the Sheraton-Chicago, which was then the Medinah Club. We were so broke we could afford to spend only fifteen cents apiece for lunch and our rent at the store was 250 bucks a month. Finally, I tell the landlord we can't make it. I tell him that unless we put in a few stools and run a saloon he's gonna own a liquor store.

"Well, he let us put in four bar stools. The very first day people were lined up three deep and we sold them liquor in paper cups.

From that day on we made money. And we kept on making money right up until the time we moved, even though we were paying 750 bucks rent at the end."

About five years ago Frank and Sam moved the Boul Mich around the corner to its present site. But the change of address did nothing to alter the clientele. The Boul Mich still draws the same account executives, public-relations consultants, radio and television personalities, commercial artists, and newspaper people it always did. Many of the veteran customers consider it a badge of honor that they have been Frank The Bank's customers since the early days. They love to sit around and tell each other stories of the good old days.Three they tell most are:

—Broadway Williams shooting his drinking companion, David Condon, dead at the bar with a blank pistol before Frank's horrified gaze.

—David Condon getting so enraged at slow service that he called the Sheraton-Chicago Hotel bar across the street and had a bell boy bring him a fifth of Scotch and mixers on a tray.

—Indiana Jimmy Fulton hanging a banner on the back wall announcing he'd be in town in another three weeks to buy all the drinks in the place. (He showed up as promised and not only bought the drinks but set up buffet lunches and suppers as well for three days.)

The thing about Frank The Bank that you must understand is that he doesn't live in the past. One look at him now as he walks swiftly through the bar area to the kitchen demonstrates that. Seconds later he is back at the bar, baskets of popcorn balanced on his arms. They will be placed at strategic points to increase thirst. Perhaps an hour later, when the checks have been cashed and the tabs collected, Frank will be serving the second course, a platter of very salty knishes—but only to those who have paid their tabs in full.

"Take one," Frank says as he moves through the crowd at the bar. "Eat up. It's good for you."

"Cut it out, Frank," says Bernie Colbeck, one of the regulars who has paid his tab. "I'm on a diet."

"Diet? What do I care about diet?" Frank screams back. "Eat and get thirsty. How can I make money unless my people are thirsty?"

With eyes alert as a jaguar at feeding time, Frank now has spot-

ted a man on the other side of the circular bar who has been signal-
ing for a bartender without success.

"Just a minute, sir," Frank shouts above the noise of the crowd.
"Jimmy Meyers! What are you doing? A customer wants a drink.
Get to work!"

Jimmy Meyers, the bartender, a native Hawaiian, has heard this
song before. Right now he is making three drinks at one time. He is
in no mood for coaching.

"Why don't you just stand there and keep your big mouth shut,"
Meyers replies. "We'll run this part of the business."

Frank's face puffs with indignation.

"Meyers, watch your step," he shouts. "You don't and I'll get
someone back there who likes to take care of my people. Serve and
be a gentleman. That's all I ask."

Meyers, who has been listening to Frank shout for twenty years,
draws a deep breath and looks to his fellow bartenders for moral
support. Their answer is a neutral shrug and a rolling of the eyes.

A party of eight customers enters the bar now, waiting at the
door. Frank quickly forgets his outburst and rushes toward them,
his face beaming. The strategy is to get them seated before they realize the place is so crowded they can't possibly be served for another
forty-five minutes. With the new group seated and not a single seat
remaining, Frank heads toward a service bar at the rear where he
will order his first drink of the day, a double shot of Crown Royal
off the top shelf with a glass of water for a wash.

Bob Murray, a regular with more than twenty years' service in
the Boul Mich, has been waiting back there for him, ready to
pounce.

"Frank," he asks now, "why is it that you talk that way about me
when I'm gone? I come in early today and the first thing I hear is
that you've been telling people I'm an egregious bore. How come?"

"Egregious?" yells Frank. "Egregious! What's egregious? I don't
even know what it means. Somebody's making up a story to get
your goat."

Murray laughs. Frank has got to be telling the truth. Murray remembers when the Boul Mich was in its old location and he asked
Frank if excavating for the new place had started.

"Excavating?" Frank replied, incredulously. "Why, they haven't
even started digging yet."

Years ago, Joseph Mitchell wrote a classic piece for *The New
Yorker* about McSorley's Old Ale House in New York City. Part of

the charm of McSorley's wonderful saloon was that the customers had grown so accustomed to being insulted by the owner that they got proud about it. That is the way it is at the Boul Mich, too, except that the customers are insulted not only by the owner but by the bartenders and waitresses as well.

Often the regulars bring in friends to serve as witnesses to these performances, driving Frank to a state of indignation by asking when he intends to buy a drink.

"Buy a drink?" Frank screams. "My job is to make money. How do I make money if I give it away? Buy a drink yourself. You want to be a big shot? Buy a drink yourself! Meyers, hurry up! This man wants to buy a round for everyone in his party."

This line of counterattack not only gets laughs but often results in the customer's actually buying the round.

As far as anyone can remember, Frank The Bank has never—with the exception of birthdays—bought any of his customers a drink. There are unconfirmed reports that he has been encountered in other spas and shown himself to be a liberal spender. But no one has ever seen it happen in his place.

The present Boul Mich consists of a large circular bar with booths for dining on either side. There is a piano bar in the corner near the door, but Frank quit hiring entertainers because, he says, they cost more money than they bring in.

(This was quite a lesson for Frank because when he ran the old Three Deuces his biggest draw was the late-evening jam sessions featuring people like Bix Beiderbecke, the Paul Whiteman orchestra players, and the Crosby brothers, Bing and Bob. Later, he served as Art Tatum's manager, taking the famed jazz pianist on a tour of England and Scotland. "They stole his contract away from me," Frank says. "They said because he was blind he didn't know what he'd signed.")

There is more than enough noise in the place anyway. Every noisemaker turns on simultaneously. The jukebox, music by Muzak, a color television set, constant clanking from a smoke-dispensing machine, and the shouting of Frank The Bank. The din is enough to defeat any ordinary attempt at conversation.

Socially, one of the big events on the Boul Mich calendar is the annual raffle on the Rose Bowl game. Chances cost a dollar each, with the profits going to the Christmas fund for Boul Mich employees. Each regular customer is ordered to buy at least one ticket. A prize of seventy-five dollars goes to the entrant who picks the slip with the correct final score. A consolation prize of twenty-five dollars goes to the entrant who picks the slip with the correct half-time score.

First prize in this year's raffle was won by John The Barber, the afternoon bartender. Second prize went to Red Maupin, the evening bartender.

It is not known what effect this will have on next year's raffle. Probably none at all. The faith of the Boul Mich regulars seems strong enough for any storm.

Despite the continual wrangling, it is rare for anyone to be barred from the Boul Mich. The only time this has occurred in recent memory was after a brief imbroglio during which one of the combatants was wounded in a sneak attack by a man wielding an attaché case.

"The guy with the attaché case is out," Frank declaimed from the other side of the bar. "Anybody who uses an attaché case as a weapon is too treacherous to drink in my place."

But even tigers mellow with age. There are days now when Frank will sit down to reminisce for a moment or two about the past. And when he does he is likely to bring up the old place and tell the story of its two doors on Michigan Avenue and the problems they caused.

His favorite concerns the day a drunk staggered in the door at the north end of the saloon only to be greeted by Frank, who told him he'd already had too much to drink and would not be served. The drunk wheeled around and went out the door. He staggered twenty feet down the street and staggered in the other door at the south end of the saloon. Frank had anticipated him. The drunk walked in the door. Frank was waiting for him.

"My God," said the drunk, "do you own every joint on Michigan Avenue?"

THE TAP ROOT PUB IS CRUSHED

Harley Budd died a little the other day. He finally lost his battle to save the Tap Root Pub.

But Harley Budd didn't go down alone when sheriff's deputies and men from the city's Department of Urban Renewal wrestled him away from his door to execute a court order to evict him from his restaurant on North Larrabee.

The fight to save the Tap Root had been waged since 1963 and more than 185,000 persons had signed petitions urging Mayor Daley to join it.

Thousands of Chicagoans are still driving around the city with bumper stickers that proclaim, "Help! Save the Tap Root Pub!"

Well, when the men from the day-labor pool came to carry out the tables and chairs and the food from the food lockers, they weren't finished when they had carried out everything inside the restaurant.

They went right on and carried out everything that was in Budd's apartment above the restaurant.

In the space of a few hours he lost a restaurant that has been seating as many as 1,200 persons at clambakes on weekends and his home, too.

The eviction notice was served because the Department of Urban Renewal is building townhouses all along the street. A shopping center will be built on the corner, but the bar and restaurant on it already has been awarded to a group headed by Donald LeBold.

LeBold is the Democratic precinct captain. Perhaps Budd's biggest problem was that he was naïve. How did he ever think Mayor Daley would join Harley Budd against a Democratic precinct captain?

Budd threw a padlock around the wooden gate leading into his place when the sheriff's deputies, backed up by a dozen policemen from the Eighteenth District, pounded on it demanding to be admitted.

Budd refused to let them in, shouting that he was waiting for due process from the courts.

"You've had due process," one of the deputies shouted back. "The court just ruled that you're out five minutes ago." With this, another deputy slugged Budd across the knuckles with a pinch bar as Budd tried to snap the padlock on his gate.

Budd let out a roar of pain and drew back from the gate as the deputies and policemen rushed through and forced him to submit.

The Tap Root Pub has long been one of the favorite eating places for policemen from the Eighteenth District and they were noticeably restrained in their actions.

The men from Sheriff Richard J. Elrod's force apparently eat at other places.

"This is what urban renewal is," Budd said as he stood in front of his place watching workmen carry out his business and place it on the sidewalk piece by piece.

"This is what they do for neighborhoods. They put up $40,000 townhouses and they throw you out like a dog. I went out and fought for my country so I could have the right to have a business. What a fool I was."

A heavy-set worker carrying a table bumped into Budd. "Come on, Buddy," the worker said, "get out of the way, will ya'. We got a job to do here and this stuff is heavy enough as it is."

"Look at that, will you," Budd said. "You don't have any rights any more. Here we have the sheriff going out and hiring day laborers at ten or twelve dollars a day to throw fellow Americans out."

Budd's eviction was made possible because the city acquired the property through condemnation proceedings and sold it to a private developer. The private developer is the precinct's Democratic captain, LeBold.

Demolition on Larrabee began in 1965. For years, the Tap Root had been the only place standing on the street between North Avenue and Armitage.

The city took away Budd's liquor license, and business actually boomed on a menu of lobsters, flown in fresh from Maine, corn, and fresh clams. People flocked to the place, either drinking root beer or bringing their own beer and wine.

A short while ago, Budd's restaurant license was revoked, but that didn't stop him, either.

He had spent nearly $50,000 in legal fees in the long battle and he wasn't about to quit.

Awhile back, Budd sat in a corner of the saloon that had stood since 1862, managing even to survive the Chicago fire.

"I feel that if you can't live as an individual in a free society you might as well give it all up.

"I think this country should have guts enough to take up arms against any taking of private property from private individuals.

"And if they don't, then I'll just have to be an individual and go by the wayside."

On Wednesday, as the workers carried out Budd's belongings, other workmen were moving a bulldozer into place close to the wood frame walls. As soon as the Tap Root Pub was empty they had instructions to crush it.

And crush it they did.

. . . AND EVEN FRITZEL'S?

For years, Fritzel's was the Toots Shor's of Chicago. I never liked the place. But this was the problem: Do you dare risk knocking a place when it's going down? Do you write a nostalgic piece about a place for which you feel no nostalgia? I decided to pass it over. But next morning, I woke up angry with myself for postponing the decision and wrote this piece in eighteen minutes. It drew more mail than any other column I've ever written.

I must be the only one in Chicago who doesn't mourn the passing of Fritzel's restaurant. What is all this we've been hearing for a week about the passing of a great landmark?

To me, a great landmark is not a place where two people go for dinner and come out with a tab for fifty dollars. A great landmark is not a place where you drive up to the door in a Fleetwood Cadillac and give the doorman five bucks to park your car illegally without getting you a ticket.

I went to Fritzel's Friday night with the idea of doing a piece on its closing. Mob scene. Television cameras all around. Long lines of customers waiting to get tables where they might be lucky enough to get their faces on the "Kennedy at Night" show on Channel 7.

In the bar, middle-aged men with toupees and mod clothes have taken a night off from their families in the suburbs and are trying to make out with the ambitious young secretaries who have stayed downtown to hunt.

"But what about your wife?" one says as she sips her martini.

"My wife, dear girl," her new friend says, "is in Lincolnwood. She'll be watching the television later. We better not eat here."

For more than a week, I've been hearing that the death of Fritzel's is a blow at the heart of the city.

A blow at the heart of the city? Am I supposed to mourn because Bennie Dunn, the former Rush Street doorman, and Howard Miller, the disk jockey, right-wing rabblerouser, will no longer have a plush place downtown where they can sit and wave to each other?

Both were on hand Friday for the closing. Howard allowed to Bob Kennedy on the television show that he used to sit in a booth

in Fritzel's to do research for the late-night interview show he used
to do on Channel 7.

That must have been a great scene. Howard Miller doing research. I thought he spent all his time trying to think up ways to
sell dusty vacant lots in Arizona.

Len O'Connor, the pundit from Channel 5, was there Friday
night, too. Kennedy asked O'Connor what he thought about it all.
O'Connor said he liked Fritzel's because it was a place where you
could come and pay your own bill.

I like places where I can pay my own bill, too. But the rest of us
in this business don't make $75,000 a year like O'Connor, so Orange
Julius is more our style.

O'Connor then added that the closing of Fritzel's showed how
badly run the city was. This, I guess, was supposed to be a fearless
attack on the Daley administration. He must be getting soft in the
head. Neither Dick Daley not Matt Danaher, that old Chicago politician, ever had anything to do with the cooking, the service, or the
prices in Fritzel's.

Over and over again through the evening, I kept hearing that
Bob Hope had eaten in Fritzel's and liked it. So did Elizabeth Taylor and George Jessel. Of course they liked it. I bet they never had
to pay the bill.

This is the big draw of places like Fritzel's. Successful business-
men bring their clients to a place where they can rub elbows with
the famous names. The famous names don't pay. The people who
want to see celebrities help pay because the prices keep going up for
the people who aren't stars.

Well, I'll say this for Fritzel's. It went down Friday night in its
own style. The celebrities were there. They all fawned over each
other. They were loud and they all uttered a lot of cheap senti-
ments about the passing of an era.

It must have been a lot like that in the first-class dining room of
the *Titanic*, too.

Chapter 12

THE PANJANDRUMS OF SPRINGFIELD

Believe it or not, they do have some honest people in the Illinois State capitol. Lieutenant Governor Paul Simon is one of them, and so are Representatives Bob Mann and Cecil Partee.

But it is always the thieves and knaves who are more interesting to write about. And how are you going to top men like Paul Powell and Webber Borchers?

PAUL POWELL'S SHOEBOX

SPRINGFIELD, Ill.—I didn't realize how depressing the Paul Powell story really is until I spent half an hour in his old suite in the St. Nicholas Hotel here.

For more than a week, I had been reading that Powell was a colorful politician with rustic humor who was loved by all.

The impression you get from these stories is that here was a lovable old man who looked and acted like the old movie actor Wallace Beery and really lived one hell of a life.

Well, if Paul Powell was happy with his life, more power to him. As far as I'm concerned, anytime you go to the wire with $800,000 in cash stashed in shoeboxes in a crummy little hotel suite, you didn't play the game as well as you should have.

I have no sympathy for Powell. For years he played the role of the wise rube who was putting it over on the city slickers, but the only one he was fooling was Paul Powell.

Powell charged onto the state payroll from the little town of Vienna, which has a population of little more than a thousand. He was a small-town guy who started out poor and decided to hoard all the money he could get his hands on. In the end it was more than two million dollars.

What a life-style he had. His suite on the fifth floor consisted of a small living room with a leather couch and two leather chairs. The bedroom was so small he had to turn sideways to walk to a closet where his money was stashed.

There was an economy-brand color television set, too. And if the former secretary of state grew tired of TV, he could always look out the window at the parking lot and railroad station across the street.

It's lucky for Powell that there was never a fire in the hotel. He had a special lock put on the door that made it impossible to open, even from the inside, without a special key.

The day Powell walked out of the hotel for the last time he did it in typical style.

Mrs. Eva Murdock, fifty-seven, the maid who had been cleaning his suite for years, came in to find him sitting in his black leather chair watching a daytime quiz show.

"I started to clean the room and he went to the closet and put on his coat," Mrs. Murdock said.

"I was working for my church at the time, seeking donations, and so I asked him if he would like to give us something.

"Mr. Powell pulled out a big roll of bills and handed me a dollar. 'I guess I can spare a dollar,' he told me."

But Powell didn't let his charity end at that point. Mrs. Murdock explained:

"Mr. Powell left, but he came right back again. 'Eva,' he told me then, 'why don't you take this piece of fruitcake and enjoy it with my best wishes.' "

Mrs. Murdock doesn't like fruitcake. But that wasn't the real reason she didn't eat it.

"My gosh," Mrs. Murdock said, "Mr. Powell had already taken two bites out of that piece of cake."

One of Paul Powell's great friends was Orville Hodge, the state auditor who went to prison after stealing millions from Illinois.

But what a difference in style. Hodge lived in the same hotel in a penthouse. And Powell went around wearing Hodge's hand-me-down shirts with the monogram "O.H." on the pockets.

Bill Nieroff, fifty-five, has been a bellman at the hotel for years. He used to take Powell's suits to the cleaners and carry his bags down to the street when Powell went on trips.

"Tips?" said Nieroff. "You have to be kidding. This was a man who knew the value of a dollar. Without fail, he used to give me two dollars every Christmas."

I talked to a lot of other people who had regular contact with Powell over the years at the hotel. Everyone of them smiled when Powell's generosity was mentioned.

I guess it gets to a point when if you're so tight that you squeak when you walk, everybody starts to believe you're a charming character.

Across the street from the St. Nicholas Hotel there is a bar called the Paddock.

The owner is Emil Saccara, who was Powell's driver until his death.

Saccara feels bad because people keep asking questions about where all that money in Powell's closet came from.

"I loved Paul Powell," he said, "and I want somebody to say something good about him. He was a great man.

"He was a humble man. Why, he'd stop on the street to talk to any bum that was passing by and give him a hearty handshake."

Paul Powell is dead and in his grave now, and those who were close to him—and they are very few in number—keep telling us that we should revere his memory.

For what?

THE MAN IN THE INDIAN SUIT

SPRINGFIELD, Ill.—Representative Webber Borchers whirled around at the sound of the buzzer. He squinted up at the scoreboard on the wall of the House of Representatives to see what bill he was being asked to vote upon.

But he was too late. Even now the results of the vote were on the scoreboard.

Borchers leaned forward quickly to press his voting buzzer, anyway. He leaned back again in disgust.

"Damn," he said, "I missed that one, I wanted to vote 'no' that time, too."

This was early Thursday morning and it was also Borchers' sixty-fifth birthday. He was wearing a rumpled gray suit and a pair of heavy woolen socks but no shoes.

Now that the necessity for voting had passed, Borchers was able to devote his attention to a summation of his colorful background.

"Don't say that I'm a gentleman farmer," Borchers said. "That's not right. What I am is a landowner. I have tenant farmers.

"Why, I bet our family owns 10,000 acres of land around Decatur and at least one-twentieth of the town proper."

Borchers took a step forward in his stockinged feet and poked a finger in the chest of his listener.

"My father was a congressman and all my relatives have been in politics since the time my earliest ancestor crossed into Illinois with the George Rogers Clark expedition.

"If there's one thing we've got, it's power, and if you don't believe me just try to go up against us. If a Borchers tells you to back off, that's just what you better do."

Borchers, who likes to refer to himself as "the most conservative member of the House," is a wiry man of medium height with steel-gray hair and an aversion to students, hippies, welfare recipients, and strangers who might try to force their way into his bomb shelter.

Earlier in the session, which was now in its final hours, Borchers had proposed involuntary sterilization for welfare recipients who had too many children.

Borchers also brought in films of the Kickapoo Rock Festival one day to show the House Executive Committee naked women, dope pushers, and the flags of anarchy that flew over the extravaganza at Heyworth, Illinois, a year ago.

It was little more than ten years ago that Borchers was cited for building a bomb shelter in Decatur without obtaining a building permit.

"I didn't get any permit," Borchers said, "because if people knew about it they might try to force their way in when the bomb dropped.

"Or they might just stand there and plead for entrance and I'd have to decide who should live and who should die."

But the bomb shelter controversy was far from Borchers' mind as the buzzer rang again for him to vote.

He moved toward his voting signal device. This time it was buried under papers. Borchers kept tossing them aside frantically, trying at the same time to see what bill was being voted upon.

Once again, Borchers was too late.

"Damn," he said. "Missed it again."

He looked up at the scoreboard to see the final vote.

"Hell, look at how one-sided it was," he said with a smile. "It wouldn't have made much difference anyway."

He turned away from his desk again and began to talk of his proudest piece of legislation.

Earlier in the session, he had succeeded in gaining passage of a bill to construct a display case at the University of Illinois for the authentic Indian uniform worn by the football team mascots from 1930 to 1967.

Borchers has a sentimental interest in the costume. He was one of the first U. of I. mascots, and he spent three weeks of his youth living in an Indian tepee while it was being made.

"Getting that suit for the University of Illinois was all my idea," Borchers said, "and it has been passed on in the same manner as the Kings of England pass on the crown jewels."

Borchers smiled.

"That's right," he said, "just like the British crown jewels. And why not? I went out and got them the last authentic Indian suit that's ever been made in this country."

Borchers got the suit by persuading a Champaign clothing store owner to put up five hundred dollars for it. Borchers then went to the Pine Ridge reservation in South Dakota to supervise the making of it.

"I got this old Indian squaw to do it," he said.

"Why, that old woman had been with the Injuns at the battle of the Little Big Horn and helped mutilate Custer's men after it was over.

"I told her I wanted a genuine war suit and I got to give that old squaw credit. She did a beautiful job.

"There were the tail feathers from thirty American bald eagles in the headdress and the skins and breastbones from a couple dozen deer in the jacket and pants."

Borchers himself first wore the Indian war suit at the half-time intermission of the Army-Illinois football game played in New York's Yankee Stadium on November 8, 1930.

On that Saturday and for many Saturdays after, Borchers thrilled Illini football fans with his nimble dances.

But now, on his sixty-fifth birthday, Borchers' nimbleness seemed to desert him as he whirled around unsteadily to cast his vote.

"Damn," he said, "missed again." Then he smiled.

"Well, I wasn't much interested in that bill anyway."

CECIL PARTEE'S BIG DAY

SPRINGFIELD, Ill.—It was 6:45 A.M. when the sunlight streaming into Cecil A. Partee's room startled him into wakefulness.

He smiled to himself before the tension began grabbing at his stomach. This was going to be Cecil Partee's big day. If everything went according to the script, he would be the first black man to be elected president pro tempore of the Illinois Senate.

Partee tossed back the sheets and put both feet on the floor of his suite in the Lincoln Tower Apartments. He stretched slowly. Then he walked to the window and looked down into the street. He was only two blocks away from the capitol.

"I'm really not nervous," he told himself, "it's just that, now that it's here, I know what an important day this is. That's it. I'm not nervous. But, God, I hope everything goes right today."

The night before, in a caucus held in the St. Nicholas Hotel here, with Mayor Daley and U.S. Representative Dan Rostenkowski present, Cecil Partee had been chosen the Democratic majority leader.

So now, in just a few more hours it would be over. Cecil Partee, at forty-nine years of age, would be one of the most powerful Democratic politicians in the state. He had come far from Blytheville, Arkansas, where his mother taught school while his father, who died when he was sixteen, worked as a cotton "classer."

"Cecil," his mother used to tell him over and over again in those days, "be prepared and try hard. Get along with people and there'll always be a place for you."

Mrs. Partee took particular interest in his classroom accomplishments since she was a schoolteacher. In fact, his mother pursued her education career for forty-five years, ending up as superintendent of schools for Mississippi County, Arkansas.

It was in 1940 when Partee was graduated from high school. At that time, black students were not accepted at schools like the University of Arkansas. So he went to Tennessee State, an all-black school.

He worked his way through school, supplementing these efforts with money earned working summers in a steel mill.

Cecil Partee smiled now as he remembered his return trip to Blytheville after graduation. It had been a good month, that June of 1944. Partee had earned his degree and so had his mother, who had been attending night and summer school classes at Arkansas State in Pine Bluff for nearly ten years.

Partee smiled because he remembered one of the big gambles of his life that had paid off.

He had always wanted to go to law school. But he had no money. And Partee knew the University of Arkansas Law School would never accept him because of his color.

Finally, the State of Arkansas agreed to do what so many other Southern states were doing at that time—keep black students out by paying their way to Northern schools of their own choice.

Partee decided on Northwestern University Law School and completed what was normally a three-year course in two years.

From there, it was a comparatively easy step to an assistant state's attorney spot and, ultimately, to the state legislature.

But Partee's future really had been settled, he realized now, thirty years before.

Cecil Partee picked up the phone.

Five rings later, the phone was picked up at the other end.

"Mom," Partee said, "I just couldn't go up to the Capitol today without calling. I just have to tell you thanks for everything you gave me."

Mrs. Bessie Partee Ivy scoffed at the other end of the phone. She told her son he was talking nonsense and that he had done it all himself.

"No, it's not nonsense, Mom," Partee said, "and I wanted to call you and tell you so."

He put the phone down then and raced for the shower.

A short time later, after donning his most conservative dark brown suit, Partee grabbed his brightly checkered overcoat from its hanger in the closet.

He stopped. And then he started to smile to himself all over again.

"Hell," Partee said to himself, "where would I be right now if the

University of Arkansas ever found out I never had the money to take that law course from them in the first place?"

He smiled to himself all the way down the elevator.

And a few minutes later he walked through the lobby door and onto the sidewalk. An icy wind was blowing. The temperature was three degrees above zero.

A cabdriver, waiting in front of the hotel, shouted to him, asking if he wanted a ride.

Cecil Partee, who would within the next three hours become the most powerful Democrat in the state legislature, declined politely.

"Thanks," he said, "but I think I'll walk. It just seems like such a beautiful day."

GOVERNOR KERNER GOES DOWN

They indicted former Governor Otto Kerner who was sitting on the U.S. Court of Appeals at the time. The day he walked into the courtroom to be arraigned he seemed bright and cheerful. Otto had always been a nice guy, if you could take that phony Oxford accent he put on all the time.

Henry Hanson, a really fine reporter for the Chicago Daily News, *had been covering Kerner for years. "Well, Governor," Henry said sympathetically, "things change, don't they?"*

"Yes, Henry, they do," Kerner said, smiling. "You've certainly put on weight, haven't you?"

It was raining. Heavy gusts of wind whipped the rain off Lake Michigan. Torrents of water, as though shot through a huge water cannon, splashed off the sides of the fifteen-story brick building on Chicago's Gold Coast.

It was 8:45 A.M. Alex, the elevator operator, had just sat down to work after wiping himself off with a towel. He had never remembered a day when he had been so wet from the two-block walk east from his bus on Michigan Avenue.

The elevator signal buzzed. Alex sighed. He wasn't ready to begin work in earnest yet. The buzzer came from the twelfth floor. It was U.S. Court of Appeals Judge, Otto Kerner, the former Illinois Governor, ready to go to work.

Suddenly, all of Alex's bad feelings left him as he saw Kerner standing there at the door, waiting with a broad smile on his face.

"That's the way it always is when you see the judge in the morning," Alex said. "He gives you that friendly smile, and right away you figure the day isn't going to be so bad after all."

The trip to the ground floor was swift.

Just before Alex opened the elevator door, he turned to give Kerner a warning.

"Better be careful when you go across the street to get your car," Alex said, "the weather's awful bad. No telling what can happen on a day like this."

Kerner nodded. Then, ramrod straight, he walked out the side door of the building to get to his car.

He took the Inner Drive south, turning west to the Federal Building, and parked his car underneath. In a few minutes he had arrived at his office on the twenty-seventh floor, giving his usual warm greeting to his secretary, Mrs. Mary Banzhof. It was 9:30 A.M.

Shortly before 10 A.M., U.S. Attorney James Thompson entered Judge Kerner's office to tell him the indictments against him had been returned.

Thompson appeared troubled later when asked how Kerner had reacted. "I'd rather not say," he said. "It's quite all right if Judge Kerner wants to comment on it. I'd rather say nothing."

"How would you expect Judge Kerner to react?" Mrs. Banzhof asked. "What would you expect?"

It was 10:50 A.M. when Theodore Isaacs, formerly Kerner's Director of Revenue, walked into the reception room outside U.S. Attorney Thompson's office on the fifteenth floor.

He was wearing a brown suit and held his brown hat in his hand. He smiled politely and his eyes twinkled through his gold-rimmed bifocals.

"I believe I'm supposed to report here today," Isaacs said.

The receptionist nodded and picked up the phone.

"Mr. Isaacs is out here," she said.

At this point, Issacs' attorney, Thomas Sullivan, appeared.

Sullivan said he would take Isaacs up to the lockup on the twenty-fourth floor until the indictments were officially announced and then make arrangements for bond.

The press conference to reveal the indictments had been origi-

nally set for 11 A.M. It was changed to 11:30 so they could be announced at the same time in Washington, D.C.

The press conference was held on the eighteenth floor. While it
was being concluded, Isaacs was already walking along the long
counter on the twentieth floor to the desk of Mrs. Helen Oswald to
sign his bond.

Mrs. Oswald had been waiting nervously.

"The only one of them I'm going to know for sure," she said, "is
Judge Kerner. I've never met him but I've seen him around the
building so much. He's been such a big man."

Sullivan signaled Isaacs where to come to a halt. Sullivan looked
at Mrs. Oswald and explained that they were there to sign a bond
for Isaacs.

People do unaccountable things under stress. Isaacs was to do
such a thing now.

"Raise your hand and repeat this oath after me," Mrs. Oswald
said of the declaration that Isaacs would make that he would appear
again when summoned.

All the time he had his hand raised and repeated the oath,
Isaacs had a wide grin on his face that he could not suppress. It was
as though he found the whole situation so unbelievable it rendered
him giddy.

The handling of a man of Isaacs' prominence apparently befud-
dled Mrs. Oswald, too.

"I'm sorry about the delay in getting the papers," she said to
Isaacs. "Now if you'll just sign . . ."

Isaacs smiled again and sat down on the very edge of a chair. He
pulled out a Parker pen with a green barrel. It was over in a minute.

"Let's not talk here," Sullivan warned. "Let's walk down the
hall."

Sullivan and Isaacs walked to the elevators. They had no comment to make to the press or anyone else.

Judge Kerner was unavailable, too. The outer doors to his chambers remained locked. No one ever knew for sure when he left the
building.

But the judge, who has always been proud that his offices in the
Federal Building were on the top floor, had prepared everyone for
that months ago.

During an investigation into another case a reporter had accosted Judge Kerner as he came through his office door on the twenty-seventh floor.

"What comment do you have to make about this, Judge?" the reporter asked.

"Up here," said Judge Kerner, looking away, "we don't make comments."

CHAPTER 13

THE PANJANDRUMS OF COOK

*Chicago's Mayor Richard J. Daley is tough and hard. He has a
reputation for ruthlessness. But he is not a stupid man and he is
more sentimental than most people know, as you will see in this
piece.*

*The Democrats re-slated Daley for his fifth term as mayor on this
day and it was a marvelous meeting because, despite how it seems
to outsiders, the members of Chicago's Politburo actually believe
each other when they talk like this.*

TEARS IN THE MAYOR'S EYES

Frank Catrambone, Sr., all decked out in his prize-winning red
slacks and armed with the mandolin he had bought for 35,000 *lira*
in Florence, Italy, was the first man into the Skylight Room on the
eighteenth floor of the Sherman House that afternoon.

Frank made it there a few minutes before the members of the
Shannon Rovers Bagpipe Band, and he was walking around playing
"Happy Days Are Here Again" for more than thirty minutes while
everyone waited for Mayor Daley to arrive.

"I play at events for the mayor and the Democratic Party all the
time," said Frank happily, in his fine Italian accent. "But today will
be the best ever, I think. He is going to run again, no?"

Frank then told everyone who would listen that he has been in
Chicago fifty-seven years, ever since coming from Calabria, Italy.

"I tell you," he said, "this man has Chicago in his heart. He likes
everybody. Maybe not everybody likes him. But the mayor, let me
tell you, he likes everybody."

178

By this time the Shannon Rovers were starting to warm up and the leaders of the Cook County Democratic Party were slowly filling up the room.

By this time, two of the party's most faithful workers, Colonel Jack Reilly and Eddie Quigley of the Twenty-seventh Ward, were passing out Daley campaign buttons.

This was a public meeting of the Chicago Democratic Central Committee and everyone who is anyone was there.

Former Alderman John D'Arco stood in the rear with his wide-brimmed hat, State's Attorney Ed Hanrahan sat in the first row at the opposite end from Cook County Assessor Parky Cullerton.

Congressman George Collins and his mentor, Izzy Horwitz, were there, as was Alderman Ed Burke.

A few minutes before the mayor's arrival Colonel Reilly called the musicians out into the hall.

"This is all wrong," Colonel Reilly said. "You should have been over at City Hall. There's no need for music now, the mayor has already announced his candidacy. We don't want any music now."

"What does that mean?" asked Frank Catrambone.

"It means go home," Colonel Reilly said. "Pack up your instruments. We don't want any music. That's what it means."

There was the sound of much activity in the corridor leading to the Skylight Room as Mayor Daley arrived, accompanied by County Board President George W. Dunne.

The meeting was called to order and only then was it clear why Colonel Reilly had sent the musicians home. The music was all going to come from the speakers' platform in one of the great Democratic Party Love-ins of all time.

Congressman Dan Rostenkowski, in charge of the meeting, called first on a Alderman Tom Keane, who cited Mayor Daley for bringing "civic pride to the people of Chicago" and for making it the "cleanest and safest big city in the nation."

Daley sat at the speaker's table with his arms folded, listening closely. He was dressed in a dark blue suit and a light blue shirt and tie. His face appeared ruddy with the wind of the outdoors on his cheeks.

"I commend the mayor for making himself available," Keane said as everyone rose to give an ovation.

George Dunne was next.

"There are many among us who like to degrade people in the

field of politics," Dunne said. "But those of us who are associated with Dick Daley in the laudable field know how great a mayor he has been."

Dunne then cited Chicago's leading role, nationally, in rodent control and lighting city streets and alleys.

"He's a man's man," Dunne concluded, "and a boy's pal."

Alderman Claude W. B. Holman, the Democrats' most important speaker on the City Council floor next to Tom Keane, came to the microphone then.

It wasn't clear why he needed a microphone. Alderman Holman is blessed with a heroic set of lungs, and if the windows had been opened he would have stopped traffic at the corner of Randolph and Clark with his message.

"Mayor Daley's detractors say a lot of things," Holman thundered, "but he keeps his light a-shinin'. They can't follow his mind so he leaves them a-sweatin' and a-pantin' a year and a half behind."

Rostenkowski was on his feet again and it turned out that the vote to have Daley run for his fifth four-year term was unanimous.

Rostenkowski and the mayor go back a long way together and the congressman appeared truly moved as he said in introducing him:

"I don't think a man of this caliber will walk through my life a second time. I give you the mayor and the next mayor of the City of Chicago."

There was another standing ovation, the fourth of the meeting, as Daley stepped to the microphone and placed his hands on the lectern.

"Thanks, Congressman Danny," he said. "Thanks, President Dunne . . . George . . . State's Attorney Hanrahan . . . Matt Danaher. They are fine boys. Great friends. I'm thankful and grateful for this honor.

"I want to say thanks first to Danny. I'm proud of him. I've known him since he was a boy and now he's one of the great leaders of the Congress. He makes you feel you've had some participation. I know he's going farther, too.

"I want to thank Parky, too, who had such a tough time in the last election . . . and to all you fine men. Tom Keane, there, who has been the general in charge of programs is another."

The mayor went on talking for perhaps ten minutes, without notes.

It was, in its way, a remarkable talk. It was a side of him that we don't see often. He talked about the right of every family to live in a decent neighborhood, about increasing the amount of money being spent on education in inner-city schools, about creating parks for ghetto children.

"We have to have parks," he said. "We don't want them running in the streets and being crippled.

"We have fine families in this city. It's not restricted to color or nationality. We have fine black families, Jewish, Irish, Polish, Lithuanian, Greek, German, Italian, Croatian . . ."

His voice choked a little then as he talked in a more personal vein.

"No one walks through life alone," he said. "My mother used to say that, God love her.

"I pledge to you as I did to my mother and dad and to my family, I'll give you all my heart, my strength, and efforts for the city I love. I hope they'll say when the time comes, 'Well, he did the best he could.'"

The mayor lowered his head then and walked back to his seat where George Dunne was waiting to shake his hand.

There were tears in the mayor's eyes. He blinked them away as he grasped Dunne's hand and shook it vigorously, all the while looking away to hide the fact that he had been so moved.

HOLMAN'S HARANGUE

Just because they seem funny to you, don't underestimate the power of the two aldermen who are depicted in the next two pieces. And Marzullo is right when he boasts he can beat you at vote-getting 15 to 1.

Minutes before Thursday's special session of the City Council began, Alderman Claude W. B. Holman got the word.

Holman is a short man with white hair but he has a very big voice. He represents the Fourth Ward and is perhaps Mayor Daley's biggest piece of rhetorical artillery.

Now he was being told he would be the first man recognized from the floor to speak out against the General Assembly's failure to vote funds for the Chicago Transit Authority.

Holman wasn't surprised.

"After all," he said, "I always speak on administration matters. All I have to know is what we're going to talk about, and I'll back the mayor.

"I'd be drawn by wild horses before I'd ever fail him."

Here it was only 2 P.M. and already it had been quite a day. In the morning Governor Ogilvie had confided to reporters that he would as soon sit down and try to talk with the Russians as with Mayor Daley.

And just before the start of the Council session, the mayor held a short press conference at which he spoke angrily of "sordid details" and the "devious maneuvers" of the Republicans and demanded that all those in his presence:

"Go out and get the truth about this thing. You're all supposed to be such great reporters."

And so now it was up to Alderman Holman. I could hardly wait because there is nobody on Mayor Daley's team who has a greater capacity for outrage. The beautiful thing about it is that the subject doesn't really matter. All the mayor has to do is wind up the Holman doll and it immediately becomes indignant.

Mayor Daley leaned back in his chair after recognizing his man and waited for the fireworks.

They weren't long in coming.

"The deceit and unadulterated hypocrisy of the Republican Legislature," Holman began, "is now exposed for all the world to see."

"By their tricky maneuvering the Republicans have raped, murdered, and killed the people of Chicago. They have sold the old, the sick, and the infirm down the river."

Holman paused an instant to catch his breath, and Mayor Daley leaned forward in his chair to make sure the alderman wasn't about to be overcome by apoplexy.

He wasn't. Now, in an even louder voice, Holman declaimed:

"This act of the Republican Legislature is the greatest frame-up since the crucifixion of Christ. . . ."

Alderman Ralph Metcalfe, who was sitting next to Holman, turned around with an astonished look. Alderman Leon Despres put his hands to his head and Alderman William Singer leaped to his feet.

The mayor smiled benevolently but his look quickly grew stern as the spectators in the gallery began to react. Some laughed, others booed, while some began to applaud and shout their support.

The mayor began pounding his gavel for order.

"You'll all be quiet back there in the gallery," he shouted. "You're not in any barroom now. Any more booing or shouting and out you'll all go. We are here to listen to a debate and to learn things."

Policemen stationed in the gallery began moving up and down the aisles, glaring at the guilty.

The Council Chamber grew silent and the mayor signaled Holman to continue.

"I'll say it again and again," Holman shouted. "It was murder, rape, and a frame-up and it was the worst thing to happen since the Crucifixion.

"I don't know whether they were full of martinis or not, but it just shows once and for good that the people down there in Springfield don't give a damn about Chicago.

"But I'll tell you right now that all the booze from here to hell won't drown out the fact that Chicago has been crucified."

With that, Alderman Holman sat down and began rocking back and forth in his chair at a furious rate. He had done his duty for God, Mayor Daley, and the City of Chicago.

In fact he had performed so well that it might be another two weeks before the mayor asks him to get indignant again.

DO-GOODERS I BEAT 15 TO 1

Alderman Vito Marzullo leans back in the high-backed leather chair in his classy City Hall office. He smiles.

"I ain't got no axles to grind," Vito says. "You could take all your news media and all the do-gooders in town and move them into my Twenty-fifth Ward.

"You know what would happen? On election day we'd beat you 15 to 1."

Vito Marzullo, who came to Chicago from his native Italy at the age of twelve, is seventy-three. He has been an active member of the Democratic Party for fifty-two years, and right now he is serving his sixth term as alderman for the Twenty-fifth Ward.

He also is the ward's committeeman, the man who dispenses the patronage jobs to his forty-eight precinct captains and to 140 other workers as well.

Vito Marzullo, this little man who sits in the plaid jacket with the American flag lapel pin, runs his ward of 22,000 registered voters with an iron hand.

"There's too much belly-aching and criticism about patronage," Vito says now. "Who ain't got it? You don't think it happens in churches and cemeteries and private industries, too?

"Who wants somebody working for him who ain't gonna fight for the policies of the leader? If I'm the boss and you don't do what I want, I fire you and what the hell's wrong with that?"

Marzullo is not angry as he talks. All of this is coming out in a soft-spoken and reasonable voice from a man who has sought political office seventeen times and has run unopposed all but one of those times.

Recently, Vito had attended a meeting of the Democratic Central Committee at which a resolution was adopted abandoning compulsory precinct work and contributions.

In some quarters this move was viewed as one that might cut into the power of the Democratic machine to deliver the vote at election time. What did Marzullo think about that?

"What other jokes you got?" Vito asks, smiling again.

"I never operated that way, anyway. In my ward we have one big dinner dance every year. We sell ads in a program for it, too, and that does it all."

Vito Marzullo leans forward and hits his right hand on his desk top.

"These do-gooders want to make a federal case out of this," he says. "The mayor don't run the Twenty-fifth Ward. Neither does the news media or the do-gooders. Me, Vito Marzullo. That's who runs the Twenty-fifth and on election day everybody does what Vito Marzullo tells them."

He leans back.

"Sure, I put a lot of people on payrolls, but everything they do for me is on a voluntary basis and it will continue that way.

"I never asked them for money.

"All we ever did was have this one dinner dance a year and it's always been successful enough to carry every bit of our expenses for the year."

Marzullo stands up and points to the four pictures on the wall to his left.

"We have the top ward in Chicago. See those four men over there? We put them all in office. That's Appellate Court Judge

Thaddeus V. Adesko on top, the others are Judge Anthony J. Kogut and State Senator Sam Romano and State Representative Matt Ropa.

"See the four men on this wall to the right? There's Mayor Daley, Congressman Frank Annunzio, County Commissioner Charles Bonk and the other man is Vito Marzullo."

Marzullo sits down. He smiles again.

"We put a lot of other judges on the bench, too. And don't ever think that these people are ingrates. They always cooperate with the party that put them on the bench whenever they can.

"You see what I mean? The Twenty-fifth Ward has a voice in every branch of government. That's a hobby we have in the Twenty-fifth. It's our way of providing service to our people."

Marzullo's ward is in the geographical center of the city stretching from Ashland to Kedzie south of the Eisenhower Expressway to the South Branch of the Chicago River.

His constituents include Polish-Americans (30 percent), blacks (25 percent), Spanish-speaking (12 percent), and Italian-Americans (5 percent).

Marzullo runs them all.

"I have office hours every Tuesday and Thursday night," he says, his eyes showing a toughness not visible until now.

"One night, these guys come in to tell me they got demands to make.

" 'You got demands to make?' I ask them. 'Who's your precinct captain?'

"They tell me they're acting for themselves and that they represent 2,000 people.

" 'You make no goddamn demands to this old man,' I told them. 'Who died and elected you guys boss?

" 'I'm the elected boss. You get out, you son of a bitches, and don't come back.' "

Marzullo's anger dies down.

"What was I supposed to do, take my pants down just because these guys come in and act tough?"

He smiles again.

"Sometimes I feel just like Abraham Lincoln. He's the one who said you can only fool some of the people some of the time.

"But my people got confidence in Vito Marzullo all of the time."

ANOTHER NIGHT, ANOTHER WAKE

*Mayor Daley goes to more funerals than any man in the city of
Chicago. This was one of the most important. It's hard to tell how
many votes a man can pick up at a funeral, but the mayor doesn't
miss a chance at getting all he can.*

Once he was one of the most powerful labor leaders the country
has ever seen.

But on this night, William Lane McFetridge lay in a gun-metal
gray coffin at the far end of a long narrow room in the Smith-Cor-
coran Funeral Home.

Out in the hall, Jerry Keenan, one of the undertakers, was explaining how McFetridge's coffin was hermetically self-sealing and
that, once it was closed, neither water, air, nor dust could get inside.

"Once that coffin's closed in the morning," Keenan said, "it will
stay just the same inside for a hundred years."

You had to wonder what McFetridge would have thought of
that. He was the son of an ice-truck driver, went to work when he
was thirteen years old, and felt lucky when they told him he would
be paid twenty dollars a month.

By the time he was forty-six, McFetridge was president of the
Building Service Employees International Union and its 315,000
members.

He took over the job when the former president, a hoodlum
named George Scalise, was driven out by Thomas E. Dewey, who
was then New York's district attorney.

McFetridge ruled the union with an iron fist for twenty years.
And when you talked about big labor in this country, the men you
were talking about were John L. Lewis, George Meany, Harry
Bridges, Walter Reuther . . . and Bill McFetridge.

It was because of McFetridge that his building service workers
supported Dewey for President in the 1948 election.

And at the age of sixty-six, it was McFetridge who undertook
the biggest project of his life—the construction of Marina City.

He supervised the use of the health, welfare, and pension funds of his union which financed the landmark, saw where the money came from, and watched where it went. Why did he work when he could have retired?

"I got a buck," he explained then. "If it were just a question of money, all I'd have to do is put on my hat and go away.

"But I had Marina City to keep me busy. I don't play golf, and one drink goes a long way these days. So I read a lot and walk a lot."

The reading and walking came to an end in Michael Reese Hospital, where McFetridge died at seventy-five.

Marina City wasn't the only thing that had kept him busy. He was president of the Park District Board and of the Flat Janitors Union (until 1967) and a member of the Chicago Police Board and the Public Building Commission. His intimate associates were the most important political and business figures in Chicago.

His basic power ran in a line from City Hall to Springfield to Washington.

The obituary notices had requested that flowers not be sent. But now the funeral home people were estimating it would take at least five limousines to carry all the roses and carnations to the All Saints Cemetery Wednesday morning.

McFetridge and his wife, Barbara Ann, lived in Marina City which is an hour-long ride on two CTA buses from the funeral home where the wake was held.

"It had to be held in a place like this," Keenan said. "There's no place downtown that has the parking space. We can hold six hundred cars out here and we're going to have at least that many.

"Why, we're making plans for at least two hundred cars in the procession going to St. Jerome's for the mass Wednesday morning."

There's irony in this, of course.

Here is a man who spent his lifetime representing people who work in old clothes and heavy-soled shoes, and the people who came to the wake stepped out of limousines and wore three-hundred-dollar suits.

The funeral chapel was jammed by 8 P.M. and still the lines kept forming at the front and side doors of the building. This was a political wake of the first order and there's an unwritten protocol to these events.

No one leaves until Mayor Daley arrives.

It was almost 8:30 when the mayor's limousine pulled up at the front door. Shortly after Daley's arrival, two of his political foes—Aldermen Jack Sperling and Seymour Simon—came in through the side door.

Sperling nodded and gave Daley a polite hello as he passed the spot where the mayor was standing in the front hall. Simon looked intently in the opposite direction.

Stopping to talk to the mayor were U.S. Appeals Court Judge Roger J. Kiley and Circuit Court Judge John C. Stamos, U.S. District Judge Abraham Lincoln Marovitz, and dozens of others.

"Hello, Mr. Mayor," said a heavy-set young man. "I'm Bib Lynch's son. Remember Bib Lynch from the Sanitary District?"

"Sure I do," said the mayor. "Happy to meet you."

The young man walked about fifteen feet away to where his wife was waiting.

"Okay," he said. "We can go now."

A well-dressed man with wavy gray hair walked by and waved to the mayor. Daley waved back, smiling a discreet funeral parlor smile.

The man walked on but his wife, still staring at the mayor, bumped into another man. She excused herself and walked away.

"That was the mayor," she said to her husband in a stage whisper. "Why didn't you point him out? I almost missed him."

In the other room of the chapel, the line of mourners was still passing quietly by McFetridge's opened coffin.

THEY DON'T STEAL VOTES IN THE TWENTY-FOURTH WARD

Here is a behind-the-scenes look at Chicago's Twenty-fourth Ward. They don't steal many votes here. They don't have to, and after reading this you'll see why. There was one positive result that stemmed from this piece. Izzy Horwitz no longer speaks to me. He kept telling me all day long that one of my bosses was a very good friend of his. They never learn, do they?

It's with people like Al Chesser that the Democratic Party's voting magic begins in Chicago's Twenty-fourth Ward. Chesser, forty, a party worker for twenty years, is now captain of the Thirty-first Precinct. On Election Day, it was Chesser's job to turn out the vote.

Late in the afternoon, with the skies turning dark, Chesser stood at his post at the northeast corner of 19th and Pulaski, waiting for registered voters in his precinct to return home from work.

"I been on the streets since 4 A.M.," Chesser said, his broad, mustached face breaking into a smile. "You know how it is. Polls open at 6 o'clock. I got to get out and put reminders on the car windows of my voters that I know go to work early.

"I got to put more of them on the gates and doors leading into the apartment buildings. I got to make sure I don't miss anyone."

After putting his reminders in place, Chesser then went to his post on the corner of 19th and Pulaski, a few feet from the Bonita Fine Foods, and taped three sample ballots to the side of the brick building.

By this time, Chesser's fifteen precinct workers were busy scouring the neighborhood, voter registration lists in hand, beginning the day-long task of knocking on doors.

"I stand at this spot every election," Chesser was saying now. "Everybody knows where I am. They all come this way and stop by so that I can give them advice about how to fill out their ballots."

Chesser's spot was in a perfect strategic position, a few feet more than the required one hundred away from the Thirty-first Precinct voting booth in a basement store on South Pulaski.

The Number 53 Pulaski bus stops on both the north and south corners, taking away and bringing back workers from his precinct of 509 registered Democrats.

Inside the polling place, another of Chesser's workers was systematically crossing off the names of registered Democrats who came in to vote. By 4 o'clock in the afternoon, every precinct worker would know which Democrats still had to be found and brought in to vote.

Nothing is left to chance by the Twenty-fourth Ward Democratic organization. It has been famous in national politics since the day back in 1936 when Franklin D. Roosevelt called it the best Democratic ward in the nation.

FDR had reason to praise the Twenty-fourth. Dominated then by a Jewish political machine, it had just given him a 26,112-to-974 margin over his opponent, Alfred E. Landon.

In those days, the golden names were Arvey and Sidney Deutsch and Arthur X. Elrod, father of Richard J. Elrod, the Democrats' entry in the sheriff race this year.

The Jews have moved elsewhere. Now the Twenty-fourth Ward is black. But here is where the magic comes in.

Political organizers such as Izzy Horwitz, now sixty, and Committeewoman Mrs. Adele Jeffe and the all-time great precinct captain, Sam Koppel, remained to teach incoming black political figures how the job gets done.

Koppel, now deceased, had a lot to teach. In the 1960s, his Twenty-ninth Precinct turned in margins like 420 to 3 over Republican aspirants.

Only five white precinct captains are left in the Twenty-fourth Ward now, but some of the real stars are black workers like Al Chesser. In 1960, for example, his precinct came up with an overwhelming vote for John F. Kennedy while the Republicans could find only five voters for Richard M. Nixon.

Tuesday was a particularly important election from the standpoint of the Twenty-fourth Ward's organization. George W. Collins, the ward's alderman and party committeeman, was running for the U.S. congressional seat in the Sixth District.

A landslide vote in the Twenty-fourth and in surrounding wards was needed to offset the expected heavy turnout for Republican candidate Alex Zabrosky in the towns of Cicero and Berwyn and send Collins to Washington.

At the Twenty-fourth Ward headquarters in an imposing old brick building on West Roosevelt that looks as though it once might have been a bank, Horwitz was talking about the congressional race.

Horwitz, short and balding, has worked in Twenty-fourth Ward politics for thirty years. He is an admitted millionaire as a result of real-estate deals, and a few years ago he stepped down as city building commissioner after it was disclosed that some of his best tenants belonged to the crime syndicate.

Horwitz denied knowledge of his tenants' activities. I have no strong feelings about the matter other than it is another one of those fascinating little bits that keep turning up in Chicago's political history.

Supporters of Alderman Collins refer to Horwitz as "The Coach," and they credit him with directing the transformation of the Twenty-fourth from the most powerful Jewish Democratic ward in the country to the most powerful black ward.

"We do it all just the same now as we did when Arty Elrod was running things," Horwitz said. "Our motto is social service. The people come first. Politics comes second."

He told how, when the Jews ran the ward, funerals were paid for, free matzohs were handed out at high holiday times, food baskets suddenly appeared for needy families, and help in getting jobs was provided.

"These things didn't just happen at election times," Horwitz said. "They happened every day of the year. Precinct captains had a duty to keep in touch with all of their people and to be on call twenty-four hours a day if help was needed."

Collins and his predecessor, the late Alderman Benjamin Lewis, have gone perhaps even further in their program.

Banquets are held for golden-age voters, Christmas parties are held for youngsters, and every summer more than a hundred chartered buses transport nearly 10,000 youngsters to the annual Lawndale picnic.

Classes are held in the organization's hall two nights each week for those who want to learn to read. The hall, with its kitchen facilities, is available free of charge to any group of ward residents just for the asking.

College scholarships are given.

Free grass seed and black earth are provided for those who want to spruce up their lawns, and free garbage cans are always available.

Collins, who is now the master of his ward's 20,000 registered voters, was sitting behind the desk in his tiny office with the telephone at his ear all afternoon Tuesday.

Collins looked like a man who knew he was on his way to Washington. He sat there smiling a lot and heaping praise on his precinct captains as they called in to report many registered Democrats were showing up at the polls.

"Hi there, Jim," Collins said into the telephone, smiling happily as though his listener were standing before him. "That's fine. Keep up the good work. You're really pouring the oil on the fire.

"You're already a winner, you know. Just keep up the good work and maybe you'll win the other prize, too."

Collins put down the phone. He stood up and shook hands. He has a firm grasp.

"The contest is a little idea we had for our precinct captains," he explained. "The captain who called in with the biggest voter turnout by 10 A.M. won a television set.

"The one who has the best turnout by the end of the day gets a free, all-expenses-paid trip to Washington, D.C."

Collins is forty-seven years old. He got his start in politics as secretary to Alderman Lewis and he became alderman after Lewis was found murdered the day after being re-elected alderman in 1963.

Collins did most of his campaigning in the Chicago wards. He went into Berwyn and Cicero only to coffee stops in homes to which he was invited.

On the wall near Collins' desk was a sign that read: "It's not the color, race, or creed but the individual who matters."

Collins glanced toward the sign and handed a political handbill distributed by his opponent's campaign committee across the desk.

"If you don't vote for Zabrosky on Nov. 3," it read, "you will wake up on Nov. 4 with a black congressman."

"I guess they kind of pushed the panic button toward the end out there," Collins said. He did not appear angry or shocked.

"But doesn't the possible bias of people in what will be your congressional district bother you?"

Collins smiled.

"We'll get along just fine," Collins said. "If you can give people the service they need, the color of your skin doesn't matter."

LAST HURRAH FOR DICK DALEY

I know now why I like this piece. It's because this was no doubt going to be the last campaign for mayor that Richard J. Daley would ever kick off.

There are some events about which no man can write quite truthfully. The legends are too strong.

A man may go to a ballgame or to a murder trial and report the end result without fear of contradiction.

But Richard J. Daley kicking off his fifth campaign for mayor of Chicago must be approached with some sense of what he has meant to this town for so long.

Daley doesn't like to hear it said, but he is the last of the powerful big-city mayors. He is the last one left with the power to throw the potential winning blow for a Democratic Presidential hopeful.

So Wednesday night when Daley opened his campaign headquarters for what might be his last campaign for office, it was no ordinary night. The thousands who poured into the lobby of the Bismarck Theater to shake his hand must have known it, too.

There was Mayor Daley, red-faced and smiling, his blue eyes twinkling, standing at the far end of the lobby under his huge campaign picture that was taken years ago.

Flanking Daley were his wife, four sons, and two daughters on one side, and his running mates, Joseph Bertrand and John Marcin, and their families on the other.

The crowd passing to shake his hand was four abreast. They extended back to the lobby door.

In the outer lobby one of those bands that constantly sounds off key was playing a tune called "Chicago" over and over.

Everyone who passed through the lobby door was handed a button that proclaimed: "Daley is the One in '71."

There are going to be some who may find hope for the mayor's opponent because there were few under thirty in the line who weren't there because their fathers hold city jobs.

There will be others who see hope because there were few black office-holders in the line and fewer people with long hair.

It is good they will have hope. No one should take that away from any man running against a four-term incumbent.

But there were other things that even an optimistic foe would have to take into serious consideration.

For one thing, the line stretched to the door for more than two hours, and the people who stood in it were those who usually get led to the best table the minute they enter any expensive restaurant.

Skip the obvious names like Alderman Tom Keane, Chief Judge John Boyle, State's Attorney Ed Hanrahan, Sanitary Board President John Egan, and Congressman Dan Rostenkowski.

Even skip landlord Charles Swibel, Harry T. Semrow and Fire Commissioner Bob Quinn and Stanely Korshak if you will.

But it's the names that usually hit only the gossip columns that show how far ahead Mayor Daley is capable of running.

Jack McHugh, who owns the construction company by that name and who built one of the Marina Towers, waited in line for twenty minutes. So did Pat O'Malley, who runs the Canteen Corporation. There were many others in this category who were pleased to attend this command performance.

All were wearing Daley buttons. Some were wearing two of them.

An overheard comment told you how much was riding on everyone's appearance—this was the distraught husband talking to his wife over the pay telephone in the theater's lounge.

"I know I promised you I'd be home for supper," he shouted. "But there's too many people ahead of me. It'll take more than an hour to get through it."

There was a pause.

"Skip it. What are you talking about? You gone out of your tree, or something? Look, there's one guy right up front with a clicker in his hand counting everybody off. And there's another—"

Another pause.

"That's all I got to say to you at this time."

The phone slammed down on its cradle. The man stomped back up the stairs to get in line to shake the mayor's hand and wish him another victory.

A little while later, after the crowd slowed, the mayor indicated it would be all right for the television cameras to move in for closeups and a little conversation that would sound fine for the 10 o'clock news shows.

It was really a hard-hitting conference.

Richard Joseph Daley was glowing now, his left arm around the shoulder of his wife, Eleanor.

"We're off to another fine campaign based on the issues," Daley said cheerily.

He shook his head when asked if he had any comment to make about charges that have been made against his administration by Republican hopeful Richard E. Friedman.

"I've never made any charges against anyone," Daley said. "I don't believe that's the way to run a campaign."

Anyone who was in the lobby of the Bismarck Theater could see how he will run this campaign.

It's a dazzlingly pure concept. You get together everybody who has any power in the town. You get them on your side and then you beat the other guy's brains out.

CHAPTER 14

LIP AGAINST LIP

PORTRAIT OF THE MOST UNPRINCIPLED MAN IN SPORTS

This is a story they tell about Durocher.
You are on a raft with him in the ocean. Durocher falls off. He
is drowning. You reach over and pull him to safety. While doing so,
you fall in. A shark comes along and takes off your leg but Duro-
cher pulls you back on the raft.
The next day you start even.

Leo Durocher, chin in the air and chest stuck out like a pouter
pigeon's, steps through the green metal door leading from the Cubs'
dressing quarters and onto the outfield grass. It is less than ten minutes before game time and another near-capacity crowd is jammed
into the antique ballpark at Addison and Clark.

Leo's cap, set squarely on the back of his head, hides his bald
spot and the Colorback on his sideburns hides the gray fringes. He
chomps steadily at the fresh wad of gum in the right side of his
mouth. At age sixty-three, or sixty-four or sixty-five—whichever version you choose to believe—Durocher's step is still light and
vaguely menacing. It still shows unmistakable signs of having been
modeled after that of one of his old idols, movie gangster George
Raft.

Leo is alone as he heads for the dugout but this is not unusual.
He spends most of his time alone. He wants it that way. He is, in
fact, never so much alone as when he is in a crowd. Maybe this is
because he has never learned how to take a back seat and blend
himself into the surroundings. For Leo must always set himself

195

against the crowd, attempting to bend it to his will. The weak he dismisses with insults and his unsurpassed mastery of the language of the gutter; the less vulnerable with carefully timed and staged displays of truculence.

The wild-eyed members of the Left Field Bleacher Bums, all decked out in their yellow construction helmets, have spotted Durocher now and they leap to their feet singing a daily tribute:

> *Give me that old time Durocher,*
> *Give me that old time Durocher,*
> . *Give me that old time Durocher,*
> *He's good enough for me.*

Hearing the singing, Leo turns to give a quick wave to the chorus, much like the tough guy on the block who is headed for a rumble.

It was "September Song" time for Durocher, the most important September he'd known in a major-league career that dates back to 1927. And he is headed for a showdown.

His Cubs—and they were Leo's Cubs—had a chance to win it all within the next month. If they did, Durocher would get some of the credit. If they didn't, he would most certainly get all the blame.

The trouble in Cub paradise is caused by the fact that Leo's style and personality are more conducive to winning sparring partners than friends. So now, after four seasons as Cubs manager, all his newly minted enemies were lined up and waiting for him to fail in the climactic hour.

It is hard to tell whether Leo was more feared than disliked. For example, there are few people who deal with Durocher on a regular basis who are willing to be quoted about him even though he is daily the most-talked-about Cub both in the press box and in the Pink Poodle, the Cubs' press hangout, after the games.

"You can't quote me," said one of the town's most prominent telecasters, Jack Brickhouse, "but I think he's the most unprincipled man in all of sports. If I had my way I'd like to see the Cubs win three straight in the World Series and then fire Durocher that night and not even give him a chance to buy a ticket for the fourth game."

"I'd love to have the deciding vote on the Cubs' board of directors," said another sportscaster. "I'd just love to see the look on Durocher's face as I voted to fire him after this season is over."

"He's a bully and a liar," said one sportswriter. "And if the Cubs do lose the pennant, you can bet he'll blame someone else. He's bush."

Not surprisingly, none of this bothers Durocher. He's been shot at before and even shot down. But he has never changed his style and never pretended to.

"I'm not coming here to win popularity contests," he said right after arriving in Chicago before the 1966 season. "And I'm not a nice guy. I haven't mellowed. I'm still the same SOB I always was. I should know. I'm the guy I'm talking about."

The wonder of it all is that Durocher was finally able to arouse the normally docile Chicago press corps. After all, this is the same group that had played Punchinello to the benevolently despotic George Halas for so long that one would have thought they'd been drained of the capacity to become indignant.

Maybe it's because Halas only insulted their intelligence (and served drinks while doing so after each Chicago Bears defeat). Durocher not only insulted their intelligence but their manhood as well.

They can't forget the time he ordered them to put out their cigars in his presence because of his sensitivity to cigar smoke. They can't forget that he made it obvious that he looks down on them.

They are strongly resentful, too, because Durocher so often made a buffoon out of former Cub manager Lou Boudreau by repeatedly swearing into Boudreau's mike during pregame tapings of the "Durocher in the Dugout" show.

And the story of the plane trip on which Durocher snatched the pipe from the mouth of baseball announcer Vince Lloyd and threw it into a toilet bowl because the smoke bothered him has been told perhaps a hundred times since it happened early this year. But never by Lloyd, who was the victim of the story. He, it turns out, is still one of Durocher's gin rummy partners.

They still tell the story, too, about another plane flight during which Durocher snatched the first page of copy from a writer's typewriter.

Durocher looked at it, glared, and then wadded the paper into a ball. "I don't like it," he growled. "Write me a new one."

It has often been said of Durocher that he will follow any route just so that it will eventually put him in a jam. It may sometimes take awhile but he unerringly finds the correct path to trouble.

That has been the story of his baseball career. The surprising thing is that anyone should have thought it would be any different in Chicago, especially since he offered to punch the editor of one of Chicago's dailies in the jaw the first week he hit town.

But Durocher didn't come to Chicago claiming he was anything but the man he is. He is tough. He is mean. And he may also be the best manager in baseball.

He proved that with the old Brooklyn Dodgers, taking them from the second division to a pennant in 1941. He proved it again in 1951 and 1954 with the old New York Giants, taking them, too, from the second division to pennants.

And now he was proving it once again in Chicago, perhaps more forcefully than ever. When he took over in 1966 the Cubs had not been out of the second division in nineteen years.

He had been here three seasons. During the first, he allowed the youngsters on the team to play and traded away valuable veterans, building for the future.

It was costly because Durocher knew the Cubs would be slaughtered. But the experience proved worthwhile for the young players. The Cubs finished tenth that first year and third the next two seasons. Now they were shooting for the pennant.

In order to understand Chicago's reaction to Durocher, you have to be familiar with the Western movie plot about the gunfighter who is hired to clean up the town. Marauders have been terrorizing this town for years. Finally, a desperation meeting of its leading citizens is held.

An old man with a beard stands to speak. "I know a lot of you aren't going to like this," he says, "but we have no choice. This has been going on for nineteen years now and unless we stop it we might as well pack up and move on."

Then he tells them he knows just the man to clean up the situation.

"Who is it?" they ask in unison. "Tell us who it is and we'll get him. We'll pay him anything if he can save our town."

"Durocher's his name," says the old man. "He takes trouble wherever he goes but he's always done the job he was hired to do."

Well, that's the way it happened. Here was the one manager that Philip K. Wrigley, the Cubs' owner, said he would never hire, but when it came down to the final hour it turned out Leo was the one man capable of doing the job.

It is easy to forget now that the Cubs were the easy marks in the league just a few years ago and that their system of rotating coaches and their athletic director furnished enough laughs for all of professional sports.

Durocher had now been here for almost four full seasons and those lean days were past. It was forgotten how much credit he deserved for making the Cubs a respectable ball club.

All the talk was about Durocher's grating personality.

So it was big news when he blasts a player at a club smoker. It was even bigger news when Durocher jumps the club for a weekend and goes to Eagle River, Wisconsin, pretending to be ill. And the social pages of the papers jingle with the stories of Durocher's fourth marriage. The wedding indeed became one of baseball's most-talked-about social events.

"This was Durocher at his best," says one writer. "He put everyone down—people he deals with every day—showing them for good and all how he feels about them.

"You see, anybody else in Durocher's situation would have invited all the writers and television and radio people he deals with every day.

"Leo didn't. Jack Brickhouse was left out and so were Vince Lloyd and Lou Boudreau. But it was even better than that because Leo did invite Ward Quaal, who is the boss of all three of them.

"That was his way of showing them that he's the boss of the Cubs and he's going to socialize only with the top echelon."

How the Cubs, players and coaches, feel about Durocher can be gleaned from the following events, which occurred at about the time of the wedding:

Several days before the event one of the Cubs—a prominent player—confided to a friend that a team revolt was imminent. "Something has to be done," he said, "because we can't win the pennant with Durocher. He just doesn't know how to handle pitchers."

The day before the wedding one of the coaches told a friend: "I don't know what to do. My wife bought a new dress for the wedding and she wants us to go. But I dislike the man so much. I told her she could wear the dress and I'd take her out someplace else."

He apparently had a change of heart, however, because he showed up at the wedding, held at the fashionable Ambassador West.

One day on the team bus heading for the airport Durocher was overheard telling his wife, Lynn, how much he would like to have the Cardinals' Bob Gibson for a pitcher.

"I suppose you'd even trade me for him, wouldn't you?" Lynn asked.

"No," replied Leo, smiling, "not unless they threw in a center-fielder, too."

But there have been interesting events swirling about Durocher for years. More than twenty years ago he was characterized by one national magazine as the "most talked about and unloved man in baseball."

It was around that time that the Catholic Youth Organization in Brooklyn threatened to boycott the Dodgers as long as Durocher was manager.

Since then he has been sued for assault and battery and for alienation of affections. He has been suspended from the game for a whole year for conduct detrimental to baseball and has been a brawler both on and off the field.

And he has always lived by the dictum handed down to him by George Raft, the screen mobster who helped Leo buy his first three-hundred-dollar suit: "To make people think you're a success, put on a big show. Make sure you are seen in the right places with the big shots. And remember, always travel first class."

Not the least of the resentment against Durocher has been caused by his preoccupation with money and his ability to make it.

It is believed that he was being paid $60,000 a year (including an expense account) for managing the Cubs. He received an additional $15,000 for performing on the "Durocher in the Dugout" show before each game and another $15,000 plus residuals for the beer company commercials he taped for that season.

Roger Kahn, who was once sports editor of *The Saturday Evening Post,* tells the story of how his magazine paid Leo $25,000 for his baseball memoirs, called "I Come to Kill You."

"Leo was very grateful," Kahn recalls.

The first year Leo managed the Cubs, Kahn was assigned by the *Post* to do a Durocher profile. "Leo was very happy to see me at first," Kahn recalls. "I told him I was going to do a piece for the *Post,* and his eyes lit up."

"How much am I gonna get?" Durocher asked.

Kahn told him that this time there would be no money involved because Kahn would be writing the story strictly from his own observation.

Durocher's answer was a simple gesture of zipping his lips to indicate that he wouldn't talk if he wasn't going to get paid.

Kahn was not dissuaded, however. He hung around with the

Cubs for more than a week, listening and jotting down notes whenever Durocher talked to other sportswriters.

Finally, Durocher exploded: "You're stealing money right out of my mouth!" he said, almost leaping up and down in anger. "You're stealing it right out of my mouth!"

He was a lonely man and a talented one, this Durocher. And it appeared that his greatest talent is for baseball and gin rummy.

He wore out every town in which he ever worked and there is no one who can tell you if he ever really had a close friend.

There were times on plane trips when Durocher sat alone for hours. On road trips he kept to his room like a hermit. His meals were sent up and he emerged only to go to the ballpark.

The players realized his attitude toward them and it made them uneasy. They knew sentiment never stood in the way of making the sound move.

After all, it was Leo himself who said:

"If I was playing third and my mother was rounding the base with the run that was going to beat my team I'd trip her. I'd pick her up and brush her off, and then I'd say, 'Sorry, Mom, but nobody beats me!' "

But they do, Leo, they do.

JERRY HOLTZMAN, SUPERSTAR

Nobody ever writes about baseball writers. That's too bad. At least one of them is also an interesting human being. Here he is. For my money he's the best of them all.

Jerry Holtzman has a typewriter in one hand, a briefcase in the other. Right now he is striding purposefully toward the player's entrance at Wrigley Field.

It is still nearly an hour before the game between the Chicago Cubs and the Pittsburgh Pirates is due to start.

This is to be a crucial afternoon in the modern history of baseball writing.

It will be crucial for Jerry Holtzman, too. Not only his longtime friendships with other sports observers but perhaps even his physical safety will be placed on the line.

Jerry has just returned from a long road trip with the Cubs. Until now he hasn't come face to face with the Chicago press, radio, and television corps.

It was just a week ago that he had defected from their lodge and taken his own stand on the great Leo Durocher controversy.

For those who missed the earlier chapters, these are the bare bones that precipitated his tense confrontation.

There had been a growing and tumultuous uproar in the media to fire Durocher as the Cubs manager.

Sports columnists, radio sports experts, television sports experts, and even television weathermen were in the act.

It was a classic example of a mob attack, with everyone finally getting up enough nerve to throw stones. Even those who write very little and spend most of their time eating the free food in the Cubs' press room were now willing to go on record against Durocher.

At this point in time it was Jerry Holtzman who had stepped to his typewriter and tapped out the immortal words:

"Fire him? . . . I'd give him a raise for putting up with the Cry-baby Cubs—all those $50,000 to $100,000 ballplayers who can't cut it any more. . . ."

With this statement Holtzman broke all the rules in the baseball writers' book of protocol.

First of all, he had written what he actually thought. Second, he had contradicted the thinking of the town's eminent sports authorities and leading freeloaders.

With this one statement, Holtzman had revealed himself to be, indeed, a dangerous man.

My problem in walking through the entrance gate with Holtzman is twofold.

First of all, I must remain close enough so that I can see what happens. Second, I must remain far enough away so that I do not get hit by shrapnel if bombing turns out to be the enemy's tactic.

The first thing you have to know about sportswriters is that they do not love each other deeply. In fact, they do not like each other very much at all. They especially do not like it when they are made to look bad by a colleague who won't play the game, who won't go along with the pack.

This, of course, has been Jerry's sin, and maybe he will now have to pay for it, I'm thinking.

"Here comes Jerry the Whip-cracker," shouts Curly Kuzma, the Andy Frain supervisor, as Holtzman marches through the gate.

Kuzma, a short man with a bald head who officiates at basketball games in the winter, has a big smile on his face.

"That was great, Jerry," Kuzma says, "just great."

So far, so good. But the next step will be more difficult—Jerry will be bearding the enemy in its own den. This is a place called the Pink Poodle.

It is where the Cubs' management serves the most vile food imaginable each day before the game starts. But despite the inferior quality of the food, the place is always packed.

The food, you see, is free. The only place that it costs money is on the expense accounts that are turned in at the end of each week.

Sitting at the first table are Jack Brickhouse, the Cubs telecaster, Harry Caray, the White Sox announcer, Bob Prince, the Pittsburgh Pirates announcer, and an unidentified man who looks as though he might be carrying a gun.

"Here comes Knute Rockne," shouts Harry Caray, as Jerry walks toward the table. "Hey, Jerry, are the Cubs gonna vote you a full share when they win the pennant?"

But there is no animosity in Caray's greeting. He seems genuinely pleased.

Brad Palmer, the CBS sportscaster, is coming at Jerry from the blind side and this looks like it could be trouble.

He reaches out and grabs Jerry's shoulder.

"Jerry," Palmer says, "you told a side that needed telling. The players and everybody are still talking about it."

Jack Brickhouse looks up from the table. He is smiling. It is that same smile you see him break into during the seventh inning telecast when his youthful relatives carry those banners around in the stands with the Brickhouse name emblazoned across them.

Obviously, Brickhouse is not going to display bad feelings, either.

Bill Frink, from ABC, comes over to shake Jerry's hand. He isn't going to bear a lasting grudge, either.

Then it hits me. They are all happy with Jerry. Incredibly, they are crediting him with turning the Cubs around in the pennant race.

Suddenly, Jerry has become a factor in the Cubs' recent surge during which they have won five of six games.

I take Jerry aside and tell him about this.

"I know," he says; "that's what I've been trying to tell you. The players and the coaches believe it, too. So does Durocher."

Then he explains what one of the Cubs people told him.

"He just came over and patted me on the shoulder last night. 'Skipper,' he said, 'ever since you wrote that piece and took over the club, we're five and one.'

" 'Keep up the good work, skipper.' "

This is like science fiction, I'm thinking. I'm having wild thoughts. I can quit my job. All I have to do now is follow Holtzman around for the rest of the season and I can write a better story than *The Year the Yankees Lost the Pennant*.

Holtzman is my key to millions in royalties. What a plot. Here's this sportswriter who sits up in the press box every day. He can make stars and destroy them. He can make managers and fire them. All it takes is a few stern pronouncements a day from his typewriter.

Jerry and I rush up to the press box and take our seats. The game begins. The Cubs look dreadful. They lose the game 11 to 6.

The game takes three hours and ten minutes to play and most of the other sportswriters are screaming they should get overtime pay because they are sitting so long.

"Jerry," I say, "I thought you had this club winning. "What do we do now?"

Jerry looks at me the way all prophets look at followers of little faith.

"Just remember one thing," Jerry says. "Victory has a thousand fathers. Defeat is an orphan."

With that he turns on his heel and heads toward the Cubs' clubhouse for a consultation with Durocher.

As he walks away he whistles a tune sung earlier by his colleagues in the press box. It's a parody of a new pop hit.

The baseball writers call it, "Jerry Holtzman, Superstar."

CHAPTER 15

ESCAPE FROM THE TOMB

"ALL AT ONCE WE SAW THESE BLUE LIGHTS . . .
THESE GOLDEN STAIRS . . .
AND AT THE TOP WAS POPE JOHNNY"

Some stories—and they are rare—build so fast and pack so much drama that they mesmerize you. In the late summer of 1963, I spent three weeks in Sheppton, Pennsylvania, covering the rescue of three miners trapped in a cave-in.

Newsmen flocked there from all over the country. The European press was there, too. Highways were jammed, especially on weekends, with cars bringing disaster fans from all parts of the Eastern seaboard. Desolate Sheppton turned into a grotesque little carnival town. Hookers set up shop. The three bars in town were packed at all hours. Business reached record proportions.

Governor William Scranton walked to the rescue area one day and talked to the miners for five minutes while thousands watched. A sculptor arrived and began doing a statue of the over-all scene. Jack Begun came from Chicago. Begun slid down a deep embankment in his blue suede shoes.

He fell on his rear but came up smiling:

"Where are these rubes?" Begun said. "They're a gold mine. I can make a million with them as a hillbilly song-and-dance team."

The story ended for us in September. It was on November 22 of the same year that Lee Harvey Oswald ended the life of President Kennedy.

I was fascinated by David Fellin. He showed so much courage all during the time he was trapped 315 feet beneath the earth with

*only a slim chance to come out alive. So, the night I watched them
pull him to the surface in a parachute harness and, as they did so,
heard him sing "I'll be comin' round the mountain . . ." , I promised myself I'd go back to see him someday.*

*I wanted to see what sudden fame had done to better his life. I
wasn't prepared to find what I did.*

It was a lonely, desolate place, and the memories it held no
longer warmed the heart.

But Dave Fellin, in his mid-sixties and wracked by emphysema,
"the miner's cough," returned to the site of Oneida Mine Number 2
in tiny Sheppton, every day.

With the autumn sun warming the back of his neck, Fellin
crouched down to stare into the mouth of the iron pipe that juts
several inches above the ground.

The pipe extends more than three hundred feet into the mine
chamber in which —five years before—Fellin and two other men
had been trapped for two weeks.

A massive rescue operation was begun with volunteers pouring in
from all over the country. Then, at 2:10 A.M., on September 1, 1963,
with thousands of spectators cheering and television cameras whirring away, Fellin and Hank Throne were lifted to the surface in
parachute harnesses powered by a huge winch.

There was dancing in the streets of Sheppton and nearby Hazelton that night. But the joy did not last and it has never returned.

The body of the third miner, Louis Bova, was never found. His
memory is preserved by a granite tombstone less than six feet from
the rescue shaft.

Fellin still lives in the tiny frame house less than half a mile from
the mine. He spends part of almost every day walking down the
gray cinder road to Oneida Number 2.

"Listen," he commands you in a raspy voice. "Listen, while I
drop this stone down the pipe. Count the seconds until it hits the
water down there."

Fellin's eyes brighten as he drops the stone. It scrapes metal as it
begins its descent. You hear it scrape again. Finally, there is a faint
splash.

"See," Fellin shouts triumphantly. "I told you it was that deep.
According to my count that was more than three hundred feet."

Hank Throne, the man who was rescued with Fellin, does not come to the mine to share this ritual. Throne, now in his mid-thirties, tends bar in Hazelton, a twelve-minute drive away. That's one reason he gets to the mine only on Memorial Day, when the local American Legion post conducts a ceremony.

But there's a better one. Fellin and Throne no longer encounter each other if they can help it.

These men, who rocked in each others' arms hour after hour to maintain body warmth during those terrifying two weeks, now hold each other in contempt.

Sheppton's population is less than eight hundred. Its families have been in the anthracite mines for generations. They work hard and they play hard and they know how to hold a grudge when they have one.

For two weeks most of these people worked around the clock without pay to save Fellin and Throne. Now they nurse a smoldering anger directed at both because Fellin hurt their pride the morning after the rescue when he told newsmen:

"If I had been running the rescue operation, I would have had us out in five days instead of two weeks."

Whenever the rescue is discussed in taverns—and it is discussed often, for there is little else to talk about in Sheppton—the question of Bova's fate always arises.

And someone always brings up the miners' tale that, after a cave-in, the smallest man is sacrificed to save the lives of the others.

Then, amid knowing nods and glances, they recall that Bova was five foot, four inches tall and weighed 120 pounds.

It's a cruel bit of gossip, and Fellin flies into a rage when he thinks about it.

"Evil men," he says. "That's what they are. Only evil men could think that I could have eaten Bova to stay alive."

Throne, who has a sardonic sense of humor, doesn't show his anger, but it's there, just below the surface.

"Why would I have eaten Bova?" he says. "I don't even like meat."

Money enters the picture, too. Fellin and Throne, it is said, profited handsomely by selling a personal account of their ordeal to The Associated Press. And Fellin profited more, through personal appearances on television panel shows.

The resentment is compounded in odd ways.

Throne is looked down upon because he is said to have spent his money wildly, and Fellin because he never spent his at all.

It is the money, too, that has come between Fellin and Throne. Throne believes Fellin got rich as a result of their two-week imprisonment, while he came out with a minimum of money, two broken teeth, a fractured finger, and frozen feet.

Fellin did not appear startled when told that Throne thinks he didn't receive a fair share of the money. Fellin stared into a tree line for several minutes as if pondering how to present his case. Then he began, speaking softly at first but building in intensity:

"You know, everybody thinks I made a lot of money. Well, I got around $2,000 from The Associated Press. I got $300 for the three television shows I was on and spent more than that going to New York to be on them. A month after the things was over nobody would pay me twenty cents for the story.

"Now about these people around here. Sure they're mad. But so am I. All I said was that if I had been directing the operation I would have dug straight down the shaft where it had collapsed instead of drilling down through the roof the way they did. I still can't believe it wasn't the way to go.

"I'm a God-fearin' man. I went through experiences down in that mine that made me even more religious. But even now I wonder what life's all about. I wonder why we're here. We know what the right thing to do is, but most of the time we can't stop the beast inside us.

"Take the two of us. If we're off on some island and there's only one piece of bread to live on, what would happen?

"Well, I'll tell you. I'd make sure that I got it no matter what I had to do.

"Now that's wrong and I know it. I should give it to you. But I can't because of the beast that's in us all. Do you get what I mean? What good is all our Christian teaching when it comes down to the crisis? I think about that a lot.

"And I think a lot about Throne, too. He was with me. He saw the same things I did. He knows he owes it to God to change his life. Has he? Hell, no. He hasn't changed at all."

Fellin stopped talking, staring at the flat table of land on which we were standing.

"Listen," he said, finally. "Let me tell you something about being down there. All the time I was there I was never scared. I was never cold. I was never hungry. And I *never* thought I was comin' out!

"I suppose if I had dynamite I would have used it that first day and ended it. Now that I'm out I sometimes wonder if it was worth it.

"One thing about it was worth it, though. It happened after we had been down there in the dark for four days. All at once we saw these blue lights, and they lit up the whole area where we were and seemed to warm us.

"Then, suddenly, we saw these golden stairs down at one end. And there at the top of the stairs was Pope Johnny. Not the handsome one you see in the pictures. This Pope Johnny was an ugly peasant and he had a wart on his ear. But he had such a beautiful look in his eyes.

"Then Hank shouted to me: 'Davie, who's that man in the gold vestments with the football helmet on his head?'

"I knew who it was, all right, but I was afraid to say so. After all, Hank wasn't a Catholic, and I had only known him a short time. I was afraid that if I told him it was Pope Johnny, then he might have got mad at me and cracked me over the head with a shovel.

"So I told Hank to follow him up those golden stairs and that maybe he'd lead us right back up to the surface. And that's just what Hank started to do. But he only got the first foot on those stairs and Pope Johnny disappeared.

"Later, when we got to the hospital, they tried to tell us we had a hallucination. They questioned us separately for hours. Then a couple of days later a navy doctor came to me and told me that we were right about Pope Johnny, after all, and that we should always believe we had seen him and not let anyone tell us any different."

It was while Fellin and Throne were in the hospital that a television camera was lowered into the chamber from which they had been lifted. It showed what appeared to be the body of a man slumped in a corner, propped against a timber post.

Excitement gripped rescue workers at the surface. Was it Bova? He had been trapped on the other side of the shaft when the cave-in occurred. Had he finally been able to work his way through the debris after Fellin and Throne were lifted to the surface? Or had he been there all along? And if Bova had been there all along, why hadn't Fellin and Throne told anyone about it?

The questions had to be resolved. A volunteer, Andrew Drebitko, was lowered down the shaft the next night while thousands of spectators waited tensely on the surrounding hillsides—just as they had done the night Fellin and Throne were rescued.

Drebitko found only a pile of clothes and blankets with a miner's hat on top of them.

Fellin often thinks about Drebitko's dramatic exploratory trip into the mine shaft. His voice trembles with emotion when he talks about it. He walked away from the rescue shaft and over to Bova's tomb, leaning on it for support.

"An awful thing," he began. "What evil men. You know, about six months later I met the man they sent down to look for Bova. I looked right in his eye and told him how evil I thought he was.

"Imagine, goin' down there to prove a thing like that! I'd never take a risk like that to condemn a man like he was tryin' to do to me.

"But not that man. He was out to destroy me. They all were. I'll never forget that."

Fellin put his hands to his head and suddenly he was sobbing and gasping at the same time, unable to catch his breath. After a while he began coughing and the exertion proved too much. He sat down next to the tomb and rested, not speaking for what seemed a long time. Then we walked slowly back up to the road to his house and said good-by.

I drove back to Hazelton and stopped in the grim little saloon where Throne works.

Throne's miner's hat rests on the back bar. On the opposite wall are action photographs of the rescue and a telegram of congratulations from President Kennedy. On another wall is a single photo. In it Fellin and Throne have their arms around each other and are smiling. It was taken shortly after the rescue.

Throne was standing behind the bar with a bottle of beer and a large glass of red wine in front of him. He needed a shave. He was wearing a dirty red shirt and smoking a small Italian cigar that he called a "dago rope."

Throne frowned when I told him what Fellin had said. Then he walked quickly to the cooler and brought back another bottle of beer. He seemed angry.

"Hell," he said, "look at it this way. Who's the one who ever got anything out of the whole thing? Fellin, that's who. Even today, people around here recognize him on the street wherever he goes. Nobody seems to remember who I am, even.

"People have told me that if it had worked out right—with all that publicity we got—I should never have had to work another day in my life.

"Heck, I'm worse off now than I was before it happened."

There didn't seem to be any way to change his mind.

Chapter 16

WHICH WAY THE WIND BLOWS

*When Bernardine Dohrn announced the Weathermen were about
to begin a bombing campaign, she sent the announcement to me on
a tape. She signed it with her initials and wrote on the outside:
"Keep running with the kids."*

*I missed out on the story because I didn't play the tape until two
weeks later.*

*I attended school at Kent State, and the shootings there took
place the day it was announced I'd won the Pulitzer. But Kent was
over then and it looked as if Wisconsin would have even more serious trouble. So I went to Madison. They really did have more trouble in Madison but the National Guard didn't shoot anything but
tear gas.*

*It wasn't until much later that the bomb went off in the mathe-
matics building and death came to Madison, too.*

*So much became confused during that time. How else do you ac-
count for what happened to a tired old man like Paul Douglas?*

WHATEVER HAPPENED TO BERNARDINE DOHRN?

Whitefish Bay, Wis.—It's beautiful here at this time of the year.
The leaves have turned. The air is crisp and clear. Lake Michigan
shimmers in the autumn sunshine just a few blocks away.

Soon, Whitefish Bay High will play its homecoming football
game against Waukesha. Posters proclaiming the event have been
Scotch-taped to the walls all over the school building.

Bernardine Dohrn, now on the Federal Bureau of Investigation "most-wanted list," went to school here for four years, graduating in 1959. Apparently she enjoyed every minute of it, including extracurricular activities like football games, the pep club, modern dance, tumbling, the school newspaper, and the hostess club.

Bernardine Dohrn, now twenty-eight years old and underground, has been the leading spokesman for the Weatherman faction of the SDS for the past year. Every time a bombing has occurred within the boundaries of the United States in that period, Miss Dohrn's name has been somehow connected with it.

The FBI describes Bernardine as a leader and an advocate of widespread terrorist bombings in an attempt at domestic revolution.

She is charged with unlawful flight to avoid prosecution for mob action, violation of federal anti-riot laws, and conspiracy, all stemming from her arrest in Chicago October 9, 1969, in Grant Park.

On that day police had to wrestle Bernardine to the ground to arrest her. People here, however, remember her only as a five-foot-five-inch-tall girl who weighed less than 120 pounds. They can't understand this new role she has been playing.

J. Harold Rose, who was principal while Bernardine was a student here, remembers her well. One afternoon Rose sat in the office he now occupies as a senior adviser and thumbed through the 1959 yearbook renewing those memories.

Rose is tall and slim. He is middle-aged and immaculately dressed. He is perfectly cast to be a school official in an upper-income suburb.

"Until this thing happened about Bernardine," Rose said, "Jeffrey Hunter, the movie actor, used to be our most famous graduate. You remember him, don't you? He played the part of Christ in that movie *King of Kings* that got such bad reviews. He died a few years ago."

Rose opened the yearbook to a page with Bernardine's picture.

"People keep coming here now to ask about Bernardine," Rose said. "I tell them all the same thing. She was a good girl, a popular one, and most attractive.

"Let me count this out for you so I have it exactly," Rose said, turning the pages and counting the number of graduates in Bernardine's class. "Yes, I have it now. Bernardine ranked fifteenth in a class of 227.

"At the close of her junior year she was chosen by the American

Legion auxiliary as the girl who would spend two weeks at the University of Wisconsin in Madison to study the meaning of democracy.

"If I'm not mistaken, I think she was also voted the most popular girl in her class."

Rose kept turning pages in the book and pointing out pictures of Bernardine taking part in various activities. In all of them, she is wide-eyed and trying to smile at the right moment.

Only one photograph shows Bernardine in a reflective moment, when she was apparently unaware the camera was about to click.

She is seated in a window sill of the school with a book in her hand. The picture is in profile and underneath the caption says: "B. Dohrn studies for final exam."

Steve French, now twenty-eight and still a resident of this community of 18,000, knew Bernardine well during the days when these photographs were being taken.

They dated steadily and it was a relationship that lasted off and on until little more than a year ago.

"Ever since people found out about me," Steve said, "they have been asking about Bernardine and whether I know where she is.

"I'm really afraid to say a lot. You never know who might take offense in these days."

Essentially, however, this is French's story. After graduation from high school, he went to college in Colorado while Bernardine enrolled at Miami University in Ohio.

It was because of their friendship that French transferred after his freshman year to Miami where Bernardine had been really enthusiastic about wanting to join a sorority and attending all the social events.

Several friends maintain, however, that it was her experience at Miami that began souring Bernardine on the system.

Her family name had been changed from Ohrnstein to Dohrn and her father, Bernard, was Jewish. For this reason, apparently, she had not been invited to join a sorority.

Shortly after Bernardine's sophomore year began, she became ill. It is not certain whether she was suffering from rheumatic fever, but she went back home for the rest of the year.

In the fall of 1961, Bernardine went back to school, this time at the University of Chicago, and her family later moved to Oak Park.

Bob Reitman, also a high-school classmate here, is another who remembers Bernardine well from that period.

Reitman, who wears a beard and is a disk jockey at WZMF-FM in nearby Menominee, talked freely about Bernardine.

"I dug her a lot," Reitman said. "She was just a pretty girl and a good girl. How would you describe her? She was intelligent, aware, and sensitive.

"I don't think there's a day that passes when I don't think about her and worry about how she's doing.

"You know, in Bernardine's first two years in high school, she was nothing to look at, at all. Then, all of a sudden she came back in the third year and she was really attractive.

"I think maybe that turned her off a little, too. Here, all of a sudden, everyone wants to give her a big play because she suddenly looks good. Before, nobody gave her the time of day."

Reitman always believed, he said, that Bernardine was a little bit smarter than the rest of the girls in her class.

"I always figured she could see through a lot of the phoniness about everything," he said.

Apparently, it was while living in Hyde Park and attending first undergraduate school and then law school at the University of Chicago that Bernardine Dohrn broke away from the system.

And it is when you talk to those who knew her at this time that you meet with refusal to talk for attribution. It is not even possible to characterize these friends too closely for fear of breaking their anonymity.

"How could Bern or anyone live in Hyde Park and not know what's happening to people?" one friend asked.

"She lived here in the white ghetto just a few blocks from some of the city's worst slums.

"People keep saying Bern didn't try to work within the system, but she did. She worked for the Cook County Department of Public Aid for a year.

"She wanted to help people but all she ran up against was red tape. Every time she tried to help someone, Bern saw the system working against everything she wanted to do for people."

University of Chicago records show that Bernardine was graduated from the U of C in 1963 and began graduate work in social sciences in the spring of 1964. Later, she switched to the law school and was graduated in June 1967.

Following graduation, Bernardine went to New York City to work for the National Lawyers' Guild, a Communist-linked group. She also reportedly traveled to Eastern Europe and Cuba.

She later returned to Chicago to work with the Students for a Democratic Society, and it was in March of 1969 that Steve French, her high-school beau, came to see her again.

French had called Bernardine's mother in Oak Park before making the trip. Bernardine's mother was upset.

"She is free, white, and twenty-one," Mrs. Dohrn told French, "and she can do what she wants. But I wish she would live within the system she is trying to destroy."

Bernardine's parents have now moved to Sun City, Florida, where they are living in retirement.

The phone rang there for a long time before Bernardine's mother answered.

"Wait a minute, please," she said. "I'll get my husband."

"Yes," he said, "this is Mr. Dohrn. My daughter? I haven't heard from her in a year. The only people I hear from now are the FBI and the newspapers.

"It's not a very pleasant way to live out your retirement, do you think?"

AFTERMATH OF A BOMBING IN MADISON

MADISON, Wis.—Christopher, his blond hair in bangs and looking slightly bewildered, walked across the freshly painted porch of his home clutching unopened birthday packages under his arms.

This was Christopher's third birthday. The tall steps of the old three-story frame were still not easy for him to negotiate without a steadying hand. Christopher lost his footing on the first step and began to tumble.

The woman from next door who was taking Christopher to his birthday party in her house quickly grabbed him and carried him down the rest of the steps. The little boy began to cry.

"We don't want the birthday boy to fall down and hurt his knees," the woman said. "Don't worry, Christopher, you're safe."

But Christopher didn't really seem calmed by the sudden attention. Perhaps years from now Christopher will recall that strange look in his mother's eyes when she told him to go next door for his birthday party.

And maybe, too, he'll remember that although his grandfather and grandmother drove all the way from South Bend, Indiana, for the day, they were not around to watch him have his birthday cake.

Finally, it will strike Christopher that the day he became three years old, his father, Robert, died in an explosion set off by people who professed they were making the world better for everyone.

Robert E. Fassnacht, thirty-three, had been working on a project in the Army Mathematics Research Center on the University of Wisconsin campus when the blast occurred.

His body was found later in a foot of water under a pile of rubble.

Gerard Fassnacht, Christopher's grandfather, sat on the wooden porch railing with his arms folded, his face set rigidly as the boy walked across the porch.

The elder Fassnacht, fifty-nine, was attempting to cope with his son's death.

"I try to live my life as a Christian," he said. "I shouldn't have feelings of this nature. My first reaction is that I would like to mop up the street with the people who did this to my son.

"That's not right, I know, but I just can't sit here and say that I'm the type of man who could walk down the street and not feel like striking back."

The elder Fassnacht paused.

"Yes," he said, although no one had asked the question, "I'm certain Christopher is three today. I remember it so well. Just three Labor Days ago my son and his wife drove him over to South Bend to see us when Chris was only a week old.

"Yes, I'm certain Chris is three today."

Now, through some strange alchemy, the elder Fassnacht was recalling the youthful days of his deceased son.

Robert Fassnacht, his father said, had decided to become a physicist while still in high school, and realized he would need a doctor's degree to get anywhere in the field.

"Robert won a Westinghouse scholarship for a project he did in high school," the father said, "and it was something I remember vividly. Robert was the first boy in South Bend to win one, and when the telegram came his sister opened it. Robert, who was always modest, couldn't believe that he had actually won."

Robert Fassnacht went on to earn his bachelor's degree at Kalamazoo College and then, aided by a Woodrow Wilson Fellowship, won his master's degree at the University of Wisconsin.

It was only a year ago that he had completed the requirements

for his doctor's degree. Monday morning, the day he died, Robert
was anxiously finishing up a research project because there were so
many other things he had promised his family he would do.

There was Christopher's birthday, of course. But there was also a
vacation trip to California to visit his wife's parents, and a move to
another home that would be much more comfortable for the family
that now consisted of his wife, Christopher, and twin daughters,
Karen and Heidi, a year old.

"I talked to Robert over the phone just a week ago," his father
said now. "He was very enthusiastic about moving and about the
forthcoming vacation."

Grandfather Fassnacht listened quietly as the sounds of singing
came from the house next door. As he listened, his eyes grew misty:

> *"Happy birthday to you,*
> *Happy birthday to you,*
> *Happy birthday, dear Christopher,*
> *Happy birthday to you."*

Now came a round of uncoordinated applause. Fassnacht shook
his head. But he did not comment on the singing. Suddenly he was
thinking about something else.

"Have I read about the bombings all across the country?" he
asked, repeating a question that had been asked several minutes earlier.

"Yes, I've read about them. I've read about them, and I've always deplored them."

"SOMETHING HAS GONE TERRIBLY WRONG"

MADISON, Wis.—I am sitting on the lawn in back of the University of Wisconsin's Student Union as I write this.

It's early afternoon and the sun is hot. But there is a cool breeze
under the trees and it is very pleasant.

I have been sitting here, staring out at Lake Mendota for some
time, trying to figure something out.

Despite the fact that the university is between semesters, there
are hundreds of students all around the lakefront area.

Right now, several are swimming off the end of the dock. Two
young guys are having a great time paddling their kayaks. Girls are
sunbathing on the dock.

Half a dozen ducks are sitting calmly on the water near shore. A dog has just leaped into the water to retrieve a stick. Off in the distance, a motorboat speeds along, towing a water skier.

Everything is so calm, so placid, here.

But in other parts of town, the Federal Bureau of Investigation and the police are still tracking down leads in the bombing of the Army Mathematics Research Center.

Way out on the east end of town, on Mifflin Street, the family of Robert E. Fassnacht, the thirty-three-year-old physicist who was killed in the blast, are making preparations to bury him.

And somewhere, the people who stole the truck and loaded it with explosives are contemplating the reactions to the thing they have done.

They are in it for good now. The man who made the phone call to police and said, "Hey, pig. There's a bomb in the Math Research Center," is in it. So is the man who drove the truck and set the clock running for the explosives to go off. And so are the others who helped collect the explosives.

This isn't marching in the streets and shouting antiwar slogans. This isn't rock-throwing or trashing. If they are caught, the charge will be conspiracy to commit murder. The fun and games are over.

That brings me back to the reason I have been sitting here at a picnic bench under a tree when I am being paid to work.

About an hour ago, the most remarkable thing happened. I had gone into Brown's Book Store on State Street just a few blocks off campus to buy a notebook.

While there, I studied the paperback book racks for some time, finally buying a copy of Richard Harris's *Justice,* a study of the contrasting uses made of the Justice Department by Ramsey Clark and John Mitchell.

It is subtitled, "The Crisis of Law and Order in America."

As I walked out of the store, I noticed a large crowd of students as well as older people gathered at the side of the building and reading a handbill that had just been posted.

No doubt it had been taped to the wall during the time I was in the bookstore because there had been no crowd there at all before.

At the top of the handbill in large black letters it read: "Why the Bombing?"

Under this was a large, high-quality photograph of the heavily damaged Army Math Center.

The accompanying text read:

We who understand and support the demolition of the Army Math Research Center must speak for ourselves because the official media have distorted the event beyond recognition.

They do not tell you that this was not any mathematics research center solving any theoretical problems, but the nation's only Army math research center whose role is to solve military problems, to design triggers for others to pull.

Their research has killed literally thousands of innocent people and has developed instruments for the delivery of nuclear and chemical-biological bombs.

These researchers shield their eyes from the fact that their work is used to keep the privileged ruling minorities in power around the world, and the press terms this self-imposed blindness "neutrality."

The media does not tell you that the bombers defended human life, not only by attacking an institution of organized murder but also by choosing time of day and time of year when the building was the least likely to be occupied—and then by phoning their warning to police 12 minutes before the actual explosion.

The police made no attempt to call the walkie-talkie-equipped guards in the Army Math Building.

They do not tell you the history that led reasonable people to commit acts of force. For a full year an increasing number of students attempted to expose the real function of Army Math and to shut it down.

At first they tried persuasion, distributing thousands of pamphlets describing the different ways that the research services the needs of the military. This led to a student demand for negotiations, but the university administration refused to negotiate.

Then followed seven months of futile protest, ranging from nonviolent marches last November to rock-throwing attacks this May. By ignoring reasoned argument and negotiation, the university's managers provoked rebellion.

By responding to rebellion with naked force they left those who disagreed with only one option—force in return. This is the background for the bombing of the Army Math Research Center, the story the news media never covered.

They do not tell you the facts that would explain the bombing and then they claim that there isn't an explanation, that it was the act of a "twisted mind."

But we are not lunatics and our actions are not wanton. We

want to live and we want to be free and if the military sup-
presses life and freedom then we must suppress the military.

It was signed, "Life Above the Trees."

As I stood there writing down the words on the handbill, I
could hear one young man who had a full beard say:

"A remarkable statement. They never once mention the fact that
they killed a man who had never done anything to hurt them."

Another young man answered: "What about all the Vietcong
we've been murdering for years?"

Those were the only two people who spoke during the time I
stood there.

I am left with several questions in my mind. First of all, who
put the handbill on the wall knowing that he or she was risking instant arrest?

Second, can it be that the people who planted the bomb are actually proud of what they did?

I have been sitting here now for perhaps another ten minutes
searching for a way to conclude this piece, but it's hard to concen-
trate.

The thing that keeps going through my mind is the title to the
first section in the Richard Harris book that I have just bought. It
reads, "Something Has Gone Terribly Wrong in America."

QUIET SUNDAY AT KENT

*"This is where it happened. This is where it can never happen
again."*—Kent State University President Robert I. White.

KENT, Ohio—It was quiet Sunday. The sun was bright. Off in
the distance, summer-school students were playing tennis.

In front of Taylor Hall, a middle-aged man with a full beard
was sitting under a mushroom-type canopy that shelters a reading
bench.

I recognized the mushroom canopy immediately. It serves as
backdrop for the copyrighted picture of the National Guardsmen as
they fired into a crowd of Kent State students May 4, 1970 killing
four outright and wounding ten.

On Sunday, the man with the beard was the only one in front of Taylor Hall. Standing there, looking at the scene, you could understand how General Patton used to feel when he said he had been at all the battles in military history.

Patton had read so much about them he could visualize the battles in his mind.

That's the way it was with me about Kent State. I read so much about that day I could stand there and see it all happening again.

But there was a terrible irony to it, too. Taylor Hall was named in honor of one of my old journalism professors. Bill Taylor. He is retired now and wealthy because he always had his hand in a lot of other things.

The irony is that the word "confrontation" was not in Bill Taylor's vocabulary. Other words were, though. I remember how hard he pounded it into his students that they should know how to spell the word "ichthyology," for example.

A journalist should know these things, he would say time and again: "An ichthyologist is a zoologist who specializes in the study of fish."

That was fifteen years ago and I've never had to use the word in a newspaper story until now.

He was strict about things like this and anyone who turned in a written assignment with a misspelled word received an automatic failing grade.

In all the time I've worked in this business I've never been rapped for a misspelling. That's why papers have copyreaders.

I never heard Bill Taylor express an opinion about politics.

The four-story building they dedicated to him in 1966 is a really fine one, but it must be dismaying to a man so apolitical as Professor Taylor that times could come to a point where students would be shot down right in front of his building.

Sunday there were university aides stationed at every road leading onto the campus, registering people who wanted to enter. They will be on duty every day until political higher-ups decide it is safe for Kent to resume normal operations.

That will be a long time coming. Sunday, one of the local papers carried a story about Sandy Scheuer, twenty, one of the girls killed during the May confrontation.

It told of the hate mail Miss Scheuer's father and mother still receive regularly.

"Well, now you know what kind of a daughter you had. Just a plain Communist," said one of the letters.

On the wall in the men's lavatory in the building where most of the liberal arts classes used to be held, there is a message scrawled in red crayon: National Guard—4; Hippies—0.

On Monday, a film called *Confrontation,* prepared by Professor Richard Myers, will be shown each hour in the Student Union. The fifty-cent admission charge will go to legal and medical funds for students involved in the May demonstrations.

"I spent a lot of time putting it together," Myers says. "And it's as objective as humanly possible. But I don't ever want to see it again."

No one who was on campus that day wants to remember any of it, but they are trapped. There is no way they are going to wipe it out of their minds as long as they live.

Glenn Frank, a geology professor who served as a mediator between the National Guard and students, is a good example.

He has been at Kent as a student and faculty member for seventeen years. A former marine, he wears his hair in a crew cut, but this apparently doesn't alienate him from the students with long hair and beards.

Professor Frank is admired by other faculty members. They feel he risked his own life in successful efforts to prevent May 4 from becoming even worse than it was.

I talked to Frank for nearly an hour. He was the first person on the scene, other than the combatants, after the shots had been fired.

Here is how he tells it:

"I was at the bottom of the hill on the other side of Taylor Hall when I heard the shots. They sounded like firecrackers—little lady fingers.

"When I got there, it was chaotic. The guardsmen had marched away, but the bodies were all around and the students who hadn't been shot were hollering and screaming profanities that I won't even repeat.

"'For God's sake,' I shouted as I moved in, 'keep back and give these people air.' It never occurred to me that some of the kids were dead. It just never seemed to be a possibility.

"Once the ambulances removed all the bodies I walked to where the National Guardsmen were now set up and pleaded with the general for time to convince the students to move out.

"The general told me I had five minutes and that then he was moving in."

Professor Frank nodded to himself as he talked, perhaps conjuring in his own mind what that would have meant.

"So I raced back up to where the students were still sitting in front of Taylor Hall.

"They weren't going to move and now another company of guardsmen headed in from another direction. Immediately, the students thought they had been suckered and that the guardsmen wanted to trap them.

"I raced toward the guardsmen shouting at the top of my lungs. I told them that if they moved in on the students they'd have to go over my body. I pleaded with them to wait.

"Then I ran back to the students and now I know there were tears streaming down my cheeks. I couldn't help it.

" 'For God's sake,' I told them, 'you've got to move. There's already been one slaughter, let's get out of here, right now.'

"Thank the good Lord they listened. There were only four or five who still refused to leave and their fellow students carried and dragged them away from the area and down to the tennis courts where it was safe."

And now, this Sunday afternoon, all the tennis courts were taken and there were another eight students sitting on the grass with rackets waiting their turn to play.

PAUL DOUGLAS: TARGET FOR A DAY

Paul Douglas is seventy-seven years old now and visibly weary. The best years are in the past. Anything in the future that turns out good will be a bonus.

Here he was on Sunday afternoon, sitting bent forward in a folding chair in the Chicago Stadium. He was alone. The position of his chair would be approximately three feet to one side of the goalie's net if the Chicago Black Hawks season weren't over.

The orchestra was playing Sir Edward Elgar's "Pomp and Circumstance" and the former Senator from Illinois appeared intent upon listening to it.

In a few minutes it would be time for him to take the stage for the University of Illinois Chicago Circle Campus commencement exercises.

By some weird, twisted thinking that only doctrinaire quasi-radicals can understand, Paul Douglas was their target for the day. His appearance was going to set them marching off into the afternoon for a commencement of their own at another location. To them, Paul Douglas is a hawk on the Vietnam war, and this insult to him was something richly deserved.

His hearing is not good, and at first he didn't appear to understand the question.

"Oh," he said, "you mean about the students. No . . . no, I don't feel badly at all. They have a perfect right to walk out of the ceremony. I don't object in the slightest."

He was smiling now and you could see that Paul Douglas hasn't grown old in the way that many people do. There are so many that have such set ideas on things and hate it when people disagree with them. But Paul Douglas was never that way before and he isn't that way now.

"This whole thing is such a serious situation," Douglas said. "I believe in mutual de-escalation in Indochina. I'm not in favor of a unilateral withdrawal because I still believe if we do that we'll lose not only Indochina but all of Southeast Asia as well."

The march to the stage by University of Illinois officials and their guests had begun now, and Senator Douglas moved haltingly to the curtain at the side of the stage.

The four detectives in their plaid sports coats continued to chew gum as they held the curtains aside so the old ex-senator could walk through and take his place in line behind commencement speaker John Kenneth Galbraith and Professor John Hope Franklin, who was also there to be given an honorary degree.

As Paul Douglas climbed the steps to the stage, he peered out into the audience of nearly 2,000 students and faculty members, many of them wearing peace symbols on the tops of their mortarboards.

He did not appear uneasy. He did appear intensely interested in what was about to take place. He has never been a man to frighten easily. Men who enlist as privates in the United States Marine Corps at the age of fifty shouldn't really be expected to wilt at the first breeze, anyway.

There was an announcement from the stage now that the students who wanted to walk out had every right to do so but their rights did not include disruption.

This was greeted by cheers from the audience, composed largely of the relatives of the graduating seniors.

Then the walkout began. Douglas peered down into the crowd, watching them go, but it was really a small army that left. Maybe there were fifty of them. They had talked a much bigger game than they were able to show.

Once they had left, those who remained stood and sang the song that begins, "My country, 'tis of thee, sweet land of liberty . . ."

Douglas stood there singing in full voice, his mortarboard removed from his head, revealing a full head of white hair with a large cowlick jutting up in the rear. He has a strong face with a large nose and even larger ears and he looks like something right out of American Gothic.

The commencement exercises lasted two and a half hours and one of the last things they got around to doing was giving Paul Douglas his honorary degree.

He stood there with a serious expression on his face as the citation was read, calling him a great educator, economist, and statesman.

In fact the only time during the afternoon when Paul Douglas seemed surprised was when Galbraith ad-libbed before giving his address:

"We liberals owe to Paul a very great deal. His greatest and most distinguished achievement was to show what enormous good intellectuals can do in politics. The rest of us have merely imitated his course."

Less than an hour after the commencement exercises ended, Mrs. Connie Singer, wife of Alderman William Singer, was standing at the entrance to the multicolored tent at Wellington and Waterloo.

She was the hostess at an outdoor party to raise funds for her husband's political thing, but what she wanted to talk about now was Paul Douglas.

Connie Singer worked in Paul Douglas's Washington office after her graduation from Mount Holyoke College and she had been worried about what might happen at the U of I commencement.

She smiled when she was told that the old senator had said the students had every right to walk out on him.

"That's so characteristic of him." she said. "He knows so much about dissent, particularly lonely dissent, because he was involved in so much of it himself.

"For years he was all alone on conservation and he was one of the small and lonely crew that fought for civil rights, and so I knew he'd certainly understand the students."

Connie was interrupted then by one of Alderman Singer's fans, but it was obvious there was more that Connie wanted to say. The fan went away and then she said:

"I can't tell you what a privilege it was for a young person to work for Senator Douglas. He has such integrity and he so respected intelligence."

Connie Singer met her husband, Bill, while both were working for the senator. Now at this party they were all having a fine time in one of those really good gatherings where the beer was icy cold and sold for only a quarter a can.

Republican Bob Mann was there, and so were Adlai Stevenson III, Alderman Leon Despres, and Studs Terkel. (It is not true that Studs is everywhere. It only seems that way.)

And wherever you turned, people kept asking whether Paul Douglas was going to make it.

He couldn't, because he is old and tired, and shaking hands under tents and drinking beer is no longer his game. The walkout at the graduation had been quite enough strain for one day.

JANE KENNEDY: ACTIVIST AT FORTY-FOUR

Maybe Jane Kennedy gave more of herself in the fight against the war in Vietnam than anyone else I've come in contact with. They finally released her from prison on this charge after fourteen months. But at last report, she still had a four-year federal term hanging over her head.

Miss Jane Kennedy, forty-four, was once the assistant director of nursing for research and studies at Billings Hospital.

Now Miss Kennedy is imprisoned in the Detroit House of Correction in a maximum security cottage reserved for inmates who are considered dangerous.

Miss Kennedy, who holds a master's degree from the University of Pennsylvania and who has taught at the universities of Pennsylvania and Kentucky and at Loyola University, recently was awarded a new honor by the warden of the prison.

"She's the most troublesome prisoner I've come in contact with in more than forty years," said Warden W. H. Bannon.

The Michigan parole board must share Warden Bannon's views. Recently, when Miss Kennedy came up for parole they decided to deny her any relief from her sentence for another eighteen months —a truly unusual holdover for a prisoner not charged with a violent crime.

Just what is it that Miss Kennedy has done? Why is she considered such a dangerous person?

Well, it's a fairly long story, but it's an important one.

The Jane Kennedy story shows what happens to people who put their lives on the line because they believe the war in Vietnam is an evil thing and that it must be stopped.

It all began several years ago when Jane Kennedy went to hear a lecture given by an antiwar priest.

"Go home tonight," the priest concluded, "and ask yourself what you have actually done to halt the war in Vietnam."

Jane asked herself that question and decided that she hadn't done anything.

So she joined a group that called itself Beaver 55. It included seven others who wanted to do something about stopping the war, no matter what the consequences might be to themselves.

The group took part in two antiwar actions. On October 31, 1969, it raided an Indianapolis draft board and destroyed all the 1-A files. A week later it went to Midland, Michigan, broke into the Dow Chemical Company plant, and destroyed computer tapes on defoliants.

Five members of the group held a press conference in Midland two weeks later—during Moratorium week—and admitted their part in the two raids. They were arrested immediately.

Jane and her four companions pleaded guilty to the Dow raid and were sentenced to serve from a year and a day to four years. They were also convicted for the Indianapolis raid and sentenced to four years each and ordered to pay $5,000 fines.

The second conviction is being appealed, but Jane is still serving time in the Detroit House of Correction for the Dow raid.

Recently, Jane and her four companions went before the parole board. David Williams, twenty, Marty McNamara, twenty-one, both of Chicago; Michael Donner, twenty-two, of Midland, and Tom Trost, thirty-seven, of St. Paul, were granted their paroles.

Jane's parole was turned down and, as it stands now, she must wait another eighteen months before she will get another hearing.

Why? Here's how Jane explained it in a letter to her brother Philip, a member of the Alexian Brothers, a Roman Catholic order, who is stationed here in Chicago:

"It is perfectly predictable in view of what is happening to the Berrigans. [Philip and Daniel Berrigan, anti-war Catholic priests, are brothers convicted for destroying draft records. Philip is still in jail; Daniel has been released for health reasons.] It is clear that there are nothing but political considerations involved. . . .

"All of the inmates and many of the personnel were astounded, because an eighteen-month flop is almost unheard of. As one matron said, 'I couldn't figure out what you had possibly done.' "

Perhaps the biggest thing that Jane Kennedy had done to show the parole board she was still "dangerous" was to smuggle out a letter to the *National Catholic Reporter* telling of conditions in the Marion County Jail in Indianapolis, where she was held for twenty-four days before being shipped to the Detroit House of Correction.

Jane's article brought about a revocation of her rights to see anyone other than immediate relatives. It also resulted in a curtailment of her right to send letters.

In her article, Jane described unsanitary conditions, poor medical service, insufficient diet, and arbitrary punishments handed out to inmates solely at the whim of prison guards.

The publication of the article marked Jane as a force to be reckoned with. She was obviously willing to rock the boat even though she was under the thumb of the very people who could easily avenge themselves without anyone ever becoming the wiser.

Jane must have known that prison authorities were not going to be happy when she wrote, for example:

Suddenly, unexpectedly, the incredible newness of danger erupted into consciousness. Four women were called out of the cellblock in rapid succession. About three dozen of us remained in the large dormitory area and waited for their return.

A half hour passed. An hour. Then murmurs.

Then came a muffled scream from the bowels of the prison. "That's Penny! Shh, listen! They're taking them to the hole."

At last our fears were confirmed. But why? What had they done? Until we learned the answer to that question, how were we to guard against being sent to the hole for the same unknowing offense? All that night we lived near the abyss of the unimaginable.

Warden Bannon expressed his exasperation over Jane Kennedy as a prisoner.

"She's always involved in mischief here," Warden Bannon said. "She keeps telling everybody she's a political prisoner. I've been in prison work more than forty years and I've never seen anything like her.

"Every time she's told something to do she always has to ask why. She's like a lot of those people who want peace and think they can tear up other people's property.

"Just the other day, she started a lot of trouble about the dentist we have here. She said that the prisoners didn't like the dentist and wanted a new one.

"It was her idea that they had a right to pick their own dentist because he was working on their teeth. Well, that's none of their business. We pick the dentist we want."

Wardon Bannon said that Jane is in a way a symbol of the things that are taking place in prisons today.

"In the old days we'd have people in here who were strictly murderers or robbers. Now we're getting these protesters in, and all they want to do is change things. Hell, they're supposed to be prisoners and here they are trying to run things. It's a lot of baloney."

Warden Bannon does admit, however, that Jane has a right to feel badly about being passed over for parole.

"I can see her side of it," he said. "The four men got paroled out of Jackson prison and she's staying for another eighteen months. I can see why she'd be a little mad. I would be, too.

"But that's the parole board's job. They do their own thinking."

According to letters sent by Jane, the parole board decided to pass her over because she gave the wrong answer when she was asked whether she would engage in similar actions in the future.

"I talked about the fact that I didn't know if I would do it again," Jane wrote, "and that I could make no promise not to because it would depend upon what was happening in society.

"I told them that I wanted orderly social change but that certain practices were totally unacceptable. Our killing one another is wrong. All else is possible if life exists but nothing [is possible] if it does not."

It apparently was for this answer that the parole board decided that Jane Kennedy was too dangerous to be released from prison in a free society.

Chapter 17

TALKING UP TO MY BETTERS

I spent two hours with Norman Mailer one day and came away with a piece not worth remembering. I'd already read so much by and about him there was nothing left to ask. But when Mailer is on, he's great—and that's how he was the day he testified in the Chicago 7 conspiracy trial.

William Saroyan and Saul Bellow are here, too. I had dinner and went to the theater with Saroyan. After being with him four hours, he tried to talk me out of writing anything he said. How do you handle that? You write it all. You are not out in the streets with a pencil and paper in your hand to socialize.

I always wanted to see Stratford and Shakespeare's house. That's here, too.

You've probably never heard of Jay Robert Nash before unless you live in Chicago. But I put Nash in this chapter because he keeps insisting he belongs. Nash, you are on your own from here on.

I TAKE IT ALL BACK, SAYS SAROYAN

William Saroyan looked uneasy. Walrus mustache, Zorba-like vitality, and all, he seemed anxious . . . on edge. The taxi was heading for the Studebaker Theater, and there'd be no turning back.

"You know, I haven't seen this play performed in thirty years," Saroyan said. "I just wonder what they've done with it. I'm anxious to see it. I don't want anyone to know I'm there. But I want to see, to sit there and watch it from a place where no one will recognize me." The play Saroyan was talking about was *The Time of Your Life,* with Henry Fonda as the star.

"I wrote this play in six days in May 1939," Saroyan said. "It's my favorite of all my plays. Before it was performed in New York, I took over as director and fired three of the stars and made everyone in the cast do things they thought were crazy. 'That idiot Saroyan is ruining the show,' they said. "I hired Gene Kelly to play the part of the dancer and fired Martin Ritt, who went on to become a good movie director. I hired George Jean Nathan's girl friend, Julie Hayden, and Bill Bendix. The show went on to win the Pulitzer Prize."

The taxi headed south, crossing over the Michigan Avenue bridge. Saroyan, who was sixty-three, wondered where all the Chicago writers were.

"Ben Hecht, of course, went out to Hollywood. He wanted to make that fast money on screen scripts. How about Nelson Algren? I used to come here sometimes and visit Carl Sandburg. Jim Farrell was here in those days, too."

"How did winning the Pulitzer Prize affect your life?" I asked.

"It didn't," he said. "How could it? I didn't accept it. The Pulitzer represents wealth. They were going to give me a thousand dollars. By that time, I had broken down all the doors. I already had a thousand. I never put up with any kind of patronage. The most important thing in the world is art. If there is any award to be given, I should give it. I should say to Ford Motor Company: 'Here! You made a nice car this year. I'm presenting you with a ribbon.' "

The taxi pulled to a halt in front of the Studebaker, and Saroyan, wearing only a suit jacket despite the cold, walked in a slightly pigeon-toed gait through the ancient theater lobby toward the ticket window. He is shorter than his photographs indicate, but with his huge mustache and large, dark eyes, he is unmistakable to anyone who has read his books and seen him on the book jackets.

A woman moved toward Saroyan, her hand extended, her eyes wide.

"Aren't you . . . ?" she began.

"I certainly am not," Saroyan said, swinging around to avoid the outstretched hand like an umpire avoiding a batter's protest on a called third strike.

"But you must . . ."

"I'm sorry, madame," Saroyan said, "but I don't know what you're talking about."

With Saroyan was a nervous press agent named Robert Fetridge from the Praeger Publishing Company. It was Fetridge's job to see the theater tickets were picked up and also to arrange appointments for Saroyan so that everyone would know he had just published a book called *Places Where I've Done Time*. A third man joined them.

"We're sending you a complete kit containing all the reviews," said Alan Edelson, the press agent for the show. "They've been very good."

The downstairs portion of the theatre was filled. The top balcony was virtually empty. "Who sits up here?" Saroyan asked.

"It used to be for college kids," Edelson said, "but nobody likes to come up this high any more. Everyone's worried about heart attacks."

Saroyan stared back at Edelson as though he were some strange engraving whose outlines were difficult to make out. The house lights dimmed. The second act began. Saroyan roamed away again.

"Is he sober?" Edelson asked. The press agent was told Saroyan had dined on blue point oysters and two glasses of ice water.

Edelson shook his head sadly. "I sure wish he'd walk on that stage and sit at the bar," Edelson said. "I'd be willing to give him ten bucks if he did that." Edelson mulled that one over in his mind. He smiled, cagily.

"Tell him if he'll walk onstage, I'd be willing to pay him fifty. Business is dead all over town. We should be selling out every night with a show like this."

The play continued. It was no longer Saroyan's play. It was now the play of a man named Edward Sherin who himself won a Pulitzer Prize for his direction of *The Great White Hope*. It was a play containing one of the most objectionable performances imaginable by an actor named Strother Martin who specializes in playing what he himself describes as "prairie scum." It was a play in which Henry Fonda moved about and mumbled like an automaton. It was a play that made three hours seem like a lifetime. It was not *The Time of Your Life*.

Fetridge headed toward Saroyan with the tickets in his hand. "We're in the first row," Fetridge began proudly . . .

"No, we're not," Saroyan roared back, looking as irate as that other man with the walrus mustache who runs Bangladesh. "I'm going up top. I'm going to the balcony. I want to see it from there." Saroyan headed for the elevator that takes people to the balcony seats, two stories up. "Let's see your tickets, please," the elevator operator said. Fetridge shrugged his shoulders. He was about to get off. Like all press agents, he is easily cowed.

"Wait a minute," Saroyan shouted. "We're going up to the top. Right to the very top." The elevator operator looked at Saroyan. He could see Saroyan was not a man to trifle with. He shrugged his own shoulders and closed the elevator doors. Saroyan charged out of the elevator when the doors were opened at the third floor, pulling on a pair of green-tinted prescription sunglasses. "Well," he said, "this is a fine old theatre. How many people do you think it seats? It must hold more than a thousand. How much do people pay for a ticket?"

Fetridge said he thought it was something like seven dollars.

"My God," Saroyan roared, "that's too damn much money. And to think they want me to take a cut in my royalties."

Saroyan found a seat in the rear row and sat down. He seemed happy now.

"I know of no spot in this theatre more appealing to me," he said. "One thing, up here you're free. Down there [he pointed to the top-priced seats in the orchestra] you're hemmed in. You're on your good behavior. People tell you to remove your hat. Remove your head. Up here, you're free."

Saroyan stopped talking. The curtain was going up. There was Henry Fonda sitting at a table in Nick's Bar. The table was at stage front. For the first time in thirty years, Saroyan was watching the play that had vaulted him to literary fame. Saroyan didn't remain seated for long. He got up from his seat and walked heavily to the aisle. He remained standing there, peering down at the stage. He stayed there for perhaps ten minutes. Then he began roaming around the back row, stopping first at one vantage point and then another, seeing how the set looked from different angles, checking the acoustics.

"There was a night, a long while back," Fetridge whispered, "that he just walked right on stage in the last act and took a seat at the bar himself. I have half an idea that's what he plans to do tonight."

The first act ended. Saroyan walked back and sat in his seat in the rear row again. Saroyan shook his head. He wasn't angry. Only sad.

"It's not for me," he said. "They've missed the whole conception.

The qualities of the people, the tone . . . But recognize, it doesn't matter what I think. And recognize, I don't say this personally. Henry Fonda. All wrong. The part should be played by his son."

Saroyan hesitated, thoughtfully.

"I wouldn't waste talent like that. I'd use it. This production looks far more like the one I threw out. It's far from what I'd ever let them lift a curtain on. But then, remember, it's not mine any more. I'm just a spectator here."

Halfway through the second act, Saroyan walked up to Fetridge and said: "I get the idea. I think I'd like to go back to the hotel now if you don't mind."

Waiting outside on the street for a cab, Saroyan said: "I always get to talking too much and forget that writers are around. Handle this right, will you? Don't say I stomped out of the theater or anything like that. Just say that I had gotten up early and I was tired and I had to get some sleep. I don't want to cause any hard feelings."

MAILER: "NOTHING TO BE SCARED OF NOW"

The Champ is sentimental about Chicago. To him it's Brooklyn with a top hat.

So Norman Mailer was happy to come back to testify at the Conspiracy 7 trial and attend to unfinished business, to pick up the strands of his scarred manhood.

Some people get angry when Mailer is referred to as The Champ. They don't agree that he's the world's best writer. They also know that his record as a fighter is awful. He never seems to win.

But Mailer talks in terms of the prize ring much of the time, and to him his appearance at the trial was his attempt to make up for "copping out" when he refused to march with his friends during the Democratic National Convention disturbances in 1968.

There was no fear in him this time.

"Nothing to be scared of now," Mailer said. "I'm exuberant. I want to get on the stand. This is a civilized court. There's nothing to worry about."

How could Mailer worry? A short time before, he and Abbie Hoffman and Jerry Rubin had gone to the posh Standard Club for lunch. Several tables away, U.S. District Court Judge Julius J. Hoffman took one look at them and asked to have his table changed. They had challenged the judge on his own turf and won.

Mailer was beautiful as he strode toward the witness stand, his shoulders rolling from side to side, his huge head of curly, graying hair propped on his squat body. It was almost as though some old Hollywood director had dressed up Rod Steiger in a Norman Mailer doll suit.

The reaction to him was unbelieveable. Even Judge Hoffman addressed him as "Mr. Mailer" instead of "Mr. Witness." Prosecuting attorney Richard G. Schultz was smiling and making it very obvious that he regarded Mailer as an author of genuine celebrity status.

Mailer's performance as a witness was flawless. He told how he had formed a good opinion of Jerry Rubin because of Rubin's "objectivity." He told of witnessing a battle between police and demonstrators at the Conrad Hilton Hotel from his room on the nineteenth floor. The language had some good touches. Asked by Schultz if he really could see the battling in the darkness, Mailer replied:

"It wasn't dark; it was twilight: It was a rare twilight and the police uniforms were sky blue. So were their helmets and some of them got so hot swinging their clubs that they took them off."

It went this way for more than an hour. Mailer talking, rolling his shoulders back and forth, jabbing his left forefinger to emphasize points.

There was a moving account of a talk he had had with Rubin months before the convention. Rubin, Mailer testified, had told him of plans to bring 100,000 demonstrators to Chicago so that then President Lyndon B. Johnson would have to be nominated under an armed guard.

"Your idea is beautiful and frightening," Mailer recalled telling Rubin, "but I'm scared." Mailer told of actual fear he had felt during the convention itself.

"David Dellinger had invited me to speak at the Grant Park bandshell," he said. "But I was at the convention to cover for *Harper's Magazine.* I couldn't get involved, get arrested. If I had been busted I couldn't make my deadline. I had to write a long piece and only had eighteen days to write it."

Then he added:

"I was in a moral quandary. A man never likes to think he does things out of the simple motive of fear."

Mailer stepped off the stand and everyone else in the courtroom was ready to leave, too. There would be a press conference and Mailer would have more to say. Down on the second floor with the televison lights on him, Mailer did not look like a man who had ever been afraid. He exudes too much confidence for that. Now he was in his element, too, and the change was remarkable.

"Judge Hoffman," he said with a smile that was more the grimace of a fighter moving in for the knockdown, "is like a fast-moving featherweight. He'd have a hundred fights and never be defeated. He'd keep that jab in your face But he'd never knock anybody down."

A man asked Mailer what he thought of Schultz, the government attorney who kept making objections to Mailer's testimony.

"You can't ask me to love a guy who keeps stickin' his thumb in my eye."

The Champ was swinging from the floor now and his claque was cheering him on.

"Mayor Daley won't admit it to himself," he said. "He'll be sick over it to his grave but the reason that President Nixon is in the White House is because the Chicago Police ran amok."

Mailer was leaning forward, perspiring at his temples.

"It's an ugly trial. It's a vendetta. These kids are cutups. They're seals. There's a gaiety about them and they're gonna laugh their way into prison."

The television lights were turned off. Mailer was on his feet, a fur coat dyed sky blue on his left arm. Moving through the admiring crowd it was astonishing to see how really short Mailer is, not more than five foot, seven inches tall. But there was one thing he had proved.

He left town with his manhood wholly intact.

THE WRITER'S LIFE IS NOT A PASSPORT

Saul Bellow sat on a folding chair on the slanted stage of Loyola University's Mertz Hall. In just a few minutes, Bellow would step to the lectern to begin one of his rare public appearances.

Bellow may well be the best writer of our time. But he is a private man in an era that has been usurped by writers such as Norman Mailer who are constantly before the public eye not only as writers but as participants and even antagonists in late-night TV talk shows as well as protest demonstrations in the streets.

We see Mailer on the "Dick Cavett Show" and know immediately that he is outrageous and witty—and even courageous. We see Truman Capote on the Johnny Carson "Tonight" show and wonder how that little fellow ever stuck it out in that Kansas town long enough to write *In Cold Blood*.

But we know nothing of Bellow other than his books and the fact that he is on the faculty at the University of Chicago. Unlike Nelson Algren, he is not mentioned in the afternoon gossip columns, and, unlike every other publicity-seeking author around, there are not continuing reports that this or that novel is about to be turned into a movie.

And so all we can do is read Bellow's books and wonder. Is Bellow really Augie March? Does he secretly feel that he would be Eugene Henderson if he only had the courage to chuck it all? Or is he Moses Herzog? And where does Mr. Sammler fit into the pattern?

"That's him," a coed in the second row said, after noisily removing her leather coat. "He looks just like his pictures. But he's better dressed than I thought he'd be."

"He's really a good writer," the girl next to her said, "but it's just that I have such trouble getting through his books. They're too deep for me, I guess."

"You should try *Sammler's Planet* if you think the others are tough," the first coed said. "I think it's out of sight. And I got all the way through it . . . almost."

An English department representative was at the lectern now and silence fell over the crowded theater. The professor explained that Bellow was one of the great names in American literature and that many of his books were considered modern masterpieces. There was a spattering of applause as Bellow walked to the lectern and promptly took a sip of water. He appeared nervous.

Bellow's hair looked almost white in the darkened theater. He is slim and his suit was well cut. Bellow dresses like a man who spends a lot of time deciding which suits he will buy and even more time in front of his closet deciding which one of them he will wear on a given occasion.

"I was going to read to you today from work in progress," Bellow said, "but it isn't working out. It's all in bits and pieces now. Besides, there's an old proverb which warns that you shouldn't show half-finished work to fools."

The students laughed good-naturedly. Bellow did, too. It was apparent the remark was more in the spirit professors sometimes adopt with students and not as an estimation of the audience's intelligence.

"So I'd like to read to you from *Henderson the Rain King* and then from *Herzog* and then I'll answer any questions you may have."

Bellow went on to explain that he had written *Henderson* with the help of a stenographer because it was overdue and he owed the publisher $10,000.

"I dictated it from 8 A.M to 1 P.M. every day," he said. "Then I'd do the dishes, do the shopping, and cook supper. After supper, I'd dictate again for the rest of the evening.

"I worked this way for an entire summer during a time of great personal difficulty. The worse things grew for me personally the more amusing I began to think the whole thing was."

Bellow picked up a copy of the book. He began reading. Eugene Henderson, the hero, is a man who decides to move to Africa where he ends up as a sacramental rain king of a primitive tribe.

> *"But if I am to make sense to you people and explain why I went to Africa, I must face up to the facts. I might as well start with the money. I am rich.*
> *"From my old man I inherited $3 million after taxes, but I thought myself a bum and had my reasons, the main reason being that I behaved like a bum."*

Bellow went on like this. He reads well and quite often his reading was interrupted by spontaneous laughter from the students. Then he read from *Herzog,* and, when he finished, Bellow was saluted with a round of applause enthusiastic enough for a political candidate or a nightclub comic.

Saul Bellow, the writer some students consider too "deep" had turned them all on by reading in person the words that are too opaque for them to understand while reading alone.

"I rather enjoyed that myself," Bellow said, his long, thin face showing the pleasure the students' approval had given him.

"The worst part for a writer," he went on, "is to reread something he has written and find that it is absolutely disgraceful. You can't get rid of it any more and you'd go mad visiting all the libraries trying to destroy it."

Bellow answered questions, even the ones that made little sense, for nearly half an hour. He explained that he tried to write every morning, that he very much enjoyed reading the novels of Henry Fielding over and over and that he didn't write anything that didn't truly appeal to him.

"If the idea doesn't wildly excite you," he said, "it's better not to go ahead. There are enough boring things being written anyway. The world is choked with them."

Finally, the question of Bellow's own career as a writer was brought up. How did it begin? Did he have any advice? It always comes down to that.

"I grew up here in Chicago in Humboldt Park," Bellow said. "There were no writers there. It was a working-class neighborhood. Later I went to Greenwich Village and then Paris and lived in cold-water flats. I smoked pot and hacked around writing book reviews.

"But there is a certain point where I realized I was becoming absorbed by the writer's life. It was then that I had to decide whether I wanted to live the writer's life or be a writer.

"It is a difficult time because there are a lot of people who would rather use the writer's life as a passport rather than go about the business of actually being a writer. It's a very attractive way of life but it wears you out for everything but living the writer's life."

Bellow answered several more questions and then begged off, explaining his throat was getting raw. When he stepped back from the lectern, the applause rose.

Bellow smiled nervously and nodded his head in gratitude. He is not an accomplished stage performer like Mailer. Saul Bellow is just a very fine writer who may be the best we'll see in our time. That ought to be enough.

SHAKESPEARE, THE KNOWLEDGEABLE AMORIST

STRATFORD ON AVON, England—"Our revels now are ended," he had written in his last play. "We are such stuff as dreams are made on; and our little life is rounded with a sleep."

He gave the lines to Prospero in *The Tempest* and the writer's name was, of course, William Shakespeare.

Each April, on the Feast of St. George, people from all over the world come to this little town where time seemingly ended in 1616 to pay Shakespeare homage.

The birth and date records on the bulletinboard in Holy Trinity Church indicate Shakespeare was born on April 23 in 1564 and died on April 25, 1616.

Peter Quennel, a Shakespearean scholar, tells us Shakespeare died of a fever he contracted following a long drinking bout with Michael Drayton and Ben Jonson, who had come down from London to visit.

I find that hard to believe. First of all, the pubs here close down from 2 to 6 in the afternoon and then close for good at 11 o'clock at night.

Secondly, it would have been extremely unpleasant for them to sit around drinking long enough in Shakespeare's house. It was a small place and they would hardly have gone out into the garden in April because it rains here every day in the spring and has for a thousand years.

Furthermore, it's a sedate little town, which at that time had approximately 2,000 residents. But, of course, that was before the Hong Kong restaurant opened on the main street. At any rate, Shakespeare is buried in a grave seventeen feet deep here near the front altar of the church, and there is a hideous bust, made of what seems to be plaster (although I know it couldn't be) hanging over it on the wall.

Carved upon the grave itself are Shakespeare's own lines: "Good friend, for Jesus' sake, forbear to dig the dust enclosed here. Blessed be he that spares these bones and curst be he that moves these bones."

To tell you the truth, I didn't actually see those lines. I couldn't because the grave was covered with flowers that had been placed there following the annual commemorative procession an hour earlier.

It was raining heavily when I arrived and I already had tromped around the town for more than an hour. I was so wet that I'm afraid if I hadn't had the admission fee, the sexton and the other elderly man who was selling the souvenirs might well have asked me to move on. A crew from the French government's television network was filming the grave site in the chapel, and they were only too happy to explain they were doing a documentary on Shakespeare's life.

"The show, it has already been on for ten years," the producer said amiably. "How shall you call it? The literal translation is 'Good Addresses of the Past.' We have already done Dickens, the Brontë sisters, Walter Scott, Oscar Wilde, and Conan Doyle."

I stood there watching them work for quite a while and it struck me once again how well dressed the cameraman was. That is something I've noticed, time and again over here. It must be that they pay the photographers more than the men who are working as reporters.

Harry Hare, sixty-nine, the sexton, stood there watching the TV men in fascination, too.

Hare, who was wearing clerical robes that drooped on his small frame, gave me a ruddy-faced grin and a nudge in the ribs.

"Look up there at that stone," Hare said.

I did. It contained the information that former parish member Dalrymple Crawford had been born on August 15, 1820, in Calcutta and had died April 24, 1871.

"Just a hundred years ago for Crawford," said Hare. "Not a soul here to put a flower to his memory."

Hare went on to explain how he had gained his present occupation. He was baptized in the church and has attended it faithfully all his life. It wasn't until he was fifteen years old, however, that he began to realize how important William Shakespeare was to Holy Trinity Church.

"I began working here then," he said. "And for more than thirty years it was my job to scrub the floor of this very chapel where he is buried. It's a very hard job. Some days, in the summer months, more than 2,000 people come here to look at Shakespeare's grave."

Hare, still quick on his feet for a man of his years, moved several feet away to put his arm on a young lady's shoulder.

"Sorry, miss," Hare said, "but I'm afraid you forgot to put your admission fee in the box when you walked in."

The young lady blushed and apologized. Hare returned, still oozing good will.

"We don't mind, at all, to have all these visitors," Hare said. "It's just that we want them to remember that they're in a church."

I left shortly afterward, walking back through the rain to the train station. Two things stood out. One was the huge portrait of Shakespeare over the main door to the town bank. The other was the Julie Shakespeare Wimpy hamburger stand.

As I walked, I kept thinking about the *London Times* article in which Professor A. L. Rowse had pointed out at tedious length that Shakespeare really was the author of all the plays and sonnets. Francis Bacon, Christopher Marlowe, and the Earl of Oxford were homosexuals, Rowse asserted, and couldn't have written plays with such a heterosexual bent.

"Shakespeare was an exceedingly knowledgeable amorist," Rowse wrote, "and a highly artistic, an ingeniously skillful practitioner of love-making who could have taught Ovid a thing or two."

Every time I think of that, I have to smile. Shakespeare was bald. You can't trust bald-headed men, I guess.

It's, of course, probably true that Shakespeare married Ann Hathaway, ten years his senior, because she had already become pregnant. It's probably also true that he deserted her and had many amours in London, where he lived for so many years. But none of that accounts for the esteem in which he has been held for centuries.

Shakespeare is remembered to this day because he could take even a subject like horror of monotony and come out with a line that goes:

"Tomorrow, and tomorrow, and tomorrow, creeps in this petty pace from day to day, to the last syllable of recorded time."

There is a line that tells all: "The life so short. The craft so long to learn."

Shakespeare didn't write that. And if you care enough about writing, it isn't necessary to explain who did.

RUNNING DOWN THE BULL

Jay Robert Nash has done it all. He has run with the bulls in Pamplona. He has studied at the Sorbonne in Paris. He has shaken hands with Hemingway and threatened to punch Big John McHugh in the nose.

Jay Robert Nash also knows everything. He has read all the good books. He has seen all the good movies. He has even written a few books of his own. Eighteen of them, in fact, none of which has been published.

He is, in short, Chicago's true renaissance man.

"All right," Jay Robert was saying in his usual charming style the other day. "You can do a story about me but don't you dare cross me. If you do, you're dead in this town. I'll bury you."

Nash, who is five foot, six inches tall and weighs less than 150 pounds, makes up for his small stature by his aggressive talk and his realistic imitation of the old movie tough guy, Jimmy Cagney.

A man who delights in taking on everyone in sight—in either threatened fisticuffs or threatened lawsuits—Nash was for a long time the editor of the monthly magazine *Chicagoland* and one of its most prolific and opinionated writers.

When Nash finally did enter the publisher's list, it was with a book that took on the Federal Bureau of Investigation.

The thesis of the book was that the FBI didn't shoot Dillinger that night at the Biograph Theater but rather a fellow named James Lawrence. The real Dillinger, Nash believes, then moved to Hollywood, living and working happily ever after under an assumed name.

"This book is powerful stuff," he said lifting a glass of beer and studying it carefully. "The heat is going to be on this thing very big. Everyone wants to serialize it.

"The only thing that bothers me is that I got myself stuck in such an amateur town with everybody wanting to write about it before it's published.

"But nobody better cross me on this thing. I've got too much time and money invested in it. Four years of my life and all my money. If they try to get in my way I'll sue them for $4,000,000."

John McHugh, a *Chicago Today* reporter, was seated quietly on Nash's left during this heady talk. McHugh was smiling now at Nash's threat to sue for $4,000,000.

"Nash," he said, "you're nothing but a little pipsqueak. Here you are, threatening the very cornerstone of the FBI and you expect everyone to sit around and take it calmly.

"You'll be lucky if the FBI isn't out here running a check on you next week."

"McHugh," said Nash, eyeing the big man with his best Cagney glare, "I warned you once before. But you won't listen. You know that three hundred acres I have in County Wicklow. Well, just forget about the ten acres I was going to give you out of the goodness of my heart. See if I care. Spend all the rest of your life in O'Rourke's saloon. It'll serve you right."

McHugh moved away, roaring with laughter, and Nash became conspiratorial.

"You know," he said, "I don't really believe in horoscopes but I'm a Sagittarius. I find out now that for my particular hour on November 26 I'm supposed to be some kind of Captain Billy Whiz Bang in publishing.

"It's strange, I suppose. But maybe it isn't really all nonsense.

"You know, there really hasn't been a good novel published in the last fifteen years. That includes Mailer, too. Everything is either obtuse like Barth or paranoid like Kesey.

"Who is Mailer, anyway? He's nothing but a staggering martyr who's been playing a role for fifteen years, sort of like Wilde was when he got out of Reading Gaol."

"Who else is there?" he continued. "Capote? He's a high-paid, highly skilled huckster and not a scintilla more.

"I learned it all from the very best. From Francis Scott Key Fitzgerald and Ernest Hemingway and Nathanael West.

"You see, I'm a very well-read man and I think the reason for it is that I have astigmatism. You see, eight-point type to you is twelve-point type to me. That's why I can read so much more.

"I've written a book now which I'm calling *On All Fronts*. It does what Capote tried to do in *In Cold Blood* and failed. It's a nonfiction novel which contains vignettes of war from 1914 to 1968.

"Everything's in it. World War I, Manchuria, the Nazi thing, Korea. And each vignette has an actual war photo to go with it. This could be my year."

Another book Nash has completed is what he calls a "very large and violent book" dealing in part with his period as editor of the *Chicago Literary Times* a few years back.

"It's called *Dust in My Hands* and a publisher in Jacksonville, Illinois, was all set to bring it out but he folded up."

Nash has virtually completed two other books as well. One is a book on crime in the Midwest. The other is a collection of interviews which he has done with literary figures in the pages of *Chicagoland*.

"The crime book can really be something. To do it right they'd have to sell it in three volumes and boxed. I've been working on it ever since I hit Chicago and it's going to be the definitive thing in its field.

"The interviews were with people like Ben Hecht, W. F. Snodgrass, the poet, James T. Farrell, Gwendolyn Brooks, Alfred Hitchcock, and Studs Terkel."

A photographer was moving around Nash now, taking pictures from various angles. Nash was wearing a tweed cap that looked as though it had come out of the prop room for *The Front Page*. But it wasn't the hat he was worried about.

"Just don't use any pictures of me with a beer in my hand," Nash said. "We authors have to maintain a little dignity, you know."

Nash then moved on to an anecdote that indicates he has an enlarged literary ego.

"Some years ago," he said, "I wrote a book that was loosely based on *Gone with the Wind*. It was about 300,000 words long. One night we were sitting around with some friends and my wife started knocking it.

"Know what I did? I threw it right in our fireplace and let it burn up. That showed that I meant business."

Nash took another sip from his glass of beer to let the meaningfulness of his valiant gesture sink through. He smiled and went on:

"Of course I let my wife know the real story a couple of days later. I still had two other copies in the back bedroom."

The thing you have to realize about Jay Robert Nash is that he apparently is not going to stop with the Dillinger exposé of the FBI.

"I have a story right now that's so big and so important it frightens even me," he said. "Not more than two days ago I found out the exact address in South America where Martin Bormann [Hitler's lieutenant] is living.

"Let me tell you something, buddy. That story is gonna hit this town like an explosion. I can see it now. Why——"

And so on into the night went Jay Robert Nash.

CHAPTER 18

CRIME AND PUNISHMENT

There are some stories that become so fascinating to you that you spend more time researching them than they are really worth. Editors tell you that all the time. "Sit down and write it," they urge. "You've worked on it too long."

The story of Roger Scannell was that way for me. Sergeant Bill Maloney of the Chicago police department had been talking to me about Roger for four years. One day, I decided it was time to call Maloney and get to work on the piece. "You're too late," Maloney said. "Roger was found hanging in his hotel room last week."

Of the other pieces in this chapter, one comes from a long personal relationship with Wally The Wiretapper. I once persuaded him to tap the meeting of the major-league baseball owners. After all his boasting, it turned out the metal walls of the Palmer House where the meeting was held would not transmit sound.

B. B. King was simply marvelous the day I spent watching him cut an album and entertain the inmates at the Cook County jail.

The fourth piece concerns the death of a South Side minister who suffered a heart attack after being falsely accused. I'll never forget the look of despair on the face of his widow.

ROGER IS DEAD

The big thing about Roger Scannell was that he was so much smarter than anyone else. For years Roger was the Chicago police department's number one stool pigeon, and he prided himself on the number of men he was responsible for sending to jail.

Roger was a burglar, too, and a premier shoplifter, and he was also a narcotics addict. He began taking heroin at sixteen, and at the end he was on methedrine, which addicts call "speed" or "bug juice."

They found Roger hanging from a venetian-blind cord in his room in a Near North Side hotel, and the police are still doubtful that he put the cord around his own neck.

But it would be an impossible task to begin seeking out Roger's enemies. There were just too many of them. He had been working to develop them for thirty-seven years.

"Let me tell you about Roger," said Sergeant Dick McKelvey of the Chicago police department's narcotics bureau. "I never found anybody on the street who liked him. He was heartless and arrogant, and he used every trick at his command to put other people down. Nobody could trust him. Time after time he turned in people who were supposed to be his best friends and sent them to jail. But then again, from our standpoint, we couldn't trust him either. Several times he tried to frame guys just to get even with them for grudges he had."

Roger was five foot, ten inches tall and weighed 170 pounds. He was a pretty good-looking guy, and if he didn't roll up his sleeves, he didn't look like a junkie. He wore expensive suits and fifty-dollar alligator shoes.

Bill Maloney, now the security chief at Arlington Park race track, worked with Roger for ten years when Maloney was a sergeant on the police force. One time Maloney and Roger were sitting in a saloon setting up a peddler Maloney wanted to arrest.

Roger's girl friend was with him at the time, and when she got up to go to the phone, Maloney asked Roger how he kept himself sure that one of his enemies didn't try to sell him a hot shot. (A hot shot is heroin mixed with battery acid or a poison. It kills instantly.)

"What do you think I got her with me all the time for?" Roger asked, smiling knowingly. "She always goes first."

McKelvey has a long memory. He still can't get over the time he gave Roger $150 of the police department's money to go into an apartment building on the West Side to make a buy. Roger went in the front door and then straight out the back. McKelvey didn't get his money back for a long time.

He also remembers the time Roger set up a former friend at whose house he had lived for six months.

"We went up there to nail the guy," McKelvey said, "and I

could see that he was honestly just as surprised as we were when we pulled the heroin out of the base of his living room lamp. I found out later how it got there. You guessed it. Roger did it."

Among the addicts, Roger was known as the man who always had a connection. He was the guy who always knew where to make a buy. They couldn't trust him, either, though. One of his favorite gambits was to take two hundred dollars from a friend to make a heroin buy and then come back with aspirin or saccharine so that the mark would end up paying for a jolt of nothing.

But people who traveled in Roger's circle don't hand over two big ones and end up with something that will relieve a headache, lightly. They waited around in alleys armed with things like knives and bottles and clubs and when Roger walked by they'd let him have it. "In the ten years that I knew Roger," McKelvey recalled, "I don't remember a single month when he wasn't beaten up at least once. I'll have to give him his due, though. It never seemed to faze him."

Roger's police record shows he was arrested for narcotics for the first time in 1952. Shortly after that his career as a stool pigeon began. Over the years he was picked up dozens of times on various charges but he never spent more than short stretches in the county jail. He was smart enough to know that he was more valuable to the cops on the street.

Maloney remembers that Roger really enjoyed playing policeman.

"He really got a bang out of turning people in," Maloney said. When it came down to the time to make the arrest, Roger would start shouting at the guy and tellin' him what a jerk he was and how it was Roger who was sending him to jail."

Over the years there must have been a lot of people in prison who remembered that Roger was the man who had sent them up there. And most of them had a lot of time to think about it. So Roger moved around a lot.

"He was a guy who never had a permanent address," McKelvey said. "He lived in every flophouse along West Madison and in every two-bit hotel downtown. Once, I remember, he spent two weeks sleeping in the back of an abandoned car."

Roger was one of the great shoplifters of modern times. The thing that made him so successful was that he had quick hands, was absolutely fearless, and also was not choosy about what he lifted.

He'd steal suits or diamonds, paintbrushes or lighter fluid. He just got a bang out of stealing because it made him feel so much smarter than everybody else. One time Roger walked into a gas station with McKelvey, and when they walked out again Roger had two cans of Simoniz under his coat.

McKelvey was astounded because he hadn't seen Roger make the move even though he was standing next to him.

"First of all," McKelvey told him, "I don't want you doin' that when you're with me. Second, I don't even know what you can do with that stuff. You don't even have a car."

Roger shrugged his shoulders.

"Now that I got the Simoniz," he said, "maybe I'll just go steal a car to go with it."

When Roger was twenty-five, his mother and father and two aunts were killed in a fire. He had been out of touch with them for years but their life savings and the insurance amounted to $50,000.

"That was a hell of a year," Roger used to say. "I shot up the whole fifty grand in eleven months. But what a time I had."

And that's the way life went with Roger Scannell. It's difficult for people who spend their days walking along Oak Street beach or taking the Northwestern commuter train to Park Ridge to conceive of the jungle he created for himself.

It was his own jungle, though, and he actually seemed to thrive in it. He lived by his wits. He took advantage of everyone he was ever mixed up with. He was just too smart. And in the end he wore everyone out.

Neither McKelvey nor Maloney nor any other policeman who ever had anything to do with him believes Roger committed suicide. But there were no witnesses and his body was in the hotel room three days before it was found. So it will go down as a suicide.

"You know what people tell me whenever I bring it up," said McKelvey. "They just give me a cold smile and say it couldn't have happened to a nicer guy."

WALLY THE WIRETAPPER

Wally Pritchard didn't realize the big guy had sat down next to him at the bar until he felt the cold steel of the gun barrel pressing against his temple. "Now you're gonna get yours," the big guy said.

"But I'm not gonna let you have it right away. First, you're gonna sit here and have one last drink with me while I watch you sweat."

Wally Pritchard was surprised, but he really shouldn't have been. He's been a wiretapper and private detective for fifteen years now, and it wasn't the first time angry people have come after him with guns in their hands. "I guess the thing that surprised me about it is that I was in one of my favorite North Side bars." Wally said. "It wasn't Rush Street or anything like that, just a quiet, friendly place."

Wally was scared.

Just as scared, that is, as he had been the night the two guys waited for him as he got out of his car and one of them shoved the barrel of a pistol into Wally's mouth. Just as scared, too, as he had been the night another guy pulled him into an alley and put a knife up against his stomach.

"But what can you do in a situation like this but wait for a chance to make your move?" Wally said. "Finally, I realize too much time is going by. The guy is only bluffing."

Wally, a little round man who once played third-string guard for St. George High in football, pushed the gun to one side and ducked back quickly, pulling his own at the same time. Suddenly, the advantage was his.

"Drop it right now and start walkin' for the door," Wally told the big guy and began marching out with him. The bartender called the police. Within minutes, Wally was back in the bar and enjoying the "last" drink the intruder had ordered for him. The thing you have to enjoy about Wally Pritchard, who is the first to admit he will never be a candidate for the Union League club, is that he doesn't take himself seriously about these things.

If Wally ever goes in the trunk or into a federal pen, both of which he views as distinct possibilities, he'll go with a smile and a wisecrack.

"Look," he says, "I've been at this thing for a long time and I don't have to work as hard as I used to because now I have a reputation and I get all my money up front." What Wally means by this, of course, is that if you want to hire him to tap a phone to get evidence for a divorce or to find out how much a business associate has on you, then you must pay his fee before Wally brings any of his $25,000 worth of electronic equipment into play.

Wally has worked for some good guys around this town who can't be mentioned and for some bad guys like Joe (Gags) Gagliano, Wee Willie Messino, and Mannie Skar, whom we can mention —even though they won't like it.

In the case of Skar, however, there's no danger. Skar represents Wallie's one attempt to change his career and become a bodyguard. The night they bumped Skar off in an alley with the fresh bag of halavah in his hand, Wally went out of the bodyguarding business for good.

"To tell you the truth I don't mind working for guys who are supposed to be bad," Wally says. "You find out right away you can trust them about money and you know where you stand with them at all times."

And yet it was two associates in this area who gave Wally his closest call back in 1959, a date which of course puts it beyond the statute of limitations. "I was working for these two guys and they get indicted," Wally says, "and so they call me in to find out what I'm gonna say when I get on the witness stand. 'Look,' I tell them, 'I gotta be honest with you. Once they put me on that stand there's no way I'm gonna commit perjury. I'll have to tell them what they ask.' "

Wally, who enjoys traveling in style anyway, was given a choice. He could go in the trunk or he could take a long vacation, all expenses paid. He went away for a year, resting in seclusion for a month in Biloxi, Mississippi, and then going on to further his career in Washington, D.C., and Los Angeles.

"With me gone, the indictment fell through. I stayed alive and protected my customers, too."

Wally is forty-four now and there have been years when he's made close to $50,000, although he is prepared to deny this and prove to the satisfaction of his three ex-wives and the Bureau of Internal Revenue that he didn't. He lives now in a plush apartment on Lincoln Park West with two television sets, two vibrating chairs, a bidet, and a de luxe bar stocked with only the finest brands. He buys a new Cadillac every six months. And before he goes out the door of his apartment, Wally always makes certain he takes a roll of ten one-hundred-dollar bills with him.

"Maybe that's the most important thing I take," he says. "In this business you never know when you're gonna get busted."

When Wally goes out to work as a wiretapper, he wears dark clothes and soft shoes ("You know, crepe soles or tennis shoes. You gotta get whatever edge you can").

"But there are times when no matter what edge you bring with you, you can't win. Take the night I'm up on Lake Shore Drive and I get into this joint to plant a bug. It's dark, of course, and I don't want to make any noise but I realize something's wrong. You know what I mean? I could sense it."

Wally found out what was wrong when the lights went on. It was another guy who was there trying to plant a bug of his own. There was one big difference between them. The other guy was carrying a badge.

"What was he gonna do? He can't bust me for wiretappin' because he's doin' the same thing and it's just as illegal for him. So I just yielded the field and went home. I had lots of other jobs anyway."

Wally, of course, takes great pride in his reputation as a wiretapper, but he isn't foolhardy about it. "Listen," he says, "if you're gonna write about me, make sure you tell them I'm only Number Two. They always said that Richard Cain was Number One and he ended up in jail. I just wanna be Number Two and stay on the street."

July 3, 1969

Poor Wally. I kept my word and never wrote that he became Number One, but that didn't stop the United State's attorney's office. They convicted Wally for a past-posting scheme at a Florida race track. He is now doing time, but I hope not too much. He's too entertaining a guy to have out of circulation.

B. B. KING PAID HIS DUES

The walls surrounding the recreation yard at Cook County Jail seem so much higher when you're standing inside. The towers with the armed guards appear more ominous.

It's a different world. Walking through the corridors, your ears are hammered by the continual slamming of iron doors and the shouted orders from guards to prisoners.

The guards are greatly outnumbered by the prisoners and so

every move they make must be a demonstration of strength. The prisoners hate the guards. The prisoners hate each other, too.

Most of the prisoners are black. A frightening number of them are there not because they have been convicted of crimes but because they can't raise money to pay their bonds while awaiting trial.

More than a thousand prisoners sat on the grass in the yard one summer day waiting for the appearance of B. B. King, the former cotton picker who many believe is the most influential blues musician in the world.

In a few minutes B. B. King would play his electric guitar and sing for more than an hour while recording a long-playing record called "B. B. King at the Cook County Jail."

B. B. was moving along the front line of the prisoners, shaking hands and talking with them. "Take my hand, B. B.," shouted one inmate, "take my hand, please. Even my mother was a B. B. King fan."

King, stocky in a bright green suit and light tan shoe boots, was smiling and showing a fine set of big white teeth.

"Right on, B. B.," shouted another man as he lifted his hand to grasp the hand of the musician. "You are just so great."

King appeared genuinely pleased by his reception, and somehow it seemed that just being able to touch his hand made the prisoners feel better. While B. B. walked through the crowd of prisoners, shaking their hands and telling them he was sorry he wouldn't be able to stay the night, one black man with a long scar on the side of his neck signaled that he wanted to talk.

"Hey," he shouted. "Come over here a minute while I tell you what I think about all this. We're not being treated right in this jail. I want you to tell people about it so they know. This thing they're doin' today is just tokenism. What do we do after B. B. King goes home? We go right back in those rotten cells. We eat the same rotten food. This jail is so overcrowded some of us don't even have mattresses to sleep on. Mister, I been here nine months and if I don't get out soon I'm gonna die."

Now, the last contingent of prisoners was being led into the yard. Some were such sad cases. One man, in his sixties, had trouble walking. Another man, whose right leg had been amputated, was pushed into the yard in a wheelchair by a guard.

Then B. B. King stepped to the microphone, electric guitar in hand, and he was talking and playing and singing. What can anyone say about B. B. King's talent at this late date that hasn't been said before? He is fine, and the things he sings about have to hit home to anyone who has ever been called upon to pay his dues.

B. B. King has paid his own dues. In the year 1956, he did 342 one-nighters. He has cut more than thirty albums and more than three hundred singles, and it's only in the last few years that he has hit the big time.

So now when B. B. King stood up there and sang the blues, those Cook County prisoners in the yard with him could sense that King knew where everything was at and that his head was on straight.

"Every day I have the blues," he sang. "Nobody loves me. Nobody seems to care."

Right then, he had hit home to every man in the yard.

"YOU TOLD A LIE AND IT COST A GOOD MAN HIS LIFE"

The well-worn Bible was on the living-room table, still open to the passage the Reverend James Jackson had been reading when the knock came at the door. His glasses were still on the table, too, right where Reverend Jackson had placed them as he got up to greet the policemen and the two seven-year-old boys who would cause his death.

Mr. Jackson, the pastor of St. Luke's Community Church, was sixty-two years old. He had done so much work with the young people in his neighborhood that it wasn't surprising the two boys would know he lived on the third floor of the old building on South Cottage Grove and that he drove a black car.

"He was such a wonderful man, my grandfather was," the young girl was saying now. Mrs. Olivia Williams, twenty-seven, was sitting in the same chair her grandfather always used when reading. It is near the window and it offered him the opportunity to look at the passing cars on Cottage Grove when his eyes grew tired from reading.

"I keep thinking that this is some awful dream," Mrs. Williams said now. "I keep thinking maybe I'll wake up and it won't be true."

But it was true that Reverend Jackson was dead, and that afternoon his widow got on a bus and went downtown to buy some new clothes to wear to his funeral. He died after suffering a heart attack while being questioned in the police building at 51st and Wentworth.

Reverend Jackson had been taken into custody after the two youngsters told police that he had kidnapped them at gunpoint and forced them into his home.

"But I haven't even been out of the house all day," Mr. Jackson had pleaded when the boys made the charge. "Ask my wife and sister. They've been with me all the time." The two women also pleaded with the policemen but it was to no avail.

The mothers of the two boys were with the police at the time, and they kept shouting terrible things at Mr. Jackson and demanding that the police "get to the bottom of this thing."

"But I've never even seen these two boys before," Mr. Jackson said over and over again. "I don't even know them. I've never held a gun in my hand in my whole life and I certainly don't even have one."

"Sorry," said one of the cops. "You'll have to come down to the station. Get your hat and coat."

Reverend Jackson was distraught, but there was nothing he could do but follow orders. He was under arrest. At the station, the mothers signed complaints charging Reverend Jackson with illegal restraint, and he was taken into a small room for more questioning.

"I don't even like to think about it," Sergeant Sam Babich said later. "It was just an awful thing. Those kids fingered him and there was nothing else we could do. They picked out his car and they knew where he lived and they told a pretty convincing story."

It was while Reverend Jackson was attempting to refute this "pretty convincing story" that he suffered the heart attack. The police rushed him to Provident Hospital but there was nothing anyone could do.

Oh, yes, there was one thing. When the boy who had been making most of the charges heard Reverend Jackson was dead he did what he could. "I think we'd better tell you we weren't really telling the truth," the youngster said. "Reverend Jackson never did anything to us. We just made up the story because we ditched school and we had to have a good excuse."

Mr. Jackson's wife was in the police station when the seven-year-olds and their parents emerged from an interrogation room and headed for the door. There were tears in her eyes, but Mrs. Jackson spoke with great control.

"Son," she said to the boy who had done most of the talking, "whatever you do, as long as God gives you life, don't ever tell another lie. You told a lie today and it cost a good man his life."

CHAPTER 19

THE NEAR-GREATS

These four pieces have one thing in common. The subjects are interesting because of their connection with people more famous than themselves. Ariane Sheppard's husband was a famous murderer. Charlie Kuhl was slapped in the face by General Patton. Sam DeStefano just happened to come to trial when The Godfather *was breaking all records in the movie houses. The Reverend Martin Luther King, Sr., had a famous son.*

"I DON'T CONDEMN SAM SHEPPARD"

She was wearing a simple white pants suit that didn't cost a dime more than $350 and her long, flowing platinum-blonde hair looked as though it had been carefully brushed within the hour.

She knew how to smile, too, and when she began talking it was with a German accent that made you wonder whatever happened to Marlene Dietrich.

Mrs. Ariane Sheppard was sitting at a table in the northeast corner of The 95th, the restaurant on top of the Hancock Center. She was talking about the final days she had spent with her late ex-husband, Dr. Sam Sheppard.

"His mind was so clouded," Ariane said, "that he had delusions. He always felt someone was following him. Sometimes he would come rushing into the house and slam the door behind him.

" 'There are two men following me,' he would shout and make me come to the window to peek through the curtain. There never was anybody there. It was all in Sam's mind."

The Sam Sheppard murder mystery is one of the classic crime

stories of our time, and I suppose that no one who was connected with it will die without the connection being mentioned in his obituary.

Dr. Sam, a young, handsome osteopath, was convicted of murdering his pregnant wife in their Bay Village, Ohio, home on July 4, 1954.

The trial provided a field day for the sensational elements of the press who fought so hard to convict him and build circulation at the same time.

They had such a field day, in fact, that the Supreme Court reversed Dr. Sam's conviction after he had served ten years in prison.

During that time, he and Ariane, who was then living in Germany, became pen pals. Ariane, a wealthy sister-in-law of Dr. Joseph Paul Goebbels, finally came to this country and married Sam upon his release. They were wed here in Chicago in the Conrad Hilton Hotel.

No one ever really begrudged the fact that attorney F. Lee Bailey had manuevered Dr. Sam's release and subsequent acquittal at his retrial.

There were many close to the situation, however, who never believed that Dr. Sam was innocent of bludgeoning his first wife to death.

Ariane still doesn't believe Dr. Sam killed his first wife, but she thinks that the ten years he spent in prison destroyed him.

"I don't condemn Sam for what happened after he got out of prison," she said now. "I just don't think he was strong enough to stand prison and, perhaps, none of us really is.

"I always tried to cover up for him when he was alive. But I talk to you about it now only because it helps explain him.

"By the time Sam got out of prison he was hopelessly lost on drugs and alcohol. How much did Sam drink? More than two bottles of vodka a day. It was a very tragic thing."

Reporters who covered Dr. Sam's second trial in Cleveland will tell you that even F. Lee Bailey never knew when Sam would get too drunk and not even bother to show up for the trial the next day.

There were constant reports, too, of Dr. Sam's beating Ariane. One night, he forced her out of a car and left her stranded on the Ohio Turnpike in a snowstorm.

"I finally decided that it had to end," Ariane said, "the time he woke me in the middle of the night and pointed a gun at my head and threatened to kill me.

" 'You've stolen money from me,' he kept shouting, 'you're a thief.'

"By that time I had spent nearly $250,000 getting him out of prison and in setting up his medical practice and buying houses for him. That night I decided I needed protection. The only way I could get it was through a divorce."

Ariane said that for the next three months she lived in hiding in a motel.

"The only time I went back to our home, even though he had left it, too," she related, "was when I was accompanied by two policemen who would walk on each side of me with drawn guns."

By this time, Dr. Sam had been out of prison almost five years. The years had not been good ones. There were two suits for medical malpractice hanging over Sam's head stemming from operations in which his patients had died.

He had resigned from the Youngstown Osteopathic Hospital staff and turned to professional wrestling. A few weeks after his divorce from Ariane became final, Dr. Sam married the daughter of his tag-team wrestling partner.

"All this time I was living in our house in Bay Village," Ariane said, "less than a mile from the home where Sam lived the night his first wife, Marilyn, was murdered. I was, and still am, very close to his brothers."

Dr. Sam died in Youngstown, Ohio, after suffering from the flu for several days. He was forty-six years old.

"When I heard he was gone," Ariane said, "I just thought that it was good. Some people are just born with a wish for self-destruction, you know."

Ariane went to the funeral. Later, she talked to the doctor who had made the autopsy on Dr. Sam's body.

Dr. Sam had told Bailey he had been injected with live cancer cells during a prison experiment and that he was probably going to die very soon of cancer.

"It was his liver," Ariane said. "He just drank so much that his liver stopped functioning. The autopsy showed that two-thirds of his brain had deteriorated and had not been functioning for a long time."

She shook her head.

"Sam was quite a man. He did pretty well for a man who had so little brainpower left, I suppose."

THE MAN GENERAL PATTON SLAPPED

SOUTH BEND—For the last twenty-eight years of his life Charles H. Kuhl tried to forget he was the soldier General George S. Patton, Jr., slapped in the face during the Second World War.

But they never let him forget. Try as Charles Kuhl might to remain anonymous, there was always someone who would revive the subject.

"Tell us about it, Chuck," they would ask. "What was the real story behind that day when General Patton slapped you? C'mon, Chuck, what really happened?"

Kuhl died of a heart attack at fifty-five. He was buried here after a twenty-minute service in a two-story, white frame funeral home.

There were perhaps fifty people in attendance. Some were there only because they had read the obituary in the papers that once again referred to Kuhl's run-in with Patton.

After the war, Kuhl had returned here to live. Many of his friends insist Kuhl never tried to get a factory job better than that of janitor because he didn't want to attract attention to himself.

Edward Nieter, thirty-two, Kuhl's stepson, said he was not told of the incident until a reporter came from New York one day to interview Kuhl.

"When the reporter left, Chuck told me that I might as well know the whole story," Nieter said. "He told me that it all happened because even General Patton didn't know what battle fatigue was.

"Chuck said that he had laid down his rifle in the front lines two times during the Sicilian campaign. The second time they sent him back to the hospital. In addition to the battle fatigue, though, he was also suffering from malaria.

"Chuck wasn't bitter about it. He knew that Patton got mad because all the other soldiers in the hospital had arms blown off and other obviously serious wounds. Chuck just wanted to forget the whole thing."

But it was Kuhl himself who gave one of the best descriptions of

Patton's attack when he wrote to his parents in Mishawaka, Indiana, the next day:

"General Patton slapped me in the face yesterday and kicked me in the pants and cussed me. This probably won't get through [censors] but I don't know. Just forget about it in your letter."

The incident was not forgotten because there had been witnesses and, further, Patton went on to slap another soldier several days later.

When the news reached General Dwight D. Eisenhower, he ordered Patton to apologize not only to Kuhl and the other soldier (who never has been identified) but to all the witnesses as well.

Patton summoned them all to his office in the Royal Palace in Palermo, Sicily. He told them about a good friend of his who had committed suicide during World War I, Kuhl later recalled.

The general explained that he was trying to slap sense into the two soldiers in the hope it might save their lives. That was the extent of the apology.

The incident, of course, later cost Patton the command of the Seventh Army.

At the time of the release of the motion-picture biography of Patton, Chuck told his stepson:

"The whole thing should be forgotten and dead. I've been trying to keep it quiet and I wish sometimes that everyone in the world would, too."

It was impossible, of course. Chuck finally agreed to appear on the David Frost television show and he even went on a tour of several cities for grand openings of the film.

"Chuck even took me to see the movie," Nieter said. "I figured that if the movie didn't have it right, Chuck would say something.

"You know what? He never said a word about it after it was over. Not one word."

A light snow was falling as the funeral service began.

The honor guard from the Disabled American Veterans Post 38 failed to show.

The minister who had agreed to conduct the service had to cancel out and his place was taken by the Reverend Edgar D. Erskin of the Harris Prairie Church of Christ.

Mr. Erskin is a patriotic young man of the cloth whose pride is a singing group of thirty-two young people called "The Patriots."

"My heart still thrills to hear 'The Star-Spangled Banner,' " Mr. Erskin told the mourners. "It still thrills to see the flag unfurl.

"This is all ours because of men like Mr. Kuhl and of men like him who served in our armed forces."

It was a short sermon and then Mr. Erskin sat down at a small organ in an adjoining room to play a medley of patriotic tunes.

Among them were "America, the Beautiful," "America," and "This Is My Country."

The service ended. It was only a ten-minute ride to the Fairview Cemetery in nearby Mishawaka.

Even though the Disabled Veterans had not been able to make the funeral, they had dropped off a flag for the coffin the night before.

Two of Kuhl's friends, Forest C. True, who is the author of a monograph on his own nightmarish experiences with German soldiers, and Gerald Kewley, a member of the Bendix Post 283 of the American Legion, folded the flag and handed it to Kuhl's widow. Then the mourners returned to their cars. Slowly, the shiny black limousines headed down a narrow winding road that led out of the cemetery.

SAM DESTEFANO IS NOT *THE GODFATHER*

Every day and every night the lines formed at the box office of the Chicago Theater on State Street and stretched, round and round, to Lake Street. In one week, more than 50,000 people went to see a movie about the Mafia called *The Godfather*.

Why? True, it has received an enormous amount of publicity in national magazines. True, Marlon Brando is the picture's star and gives his most convincing performance since *On the Waterfront*. And it is true that the book was the number one best seller for more than a year.

But none of these things individually, nor even all of them combined, are enough to have made all those people shiver in the cold, waiting for a chance to pay four dollars to get into a movie.

Wasn't it just the other day we were being told movies were finished and television had taken over?

Perhaps we're more romantic than we think we are. *The Godfather* shows us the family of Don Vito Corleone in an almost heroic light. Why should we dislike or fear them? The old don, portrayed by Brando, sees to it that a girl's honor is avenged. He refuses to traffic in heroin. All he wants to do is run profitable operations based on gambling, liquor, and women.

All we see of the old don is a man devoted to his wife and his sons, a man interested in seeing that they are provided for after he is gone. And this is the beautiful part of the whole thing. We walk away from the movie house with sympathy and admiration for the Corleone family. We are even pleased that the don's son, Michael, played by Al Pacino, has been able to establish himself as the new family leader by engineering the simultaneous murder of all of the family's enemies in a single swoop.

"My father is no different from any other powerful man," Michael Corleone says at one point in the film.

And then after the opposition has been gunned down, Michael says: "Today, I have handled all the family business."

The business is murder. But we are not frightened by it because the only people we see getting killed are rival mobsters. Only the gunmen get killed in this film. They are portrayed almost as soldiers. We feel they knew they faced terrible risks all the time. And not one of them dies a coward.

It's magic. No wonder we walk away feeling a sneaking admiration for the Don Corleone family and by extension for all crime syndicate hoodlums in Chicago as well.

I would have believed it, too, if I had not watched Sam DeStefano in action in the U.S. District Court recently. DeStefano, often referred to as the clown prince of the Chicago crime syndicate, was on trial for threatening the life of a government witness in a narcotics trial.

DeStefano served as his own lawyer in the case. He did lots of flamboyant things. He waved thousand-dollar bills in the air. He complained continually that he was ill of five terminal illnesses and didn't want to spend the rest of his life in jail.

DeStefano, sixty-three, portrayed himself as a warm-hearted grandfather (a term he used often) who only cared about spending time at home with his family.

"I have all the money I want now," he told me one time after court had recessed. "All I want to do now is stay home and enjoy my family."

Beautiful. It's a great story. So warm. So moving. It's American as apple pie. Sam DeStefano, the friendly grandfather who made all his money in the bail-bonding business now wanted to live peacefully at home wearing the same pink slippers he wore to prance around the courtroom every day.

DeStefano knows about the inside of prisons. Before being convicted in this latest case, he had served time for bank robbery, black marketing, rape, and perjury.

One day, a few years back, he found it necessary to take the Fifth Amendment 337 times as Charles Siragusa, head of the then Illinois Crime Commission, went after him.

DeStefano took the Fifth when asked if he had been responsible for hanging one of his juice-loan collectors from a meathook in the celler of DeStefano's house, beating him with a baseball bat, and putting a blow torch to his face.

DeStefano even took the Fifth when asked if he had murdered his own brother.

On the day I talked with DeStefano he was happy to talk about threatening the government witness.

"Look at me," he said. "Is anybody afraid of me? But when I walked into that elevator and saw this guy that day he was so scared the blood rushed to his brain and the eyes fell out of their sockets."

DeStefano's line of thought switched. His eyes lit up.

"Come to think of it, there are a lot of judges I'd like to meet in an elevator. I'd let my presence be felt, you can be sure of that."

Then he went on about the man whose life he was accused of threatening.

"I never knew this creep and besides when I was in the joint [prison] I heard he was using my name to do things on the outside. He was a snake around my family. He thought I was gonna die in prison.

"He never thought Sam DeStefano was coming back out, but I'm out. And I pay my debts. I want what belongs to me. I ain't gonna die until I pay my debts."

One thing Sam DeStefano did that day was unforgettable. He is almost brilliant in the role of the clown and he had the crowded courtroom convulsed in laughter many times.

But one time, halfway through the afternoon session, DeStefano got out of his chair at the defense table and walked to the wastebasket. He turned his back to U.S. District Court Judge Richard B. Austin and looked out over the crowded courtroom.

DeStefano's comic mask was gone. There was a look of contempt in his eyes. Then he bent his head down and spat in the wastebasket. Four times in succession. I had never seen that done in a courtroom before.

There is a difference between Sam DeStefano, the grandfather, and Vito Corleone, the Godfather. One is real. The other is fiction.

"MARTIN LUTHER KING, JR., IS NOT DEAD"

The Reverend Martin Luther King, Sr., came walking up the aisle of the First Methodist Church of Evanston, his shoulders rolling with every step.

His son's shoulders used to do that, too, when he walked, and now, with the television cameras whirring and the church jammed to the doors, it was easy to note the similarities between father and murdered son.

The audience was predominately white and seemed eager to be receptive in the same way white audiences had been for his son in the summer of 1965 when he spent so much time in Chicago, campaigning for brotherhood.

This was to be a tribute to Dr. Martin Luther King, Jr., on the first anniversary of his death, and, eerily, it was starting out like a television tape of one of those meetings from four years ago.

The only difference was that the Reverend Ralph Abernathy and comedian Dick Gregory weren't there to warm up the crowd as they did in those days.

The Reverend Mr. Abernathy has lost about fifty pounds and he no longer tells jokes. Gregory was in Cook County Jail and he isn't telling jokes either right now.

The Reverend Martin Luther King, Sr., is a tiny round man with white fuzzy hair, and when he gets to the pulpit you can see that he's spent a large part of his sixty-nine years working from one.

His accent and his timing are the same as his son's, and he, too, has a faint lisp when he pronounces the letter 's.'

His eyes had seemed to grow moist earlier when Mrs. Mary Gurley, the magnificent soloist from the Ebenezer Baptist Church, had sung one of his son's favorite hymns, "When I Survey the Wondrous Cross."

He had quickly put one hand to his eyes while Dr. Dow Kirkpatrick, senior minister of the church, had read the advice the assassinated civil rights leader left for any future eulogist:

"Tell him not to talk too long . . . Tell him not to mention that I have a Nobel Prize—that isn't important.

"I'd like somebody to mention that day that Martin Luther King tried to give his life serving others . . . Martin Luther King tried to love somebody . . ."

Now it was just one year to the day since his son had been killed, and the Reverend Martin Luther King, Sr., walked slowly to the pulpit in the silent church.

"I never thought it would come to the point where I could cry so easily," he said. "I suppose I'm getting old.

"You know, I get threats of all kinds every day, and you've got to believe they'll do what they say because they've already done it once.

"My head is bloody but unbowed, and I speak between tears when I think about this."

The old man halted deliberately, making sure his audience was paying attention to his every word.

Then he began again in a shout.

"Martin Luther King, Jr., is not dead. He is living. He's serving every day . . . He can't die. . . ."

The father kicked the pulpit in anger, making a noise that could be heard in the last pew.

"You know somethin'," he said now, eyes shining. "The devil is tryin' to make me hate somebody. That's when I had to stop cryin' and write ol' brother devil a letter.

"I'm gonna take what strength I have left, I told him, and go around this country and tell them that I love God and that I love men and I want you people here to do the same."

His sermon lasted an hour. Sometimes he showed the erudition for which his son was famous. At other times he played the role of the country preacher, clowning and shouting at his flock.

For a finale, he walked off the pulpit and down into the middle aisle to shout in the ears of several staid Evanstonians, who, surprisingly, seemed to love it.

Then, too soon it seemed, it was over, and at the old man's directions the entire congregation—whites and blacks—were standing, arms entwined, and singing "We Shall Overcome."

It is a very moving song, and there are many people who can't sing it without tears coming to their eyes. This is the way it was this night, with the entire congregation swaying to the music and the Reverend Mr. King and Dr. Kirkpatrick and the choir swaying near the altar.

It made you think of a night about five years ago, when Martin Luther King, Jr., had a crowd of more than 9,000 doing the same thing on the Winnetka village green.

"I think he's going to be able to do it," a man had said that night. "I think that Martin Luther King, Jr., is going to be able to bring sanity to this world, after all."

He didn't make it, of course, and in fact a couple of days later when he led a march of thousands to City Hall, Mayor Daley was tied up with other business and unable to meet with him.

But perhaps his father's philosophy had prepared him for that.

"Thank you so much," the old man said in closing. "Be sweet. Keep the faith. And keep . . . looking . . . up."

CHAPTER 20

EVERYBODY INTO THE GAME

About halfway through this piece the Falstaffian figure of Minnesota Fats enters the stage. He is past his peak now and the real hustlers kept walking past him as though he had never existed. He can't shoot pool with the best any more, but his mouth moves just as fast as it ever did.

IN WHICH MINNESOTA FATS COPS OUT AND THE RED RAIDER TAKES A FALL

JOHNSTON CITY, Ill.—The pool hustler dwells in a subterranean world of stealth and anonymity. The true hustler hates to give his real name. The sight of a camera prompts him to excuse himself from the room.

It must be that way. In order for the hustler to survive, he must often spend three days in a strange town losing game after game for two and five dollars a crack. Then he's all ready. On the fourth day his mark will finally get up the courage to bet $1,500 on one game of straight pool.

That's when the hustler stops smiling, chalks his cue with extra care and runs a hundred balls off the break. This done, he picks up his winnings, announces he's going to the men's room to wash his hands—and disappears.

All hustlers are supreme egotists. Each believes there is not a man living who can beat him when his stroke is right. Each year more than 150 of them gather in this tiny coal community to compete in the annual Hustlers' Tourney sponsored by George and Joey Jansco.

This year's tourney lasted four weeks. Corn Bread Red was there. So were Weenie Beenie and Boston Shorty, Omaha Fats, Minnesota Fats, Daddy Warbucks, Tugboat Whaley, the Red Raider, Cicero Murphy, Handsome Danny Jones, and Ugly Prichett.

Maybe they figure they are all safe from public scrutiny here. The population of Johnston City is only 3,800 and it is located a mile north of Dog Walk, nineteen miles northeast of Wolf Creek, and thirty miles west of Muddy. It is hardly the crossroads of the nation. Individual champions were decided in one-pocket, nine-ball, and straight pool. Each of these competitions took a week to complete, with the winners in each division meeting in a round robin to determine the winner of the $20,000 final event.

As always, it took place in a small building which has a specially constructed pit with two tables surrounded by inclined grandstands. The building is part of the Jansco recreation complex, which includes a restaurant, a night club, a billiards club that is open twenty-four hours a day, and a golf course. Some of the biggest money changed hands not during tourney play, but over in the billiards club, where hustler went against hustler with their backers' money exerting all the pressure.

The night everyone went away remembering best, however, was the first night of nine-ball competition. It pitted Corn Bread Red against Boston Shorty and the Red Raider against Kazuo Fujima, the national champion of Japan. Nine-ball is a classic hustler's game. The hustler prefers it to straight pool and any of the others because it can literally be won in seconds. Only the first nine balls are used. They are racked with the one-ball in the point of the diamond and the nine-ball in the center. The object is to sink the nine-ball and this can be done at any time in combination with another ball. The player who wins eleven games first wins the match.

The stands were packed as George Jansco, a tiny barrel of a man, stepped to the platform to explain there would be a slight delay in the start of the first match because Corn Bread Red had not yet arrived. "He played next door for twenty-four straight hours," Jansco explained, "and when he was finished he carted off $1,700. But he figured he'd need an hour's nap before coming back for the tourney."

Boston Shorty snickered at the explanation. His real name is Larry Johnson, and he got his name because he stands five foot two. He is bald and suffers from acne, and he could make a living in the movies playing wheel man for a million-dollar robbery ring.

"If he isn't here on time," shouted a voice from the stands, "then forfeit the game to Boston Shorty. Come on, Jansco, you know the rules."

The voice was that of the Red Raider, whose real name is Jack Breit and who comes from Houston. But before any action could be taken on his demand, Corn Bread Red himself appeared in the doorway. Corn Bread Red's real name is Billy Burge. He comes from Detroit, and he has been considered one of the world's best nine-ball players for the last seven years. He was wearing a blue sport coat with blue slacks and a blue turtle-neck shirt underneath. He has red curly hair and there is a long scar on his left cheek.

"Hold it a second and I'll be with you," shouted Red. "Just have to get an eye-opener first." He walked over to the bar where he was handed a glass of straight whisky poured over two ice cubes. He brought it with him to the table.

The match began and now all you could hear was the clip-clopping on the floor of the leather-healed shoes worn by both contestants, the screeching of the chalk on the cue sticks, the click of the balls as they collided, and the rumble as they rolled under the table.

Corn Bread Red took an early lead, and this apparently annoyed the Red Raider.

"What's the matter with Boston Shorty?" he said. "The other day he played me and he must have been on pills. He could have beat Willie Mosconi. Now look at him. A man who makes shots that bad doesn't even belong in this tournament. Boston Shorty ignored the taunt. He had been trailing 4 to 1, but came back to tie the score at 4-all.

"So that's the great Corn Bread Red," said the Red Raider. "He doesn't look like much to me. The way this thing is going, I'm gonna probably send everyone here out of Johnston City on scooters. In fact, when it's all over, I may be in the used-car business. Moochers like these guys couldn't go for nuthin' without a backer. Why, if it's their own money, they wouldn't bet fat meat was greasy."

It wasn't Boston Shorty's night. Corn Bread Red finished him 11 to 4 and now Jansco was on the stage again.

"Introducing Mr. Kazuo Fujima, the national champion of Japan," he said, and there was a polite round of applause. "Also introducing," he said, "one of the most highly rated nine-ball players in the world, Mr. Jack Breit of Houston, Texas."

An enthusiastic round of applause followed, and now there was a rush to the rear of the room where a man was taking bets. The Red Raider was such a big favorite against his unknown opponent that virtually no money was bet on anyone but him. Fujima stands five foot tall, weighing less than a hundred pounds. The Red Raider is six foot two, and weighs 225.

Fujima was impeccably garbed in a funeral black suit, a white shirt, and dark tie. The Red Raider wore a brown sports coat with a light-brown shirt buttoned to the collar. He was wearing Hush Puppies.

Fujima earned the right to break first. He sank the nine-ball on the break and the crowd responded approvingly. The Red Raider shrugged and smiled condescendingly at the beginner's luck. He leaned over the table now, sighting the lead ball for his breaking shot. But the shot left the one-ball unguarded.

Fujima sank the one-ball and ran the table to take a 2-to-0 lead.

The Red Raider shrugged again, but this time he did not smile. There was a rustling in the crowd as a loud voice boomed in the rear of the hall. It was Rudolph Wanderone, sometimes called New York Fats, and at other times Minnesota Fats, Chicago Fats, or even Hollywood Fats.

Minnesota Fats is a retired hustler now and makes his living from royalties on billiard equipment. Anonymity is the last thing in the world he seeks. Television cameras and men with pencils and papers now serve as a magnet to him.

"I just turned down a great role in the television show 'Ironside,' " he said. "I didn't have the time. So I told them to give it to Keenan Wynn. He's a friend of mine. ABC is comin' down to my house to do a special on me in the next few weeks. Another outfit wanted to fly me to New York to do a commercial that would take me about five minutes. They wanted to pay $5,000. But I don't have the energy. I'm tired."

Fats looked tired. He is no kid any more. His hair is brown, but there are big splotches of gray. His waistline is fifty-four inches. It must be a job to carry it around.

A man with a pool cue walked over and suggested a game of eight-ball if Fats would spot him two balls. Fats reacted with indignation.

"Look, punk," he said, "I was shootin' pool before you knew what popcorn was. I'm forty years older than you, I've been up three days and three nights, and you want two balls. You don't want to play. You wanna stick somebody up." The man laughed and walked away.

"You know," Fats continued in the wake of his verbal conquest, "I used to sit in Bensinger's in Chicago and wait for little punks like that to get good enough to want a piece of the Fat Man. Then, when they'd come up with their proposition, I'd make sure we had a good crowd and knock them little punks right into the bleachers."

There was a roar from the crowd now Fujima had just won his tenth game and was leading by two. He needed only this final game to win. The Red Raider, obviously nettled, slammed the heavy end of his cue stick into the wooden floor. Then he approached the table to break. Once again, he left the one-ball unguarded. And for a final time, Fujima ran the table.

As Fujima walked back to the front of the table, the Red Raider's massive figure loomed over him, barring his path. He extended a huge paw to his tiny adversary.

"You play pretty good," the Red Raider said. "Pretty lucky, too." Then the Red Raider turned and walked away—straight into the office of George Jansco, the tourney director.

"Well, I'm through with you creeps," the Red Raider said. "Who was that creep you had racking up them balls so that little Jap could sink the nine-ball on the break four times? I'm gettin' out of here tonight and headin' back to Houston. I can make two hundred dollars a day hustlin' there without any trouble."

He turned and walked out of Jansco's office. Jansco sat there smiling.

"That's the way it is with hustlers," he said. "Every time they lose, it's the rules, the lights, or the tables. First thing they want to do is fight or play million-dollar freeze-out. An hour from now he'll be over it. He'll be back playing again tomorrow. Who knows, maybe he even lost that match on purpose to set up a mark."

Jansco was right in one respect, at least. The Red Raider stayed on for another week. And that very night he picked up $1,300 in a game with a mark who thought the Red Raider couldn't play nine-ball very well any more.

As it turned out, the tourney was a satisfying event to many. Handsome Danny Jones from Atlanta took away $3,600 for winning the all-around title in a play-off with Boston Shorty. But the biggest single winner was the biggest hustler of them all, a young man named Fast Eddie Allen from Burbank, California. Fast Eddie, who also is called The Angel in the Outfield because he brings attractive young girls to watch him play, reportedly earned more than $10,000 in pickup games with the other hustlers in the billiard club.

"Can't understand it about Fast Eddie," said Jansco after the tourney ended. "He didn't do very good in tourney play at all. With all those people watchin' he seems to get very bashful. But when he was playin' those other hustlers for big money, he didn't seem bashful at all. "When the money was on the line, he showed what it really means to be a hustler."

CHAPTER 21

CONSPIRACY 7 CLOSE-UPS

The Conspiracy 7 trial that began in Chicago on September 26, 1969, and ended February 20, 1970, was a memorable series of courtroom confrontations, high jinks, and heartbreak. At the start, most of the large press corps in attendance were fascinated by the zany antics of the defendants. It ended with many of the reporters passionately sympathetic to them as human beings if not complete allies of their political goals. Perhaps the words of Pascal describe the transformation best: "We know the truth, not only by reason but by heart."

The trial has been dealt with at great length by others. What follows are a few moments, not only from the trial but its aftermath, that will stick in my mind as long as I live.

Read the first piece about a girl named Nancy and then ask yourself if you can ever look at her husband again and consider him a total buffoon.

NANCY WITH THE LAUGHING FACE

The car glided into the right-hand lane and left the Eisenhower Expressway, slowed, and then turned south on California. Nancy sat on the passenger's side, her right arm out the window, catching the breeze. She was smiling.

"Nobody ever knows when they start out where their lives will lead them," she said. "Take me. I grew up in Brooklyn. When I was ten my family moved out to East Williston, Long Island, and I went to a really good public high school. It was called Wheatly High. It was all white and I was into everything. I was a cheerleader and the star of the field hockey team. I played the clarinet in the marching band, and I was very good at folk-singing and guitar-playing."

The car stopped for a red light.

"Are we going the right way?" Nancy asked. "I want to make sure I get there on time, you know. I haven't seen him in a long time."

Assured that Cook County Jail was less than ten minutes away, Nancy relaxed.

"You know, I used to read a lot in high school. I remember how much I loved Salinger and *The Catcher in the Rye.* I liked Camus, too, especially *The Rebel,* and I was really in love with Bob Dylan. There's one place where I've changed, I guess. Now I only like Bob Dylan and I dig the Rolling Stones and Creedence Clearwater Revival. I'm cooling off on the Beatles.

"Well, to get back to what I was saying. I had gone to this square high school, and now I wanted to go to a big state school where I could see what was really going on. I could have gone to Radcliffe or Smith, but I wanted to go to the University of Wisconsin, and since my grades were so high I had no trouble."

That was 1961. By the time Nancy had graduated with a major in psychology in 1965, she had established herself as being close to a straight-A student as well as a political activist.

"While I was up there I think I read all the books of Herman Hesse. It wasn't Hesse who did it, but I kept getting more and more political. I did all kinds of liberal things. I wanted to go to Mississippi to work with the black people one summer, but my parents wouldn't allow it. Instead, I went to Cleveland and worked in the ghetto there. Up in Madison, I worked, in my free time, in a children's diagnostic center."

Nancy smiled and her brown eyes widened.

"You see," she said, "I tried to work within the system."

The car had been parked a block away from the jail. Nancy could see the tall concrete walls as she headed toward the meeting with her husband.

"I'm nervous," she said. "You never know what's happened to a person's life in jail. You're always concerned about what you're going to hear."

Three tall black men with red tams walked past us on the street.

"They must be the Blackstone Rangers," Nancy said. "I remember seeing those same berets at Fred Hampton's funeral."

There was still time before visiting hours would begin, and now we were sitting in a dingy restaurant drinking diet sodas.

"So after Wisconsin, I went out to Berkeley and began working on my master's in psychology. I was very into political psychology, and I'd do things like work with black kids. It was my job to interview them and find out why they were smacking their white teachers. I didn't have to be a psychologist to know the answer to that. They were doing it because their teachers were racists. I'd tell them to go out and join SNCC."

We were out of the restaurant now and walking through the Criminal Courts Building, through the back yard and into the front door of the jail where relatives of the prisoners wait in line to be identified and searched.

Nancy was possibly twenty-fourth or twenty-fifth in line.

"It was in Berkeley that we met," she said. "He was really into the antiwar effort. It was a group called the Vietnam Day Committee and it was great. We'd all sit around and rap and drink beer. This was all before the hippies and Haight-Ashbury, you know. They were planning big marches to places like the Oakland Army terminal and thinking about stopping the troop trains. I remember the first time I saw him.

"He had a small mustache and he looked like a classical anarchist bomber and he had twinkly eyes and he was always laughing and I liked him immediately."

Nancy was at the door to the jail now and in minutes she would see her husband.

"You know," she said, "when we tell people that we're really not married and just living together, we're really putting them on. Maybe we shouldn't do it, but we know how uptight it makes everyone, and I guess that's why we don't stop. Let me tell you something. I wouldn't want him any other way. To me he's always been very brave and beautiful. They talk about him getting rich now from his book, but I know he's going to do things with it to help people. I really do."

The door opened and the jail guard said:

"Your name and the prisoner you have come to see?"

Nancy held out a white envelope addressed to her, and her passport, and for the first time she did not look quite so self-assured.

"My name is Nancy Rubin," she said in a soft voice, "and I'm here to see my husband, Jerry Rubin."

ABBIE'S CHRISTMAS PRESENT

I went to see Abbie Hoffman in the hospital on Christmas Day. I knew how much he professed to hate Establishment values, so I brought him a present—a binder for taking notes in court.
Do you know what? He was really pleased by it.

Abbie Hoffman was propped up in his Michael Reese Hospital bed with an oxygen mask over his nose and mouth.

Abbie was suffering from what he insisted was bronchial pneumonia. He had just been examined by a doctor for the U.S. government to determine when he could retake the witness stand in the Chicago 7 Conspiracy trial.

He pulled off the mask and placed it on a table at the side of his bed. There was a mischievous smile on Abbie's face, the kind that's always there when he has come up with a bright idea.

"I hear Judge Julius [Hoffman] is gonna bring me into court Friday right on this bed to testify," Abbie said, pleased at the thought of it all.

"The last time I remember that happening was when they brought my neighbor up in Massachusetts, Bernard Goldfine, into court on his bed to testify about all those vicuña coats he had been giving to people in the government."

Abbie was asked whether he would mind going into court on his bed.

"Mind!" he said. "Like man, that would be out of sight. Can you just see me in there, flat on my back, talking to that jury through my oxygen mask?

"Like I mean, how can anyone go see a play or a movie after this trial is over? It's been the greatest, and the next witness I expect they'll be calling will be Mies van der Rohe, the courthouse architect, back from the grave, to complain because our lawyers have been leaning on his rostrum."

This was the second Christmas in a row that Abbie had been in the hospital.

"Last Christmas I was in Albert Einstein Hospital in New York City," he said. "I developed hepatitis in a Washington, D.C., jail, for which I'm now suing for $300,000. If I win the suit it will be a whole new ballgame."

Abbie began coughing and one of two interns sitting at his bedside moved in to put the oxygen mask over his face again.

"What a way to fight the government," Abbie said, just as the mask was being placed in position.

A few minutes later he was back up again, propped on the pillows, listening politely as the interns urged him not to talk anymore.

"I don't understand what Judge Hoffman's hurry is," Abbie said. "This trial is gonna last until 1984 anyway. I'm in no hurry. You know, I've been in court at least once a week for the last five years, and I've got four or five more trials ahead of me."

"Does all this get you down?" one of the interns asked.

"Get me down? Like man, I'm ready to take the bar exam next month."

A different Abbie Hoffman made an appearance at this point. The clowning stopped and he started talking about his early days as a civil rights worker in the South.

"You know," he said, "I've been beaten up badly more than twenty times by the police. I've got scars all over my head and buckshot wounds all over my body. Most of that came from places like McComb, Mississippi, and Yazoo City, Mississippi.

"It was in Yazoo City in 1964 that I went through a red light and the sheriff stopped me. The only thing about it was that town didn't have a red light. That's what I tried to tell him in a nice way.

"'Are you trying to tell me my eyes are bad?'" he answered, "and right away I knew it was going to be heavy.

"I was right. They threw three of us in jail and then they gave the other prisoners pints of liquor and told them that we were civil rights workers and that if they beat us up they'd go free.

"Well, they beat us up for seven hours. The sheriff was true to his word. He let the guys who beat us up go free and then he threw us civil rights workers out into the gutter."

Abbie remembers, too, what happened to local Southern lawyers who tried to help the civil rights workers in their court appearances at that time.

"Once they'd get in the action with us," he said, "it was like the next step for them to get rode out of town. Freedom is like leprosy.

If you try to touch it you'd better watch out. Next thing they'll say you're running around trying to start riots."

THE FREAKING FAG REVOLUTION

Thomas A. Foran, the United States attorney who led the prosecution, was an interesting case. He grew to feel that he was being made a target for ridicule by some members of the press. He wasn't. It was just that the defendants provided us with so much better copy.

Several weeks after the trial I noticed an item in Irv Kupcinet's column in the Sun-Times *that Foran was going to give a speech to the Loyola Academy Boosters Club and that he would discuss the trial.*

He hadn't talked about it publicly before, and I decided to go out there and sit in a rear row, wearing a blue blazer and gray flannel slacks, which is what everybody wears who goes to booster club meetings all over the world.

Foran spoke with brutal frankness, and for almost an hour the bitterness pent up inside him came out. Incredibly, I was the only writer on the scene. The next day, when Foran was questioned about the quotes, he said: "Fitzpatrick always has been out to get me."

He did not deny a single quote then except to point out that he had concluded his talk by saying: "They look at us like we're dinosaurs when we talk like that . . . and maybe they're right."

I left out the last part, he charged, to make him look bad. I left it out because it was drowned out in the cheering—if that's what he said.

Later, Foran tried to get the Democratic nomination for governor. By that time he was willing to say the whole speech had never happened. But that's not surprising when a guy wants to be governor.

Now U.S. Attorney Thomas A. Foran was in his element. Sitting on the edge of their seats, listening in rapt attention and nodding agreement all the way, were some two hundred members of the Loyola Academy Boosters club in Wilmette.

No one in Wilmette is prejudiced. They even made it plain that a black photographer was welcome to stay and take pictures . . . after he was searched for weapons, that is.

In this cozy atmosphere, Foran spoke out bluntly, for nearly ninety minutes expressing contempt for the Chicago 7.

"Bobby Seale had more guts and more charisma than any of them," Foran said, "and he was the only one I don't think was a fag."

Coming in for hard knocks were defendants Abbie Hoffman, who Foran said was "scummy but clever"; David T. Dellinger, who he said was a "sneak and uses people like a ventriloquist"; the defense attorneys, whom he called "mouthpieces"; and some members of the press.

Referring to the defendants and Seale, who was on trial with the 7 until U.S. District Court Judge Julius J. Hoffman sentenced him to prison for contempt of court, Foran continued:

"They [the defendants] used that kid as though they were masters of the plantation. They used him so grossly and so callously that I can't see how the news media couldn't see it."

Foran said that the day Seale was severed from the trial he indicated to Foran that he knew he had been used, too. "He came to me and he said: 'Hey, Tom, it looks like I got caught in Whitey's den.' "

Foran said his feelings about this were buttressed by a remark that Jerry Rubin made to him one day in the corridor.

"Hey, Tom," he quoted Rubin as saying, "if we didn't have the niggers for an issue, where would we find new niggers?"

Foran said the binding and gagging of Seale because of his courtroom outbursts was "the most horrible sight I've ever seen in a courtroom."

"That can't go on. We're going to have to put them in another room and use television. We can't do that any more."

Foran explained his reference to defense attorneys William M. Kunstler and Leonard I. Weinglass as "mouthpieces":

"There's no greater insult I can give them. They were like doctors who take out gall bladders when there is nothing wrong with the patient. They have no sense of professional responsibility. They were incredibly unprofessional and they deserved what they got."

Foran also struck out at sections of the press for what he said was biased coverage of the trial and the disorders at the 1968 Democratic National Convention that spawned the proceedings.

He gave his listeners an insight into what caused the Chicago police to beat demonstrators at Michigan and Balbo in front of the Conrad Hilton Hotel during the convention.

"I was sitting there in my car," Foran said, "and I remember that it was 7:49. I called in over my radio phone and told my office the place was ready to blow.

"A short time after, it did. For eighteen minutes the police moved in and got even for what they had been taking from the demonstrators for three days.

"After that the police felt great. They were smiling and waving and you could see it was a great psychological thing for them."

Foran halted for an instant and smiled.

"You know," he said, "I think that even the demonstrators felt better after that was over, too."

He was particularly critical of National Broadcasting Co. news coverage of the trial which he called "an absolute disaster."

He also chastised columnist Nicholas von Hoffman of the *Washington Post,* some of whose comments about the trial appeared in the *Sun-Times.*

"He's not a reporter," Foran said. "He's a participant in the New Left movement and everyone knows it. The other newsmen should band together and get rid of him."

(Reached at his home in Washington, Von Hoffman commented:

"If Foran really meant all that he said in his unfortunate speech, and if it's all true, he has proven the most extreme allegations of the defendants and their lawyers.

"The man he exhibited tonight making that speech is someone we should all feel sorry for, because he is consumed with guilt and anger for having had to take part in the trial—he's totally ripped up inside.

"Foran is a better man than the speech he has given.")

Foran told his audience, which received his remarks enthusiastically, that the New Left movement had made a special effort to infiltrate the college campuses and the news media.

"I think they've done a pretty good job at both," he said.

Foran expressed particular annoyance at newspaper coverage of his cross-examination of Rennie Davis.

"It was the hardest cross-examination I've ever had," Foran said. "That kid is smart as a whip, but after two-and-a-half days I got him to admit he had come to Chicago to discredit the government.

"What happened was typical of the press coverage; it never got in the papers or on TV. Instead all they wrote about was Norman Mailer, who took the stand next."

Mailer also came in for a few brickbats.

"By the way," Foran said. "Mailer is an utter jackass. He walked around like this [Foran mimicked Mailer's arms-akimbo walk] and he talked just like an idiot."

Foran kept one hand in his pocket virtually all the time he talked to the Boosters, an organization of fathers of Loyola students who attend all the football, basketball, and wrestling competitions to cheer their sons on.

Foran stood on the basketball court as he spoke to the members, who sat in the stands.

The only times he deviated from this stance were when he walked about mincingly or gave limp-handed waves in describing defendants or members of the press.

Foran's son is an outstanding high-school football player. He pointed out that it was only his attendance at the school's games on Sunday afternoons during the fall and wrestling matches ever since that had helped him maintain "my sanity" during the trial.

Foran said that it had been a "superhuman effort" for him to keep his temper in the courtroom for the duration of the trial.

Foran said that he had been continually subjected to insults by Davis.

"I was his man," Foran said. "He'd sit near me and keep whispering insults to me all day about my sexual prowess."

Foran said Richard S. Schultz, the other prosecutor, received a torrent of abuse daily from Jerry Rubin.

"Rubin is a baby," Foran said, "a kid who is very conscious of his Jewishness. Schultz is Jewish, too, and so Rubin would fire filth at him, *sotto voce,* so the judge couldn't hear.

"He'd keep telling Schultz he was going to be the first Jew Nazi. I'm amazed that Schultz didn't belt him one. You know the papers kept calling Davis the boy from next door. I'll tell you one thing. If he had lived next door to me I would have fixed him."

Foran also criticized chief defense attorney Kunstler for his habit of promising the arrival of "name" witnesses.

"He'd stand up there and he'd say that God was his next witness or that he had the President of the United States under subpoena. It seemed like every witness they had was a celebrity."

Also criticized by Foran was the defense's attempt to put the Reverend Ralph David Abernathy on the stand.

"They made damn sure they got him out of town," Foran said, "so he couldn't testify because they knew he had nothing to add to the case. They just wanted to use him."

Foran closed with a call for action by parents to save the younger generation.

"We've lost our kids to the freaking fag revolution," he said, "and we've got to reach out for them.

"Perhaps because we came through the Depression we've become too materialistic with our two cars to a family.

"Our kids don't understand that we don't mean anything by it when we call people 'niggers,' " he concluded. "They look at us like we're dinosaurs when we talk like that."

At this point, Foran was interrupted by a standing ovation from the members of the Boosters Club.

ORDER IN THE COURT

I keep running into Bill Kunstler. And every time I see him I think of that day in court when Dave Dellinger was sentenced for contempt. I also think of what he said the day after Judge Hoffman passed the sentence for contempt. "Yesterday, I felt such a deep sense of utter futility that I could not keep from crying, something I had not done publicly since my childhood . . . but I am not ashamed of my tears. Neither am I ashamed of my conduct in this court. . . . If I have to pay with my liberty for such representation then that is the price of my beliefs and sensibilities."

Sitting there in the courtroom, taking notes as Kunstler spoke, tears came to my own eyes. It was so moving, in fact, that when Kunstler went downstairs to give it again for the television cameras, I cried again.

The cuff on the right leg of David Dellinger's green slacks had flopped over. His brown tweed coat needed pressing. On his right wrist was a white band like those on patients in hospitals. But Dellinger's had come from the Cook County Jail.

The jury had just left the courtroom to begin deliberation and now U.S. Distric Court Judge Julius J. Hoffman began reading the speech he had prepared about what he refers to as the "contumacious conduct" of the Conspiracy 7 during the five-month trial.

It was a surprise to the defendants but they didn't seem afraid. Abbie Hoffman put his tan boots on the table. Jerry Rubin started laughing and taking notes.

So did everyone else at the defense table. Over at the prosecution table, Assistant U.S. Attorney Richard G. Schultz put one hand over his mouth and suppressed a smile. U.S. Attorney Thomas A. Foran turned his back on the defense table and rested his head on his right hand like a man passing time in the public library.

The judge's style during the lengthy reading of his charge to the jurors had been given with marked intonations in an effort to make sure they understood every word. His head had bobbed back and forth for emphasis on some points and from side to side on others.

But now it was changed. The delivery was different. Now Judge Hoffman's voice was strangely flat as he began reading the citations against Dellinger.

In the front row of the courtroom on the left-hand side, Dellinger's two daughters, Tasha, twenty-two, and Michelle, thirteen, sat ashen-faced.

The citations for contempt against Dellinger seemed to go on interminably as many listened with growing disbelief.

By the time they reached fourteen, Rubin had stopped laughing. His face was blank. Abbie's feet were on the floor and he was sitting with his eyes shut. Chief defense attorney William M. Kunstler wrote feverishly, keeping up with the judge's citations.

At the count of twenty-six, Rubin left the table and walked to the men's room, which is just off the side of the court in a lockup.

"Right now," he said, "the score is 26 to 0 and we're losing."

Judge Hoffman reached twenty-eight and stopped. He called for a recess, and the defendants, stunned now, announced they would hold a press conference.

By the time Rennie Davis, Abbie, and Rubin reached the second-floor press room, it was jammed with television cameras and radio microphones.

If you have been around them for any length of time at all, it is important to hear what they say at these events because they generally are warm-ups for what Judge Hoffman will hear at the next session.

So it was here that Rennie Davis said for the first time that the judge had destroyed the jury system. And Abbie said the things he would later say to Hoffman after he was sentenced late in the afternoon.

As they left to go back upstairs, Abbie hugged his wife. Rubin hugged his, too, in the belief it would be for the last time for a long time.

Back in the courtroom, Kunstler, dressed in a dark blue suit and white shirt, made an impassioned speech that cited Dellinger's right to remain free. The judge overruled Kunstler and now it was time for Dellinger to stand up and make a statement if he so chose.

Dellinger, fifty-four, a Yale man, scholar, and lifelong pacifist, has made many speeches in his day. But this would be one of his most important.

He stood erect and placed both hands deep into the side pockets of his trousers. The flopped-over cuff had still not been pulled up.

"I hope you'll do me the courtesy," Dellinger began, "not to interrupt me while I'm talking."

Judge Hoffman would make no such guarantee but asked for Dellinger's respect as he spoke.

"The facts don't always encourage false respect," Dellinger said.

Then Dellinger, his voice quaking with emotion, began talking about the war in Vietnam and racism.

"I don't want to talk politics with you," Judge Hoffman said.

"You've tried to keep it out of this trial and these are the two burning issues," Dellinger said.

"I'll ask you now to sit down," Judge Hoffman said. But there was no acid in his tone. Judge Hoffman seemed tired.

Dellinger took his hands out of his pockets now, and he had the determined look that men get when they're about to jump off a high diving board for the first time.

"Sure," Dellinger said, "like good Germans we're supposed to support the evils of our decade. Now like good Jews we're supposed to go quietly and politely to the cremation camps.

"Like poor people and women and those without formal education, like lawyers who won't stay in their place. . . ."

The marshals were moving in, urging Dellinger to stop talking, but they didn't want to lay hands on him despite the judge's order.

They have been with Dellinger in this trial nearly five months and it was no secret they had enormous respect for him.

As Dellinger continued to talk in a tone growing more desperate by the sentence, the sounds started coming from the spectators' gallery, where his daughters and the members of the Conspiracy defense staff were sitting.

The marshals were moving in that direction, too.

"This is a travesty of justice," Dellinger shouted, "and you know the records will condemn you, not us."

Abbie Hoffman was leaning forward at the defense table. So was Rubin. Kunstler was looking across the table at Dellinger as though transfixed.

Foran still had his head in his hand. Schultz wasn't smiling; just staring.

"I sat there and heard Foran say terrible things about me yesterday," Dellinger said. "Now I will not be quiet. The people won't be quiet."

What happened at this point is difficult to describe. It came from all directions and everyone seemed powerless to stop any of it.

In the spectators' section, the marshals had moved in on Dellinger's two daughters, who were shouting and screaming at the judge.

A man leaped over several rows and onto the back of one of the marshals. One marshal who stands six foot, six and weighs more than three hundred pounds had waded into the section where the girls were.

He seemed like an embarrassed elephant because the first thing he did was begin tripping over bodies on the floor. The marshal is really not a vicious man and now he was trapped in an impossible situation where he was made to appear the biggest bully since Goliath fought David.

Dellinger, seeing what was happening and hearing his daughters screaming, leaped to his feet again, with two marshals around his back.

"Leave my daughters alone!" he shouted. "Leave my daughters alone!"

"Tyrants!" someone shouted.

Another marshal, stationed near the judge's bench, said loudly to himself: "Where are the other marshals? We're supposed to have enough men to handle this."

Somehow Dellinger broke free and was in the front row wrestling with the marshals there, as were Abbie Hoffman and John Froines.

Judge Hoffman just looked down into the scene of tangled bodies and shouts with no expression. It was impossible to tell whether he was angry, frightened, or just puzzled.

Neither Foran nor Schultz made a move.

But now the most remarkable scene of all took place and it will stick in the minds of those who saw it for a lifetime.

Kunstler, seeing the uproar, stood and looked toward the judge. Tears streamed down his cheeks.

"I hope you're satisfied," he said to Judge Hoffman from the lectern. "All my life has come to nothing."

Kunstler moved forward now to the bench in front of the judge's desk.

His arms were stretched forward with the palms up. The arms were stretched out so far that there were at least four inches of his thin, pale forearms showing.

It was hard to hear Kunstler speak over the uproar and the sounds of bodies banging against the courtroom door as they were being hustled out.

"You've destroyed my life, Your Honor," he said, voice choking. "I plead with you. I beg you to come to mine now. Put me away too. I don't want to be here any more."

Kunstler wasn't the only one with tears. Men and women all over the courtroom, on both sides of the political spectrum, were having trouble seeing, too.

Leonard Weinglass, Kunstler's assistant counsel, moved beside his colleague. He grabbed the taller man's arms and led Kunstler back to the defense table.

Kunstler sat. He dropped his head on the table and sobbed. At the other end of the table, Abbie Hoffman's head was sunk on the table, too.

And now the silence over the courtroom was so awesome that the sound of the heating unit could be heard in the next room.

In the silence, Jerry Rubin ran three steps toward the judge's bench and shouted: "Heil Hitler! Heil Hitler! That's how you should be greeted."

Dellinger was back in his seat now, too.

In a low, resigned voice, he said:

"Well, you've preserved law and order in Chicago, judge."

KUNSTLER REVISITED

*Sometimes, when you really grow to like a guy you write about,
the piece comes out like this one after a meeting with Kunstler in
New York nearly two years later.*

NEW YORK—The glass door at the corner of Ninth Avenue
and Forty-second Street is locked. You can't get in unless someone
pushes a buzzer from upstairs.

The letters across the door say: Center for Constitutional Rights.

The buzzer rings. You climb the long flight of stairs to attorney
William Kunstler's office.

There is a cork bulletin board on the wall to your left as you approach the receptionist. On it are notices informing that you can
hire John Froines, Abbie Hoffman, Tom Hayden, Dave Dellinger,
and others as speakers. The price is negotiable.

There is also a Jules Feiffer cartoon about U.S. District Court
Judge Julius J. Hoffman. It is yellowed with age.

There is another cartoon from *The New Yorker* magazine. It
shows a fat, well-dressed guy talking on the telephone in an opulent
office.

The caption under the cartoon reads: "I'm afraid I'm not the
Jerry Rubin you want. However, lots of luck, power to the pigs,
and soon."

This is where Bill Kunstler works these days—that is, when he is
in town. The former chief defense counsel for the Chicago 7 or 8, or
whatever, is so busy defending so many apparently lost causes that
he doesn't remain in the city that often.

My one memory of Bill Kunstler's appearance at the Conspiracy
trial was that he always appeared to be so tired. Well, he looks to
be even more tired now. Gaunt if you will, with sad, sunken eyes.
Henry Fonda would have to go without sleep for three months to
undertake the role.

Kunstler is sitting there now and he's remembering the role he
played in the horror of the Attica prison rebellion. Really, he's remembering how it was on the morning that the guns began firing.

"It was the worst day of my life," Kunstler says. "I knew so many of those prisoners. I'll never forget standing outside the prison wall and hearing the popping noises of the guns. B yard, where it all took place, was far away from the main gate, but you couldn't mistake the sound. You stood there and knew they were killing people."

Kunstler hesitated briefly but there is such a mellifluousness to his voice that the sound seems to echo until he picks up again.

"After it was over, my wife and I were walking down the road, away from the prison. She had been farther away from the wall than I and had been badly affected by the gas.

"As we walked down the road a car with four men in it came at us. They made a feint as if to run us down and I could see they all were laughing.

"I don't think now that they really meant to run us down, but we leaped off the road as they sped by. After that a minister drove up and he gave my wife and me a ride all the way to Buffalo.

"I think perhaps that it was much like when my father died. There were times for the next two days when I just sat alone without being able to speak, with the tears running down my face.

"And it wasn't until the word finally got through to us that there were no cut throats and no emasculations that I realized this was not a time to be oversentimental, that is was time to get back in the fight because there was work to do."

He looked up and smiled, that same sad smile that he always has ready to give to anyone who approaches him in friendly fashion. It's a smile that tells you the world is all screwed up but let's get our act together and fight the battle anyway.

"You know, I've never told anyone this, but I suppose you can use it if you will," he said. "I think about it a lot.

"Since the end of the Chicago trial I've already become a grandfather twice. One of the children's names is Jessica Monroe. The other is Daniel Philip.

"I'm a member of the Berrigan brothers' defense team, you know, and I go to visit them in prison at least once a week.

"Well, one day I brought little Daniel Philip with me to see them and they both blessed the child for me in an ecumenical ceremony. Sometimes, when I think things are going so badly, I think about that day and how happy it made me."

Bill Kunstler shook his head.

"You know," he said, "we reach a point when we are prepared to go to jail with our clients. Lots of better men than me have gone in the past. I'm prepared to go myself now if I must."

He smiled again . . . sadly.

DELLINGER: "I'LL MISS THE OUTSIDE"

I saw Dellinger shortly after this. Somehow, the sight of Dave Dellinger, soaking wet and slogging through the mud near the Washington Monument, seemed right. I really think he's a patriot, in the classic sense. Someday maybe even our courts will realize this.

WASHINGTON—"Sometimes when I wake up in the morning tired, I think about the idea that I'm probably going back to jail," David Dellinger said.

He smiled dryly.

"I suppose it's at times like that, when I'm tired, that I think I'd rather not have to go. That's when I know how much I'll miss the outside."

Dave Dellinger, fifty-six years old, is free on appeal after being sentenced to serve five years after being found guilty in the Chicago 7 Conspiracy trial on charges that stemmed from the street battles during the Democratic National Convention of 1968.

He has also been sentenced to serve two and a half years for contempt of court by U.S. District Court Judge Julius J. Hoffman, but that sentence is to be served concurrently if Dellinger's appeal fails.

Dellinger was standing in drenching rain about a hundred yards from the Washington Monument as he talked.

He was down here to head a peace rally that had just been postponed because of the rain. He was soaking wet. Standing in a sopping green suit, his shoes waterlogged, and his sparse gray hair hanging over his ears and down his forehead, he looked like a man who needed a dime for a cup of coffee.

"People tended to be too optimistic about our case," Dellinger said. "Wherever I went they'd tell me they were sure the Supreme Court would declare the conspiracy law null and void.

"I was never that optimistic. For more than a year, it has been clear to me the government was dragging its feet on our appeal, waiting for a change in the makeup of the court.

"Now they have it with these two new appointments. I just assume that we'll all be going off to jail for a while in the not-too-distant future."

Dellinger headed for his car, walking through puddles of water six inches deep without any effort to avoid them.

"This won't be the first time I've been in jail," he said. "I served three years during World War II for opposing that one, too.

"I found out that time what it's like to be in prison. Life doesn't change that much. Once you get into prison you find it doesn't make that much difference to you."

Dellinger smiled sadly as he bent over to open the door of his rented car.

"They kept warning me about how terrible it would be in the hole," he said. "Well, it didn't take me long to make solitary. Once I got there, I found that really didn't change things much, either.

"I have a lot to tell you, I found a lot of human dignity among prisoners. You know, when you're in prison, your civil liberties are taken away and the restraints on your jailers are removed, too.

"But still, you find a solidarity and comradeship among prisoners that is heart-warming. I met some of the most wonderful people I know in prison."

We drove away from the Washington Monument, heading downtown.

Dellinger continued to talk as he drove.

"All of the [Chicago 7] defendants, with the exception of Tom Hayden, held a reunion just a week ago up at Bill Kunstler's house in Mamaroneck, New York.

"It was a wonderful party. It was particularly great because we rediscovered that for all our differences there is still a lot of love and happiness among us all."

Traffic was heavy. Driving in a strange city was proving difficult, and Dellinger interrupted himself at this point to ask if any of the three young people in the back seat knew if we were heading in the right direction.

"Do you remember how we all tried to present Bobby Seale with a birthday cake during the trial and the marshals stopped us?" he asked.

"Well, Bobby was the last one to arrive at Kunstler's house for the reunion. We all waited in another room for him to get settled.

"Then, all of us—Abbie Hoffman, Jerry Rubin, John Froines,

Rennie Davis, Lee Weiner, and myself—came through the door into the living room with a birthday cake with lighted candles for Bobby.

"We all burst out singing. It was a wonderful moment. Bobby was obviously pleased and embarrassed and grateful all at the same time."

We kept driving through the heavy rain and the traffic and Dellinger continued to talk about his codefendants, bringing their activities up to date.

Nobody has seen much of Hayden, who has been living in California. But all the others are in constant touch with each other.

Dellinger, Davis, and Froines are leaders of the People's Coalition for Peace and Justice that is starting a new peace offensive.

Dellinger and Davis live in New York, but Froines is scheduled to begin teaching college in Boston soon.

Hoffman is depressed because he has been attacked so often by other members of the left who believe he has made a lot of money from the movement.

Rubin is living in New York, too. Weiner is teaching at Rutgers University in New Jersey, but living in New York.

We had been driving for more than ten minutes and Dellinger pulled the car to the curb and stopped.

He smiled.

"Look where we are," he said. "We're back at the exact same place we started from. There's the Washington Monument again. We've gone in a circle."

He laughed softly.

"Do you suppose there's some meaning in this for us all?"

THE SYSTEM WORKS AFTER ALL

And it all ended like Greek theatre. Only this time the deus ex machina *that lifted the would-be victims from seemingly certain defeat was the United States Court of Appeals.*

The Appeals Court tossed out the convictions of the five defendants who were convicted and they blamed the whole fiasco on Judge Hoffman and Tom Foran.

So it goes.

This should be an easy piece to write. The Chicago 7 Conspiracy trial verdict has been reversed. The system works. Judge Julius J. Hoffman and Thomas A. Foran, the dandy little federal prosecutor, have been slapped on the wrists.

Let's all be happy and rejoice. The Republic is safe.

Now Judge Hoffman can add the names of the three judges of the U.S. Court of Appeals to the list of those who are biased against him.

Now perhaps Foran, who is also hypersensitive to criticism, will say that the three appeals court judges were out to get him. In the past that has been one of Foran's favorite ripostes when asked to comment about newspaper accounts he deemed unfavorable to him.

But this piece isn't really easy to write. Judge Hoffman and Foran offered little reason for anyone to respect their conduct during the nearly five months of the trial. Judge Hoffman held the cards and he played the role of the martinet.

As head of the prosecution team, Foran had the evidence for a conviction but he blew it.

That is why this piece isn't easy to write. Judge Hoffman and Foran are such easy targets now. That is why it's important for us to remember and never to forget what they almost got away with.

This is how the three-judge panel concluded section VIII of their decision, the portion dealing with the "demeanor of the judge and prosecutors:"

"We conclude that the demeanor of the judge and prosecutors would require reversal if other errors did not."

The defenders of Judge Hoffman and Foran will be quick to point out that it was the unruly conduct of the defendants that provoked the reactions of the judge and prosecutor.

This defense doesn't hold water with the appeals panel.

"There are high standards for the conduct of judges and prosecutors," the ruling states, "and impropriety by persons before the court does not give license to depart from those standards."

Newsmen who covered the trial regularly were appalled by Judge Hoffman's cavalier attitude, his incredible vanity, and by a bias against the long-haired defendants that was so blatant that it defied belief.

Every day there was another sarcastic remark leveled at either the defendants, their attorneys or their witnesses. This was not lost on the Appeals Court panel, which wrote:

"Out of the several hundred readily identifiable comments of such character in the record, more than 150 were made in the presence of the jury."

The Appeals Court goes on to cite several instances.

From the start Judge Hoffman made it plain that he resented the fact that William Kunstler, the chief defense counsel, was a New Yorker and that Leonard Weinglass, his assistant, was from Newark.

There was the day that Kunstler complained to Judge Hoffman that reproduction of a tape being presented in evidence was not accurate because of the volume at which it was being played in the court.

"It isn't like the New York Symphony that you may go to when you go back home," Judge Hoffman said.

Another day, Kunstler mentioned the distance between two points in Chicago. Judge Hoffman smiled acidly and reminded Kunstler that he was a "visitor" in Chicago.

On another occasion he told Weinglass that he must be mistaken about something Weinglass said about Chicago because "he was thinking of Newark."

There were so many ugly little scenes. There were so many of them they became lost under the impress of all the ugly large scenes enforced day after day by the might of as many as nineteen federal marshals in the courtroom to keep order.

There were all those days of subzero temperatures when young people were forced to stand outside in the street to wait in line while Judge Hoffman's society friends were escorted inside and ushered to the best seats in the house.

One day J. Anthony Lukas of the *New York Times* was tossed out of the courtroom because one of the marshals decided it was illegal to carry a book into the courtroom.

Another day, Jim Singer, who covered the trial for *The Sun-Times,* and myself were arrested, fingerprinted and tossed into jail. Our crime? We attempted to walk down the hall to get to the press room.

That hallway had been declared off limits just three minutes before.

The police state is always only minutes away.

But Judge Hoffman's pecking away at Kunstler and Weinglass never ceased. On the last day of the trial when Judge Hoffman sentenced Weinglass for contempt he made a point of referring to him as "Mr. Weinruss."

Judge Hoffman had done that all during the trial. Weinglass had corrected him every time. On that last day, Weinglass just shook his head. He didn't bother to attempt to correct the trial judge again.

The three-judge panel notes one day that Kunstler objected to restrictions being placed against his leaving the courtroom:

KUNSTLER: "There is no way we can conduct a defense under these circumstances."

JUDGE: "I don't know about a defense, but you are doing some conducting. . . ."

Another time, Kunstler argued about a ruling that evidence was "hearsay." Kunstler said he didn't understand.

Judge Hoffman silenced him with: "You will have to see a lawyer, Mr. Kunstler, if you do not understand it."

Judge Hoffman always made it evident that he considered Weinglass, the younger of the two attorneys, to be an inexperienced lawyer.

Once, Weinglass argued that he believed he had been asking proper questions for the purpose of impeachment, the three-judge panel notes.

I remember the day well. Judge Hoffman glanced down from the bench. There was a tight little smile on his lips. Then he glanced ever so slightly over toward the jury box and said:

"I would like to preside over a class in evidence, but I haven't the time today."

There was another time when a similar situation arose with Kunstler. The Appeals Court notes that, too.

"I will be glad to tell you, privately, how to do it. I haven't any right in a public trial to give you a course in evidence."

There is all this to it and so much more.

If just once, Judge Hoffman had shown a spark of humanity toward the defendants, this would have been an easier piece to write.

But he never did. Now he must pay the price. The members of the Appeals Court, the men whose respect he must desire most, have now told Judge Hoffman that he was all wrong. All the way.